CREATED BY **JOSS WHEDON**

JORDIE **BELLAIRE** DAVID **LÓPEZ** SAS **MILLEDGE** RAÚL **ANGULO**

Buffy the vampire slayer™

VOLUME TWO **ONCE BITTEN**

BOOM! STUDIOS

Series Designer
Michelle Ankley

Collection Designer
Scott Newman

Assistant Editor
Gavin Gronenthal

Associate Editor
Jonathan Manning

Editor
Jeanine Schaefer

Special Thanks to **Sierra Hahn**, **Dafna Pleban**,
Becca J. Sadowsky, and **Nicole Spiegel**
& **Carol Roeder** at Twentieth Century Fox.

BUFFY THE VAMPIRE SLAYER Volume Two, February 2020. Published by BOOM! Studios, a division of Boom Entertainment, Inc. Buffy the Vampire Slayer ™ & © 2020 Twentieth Century Fox Film Corporation. All rights reserved. Originally published in single magazine form as BUFFY THE VAMPIRE SLAYER No. 5-8. ™ & © 2019 Twentieth Century Fox Film Corporation. All rights reserved. BOOM! Studios™ and the BOOM! Studios logo are trademarks of Boom Entertainment, Inc., registered in various countries and categories. All characters, events, and institutions depicted herein are fictional. Any similarity between any of the names, characters, persons, events, and/or institutions in this publication to actual names, characters, and persons, whether living or dead, events, and/or institutions is unintended and purely coincidental. BOOM! Studios does not read or accept unsolicited submissions of ideas, stories, or artwork.

For information regarding the CPSIA on this printed material, call: (203) 595-3636 and provide reference #RICH – 874132.

BOOM! Studios, 5670 Wilshire Boulevard, Suite 400, Los Angeles, CA 90036-5679. Printed in USA. First Printing.

ISBN: 978-1-68415-482-1, eISBN: 978-1-64144-640-2

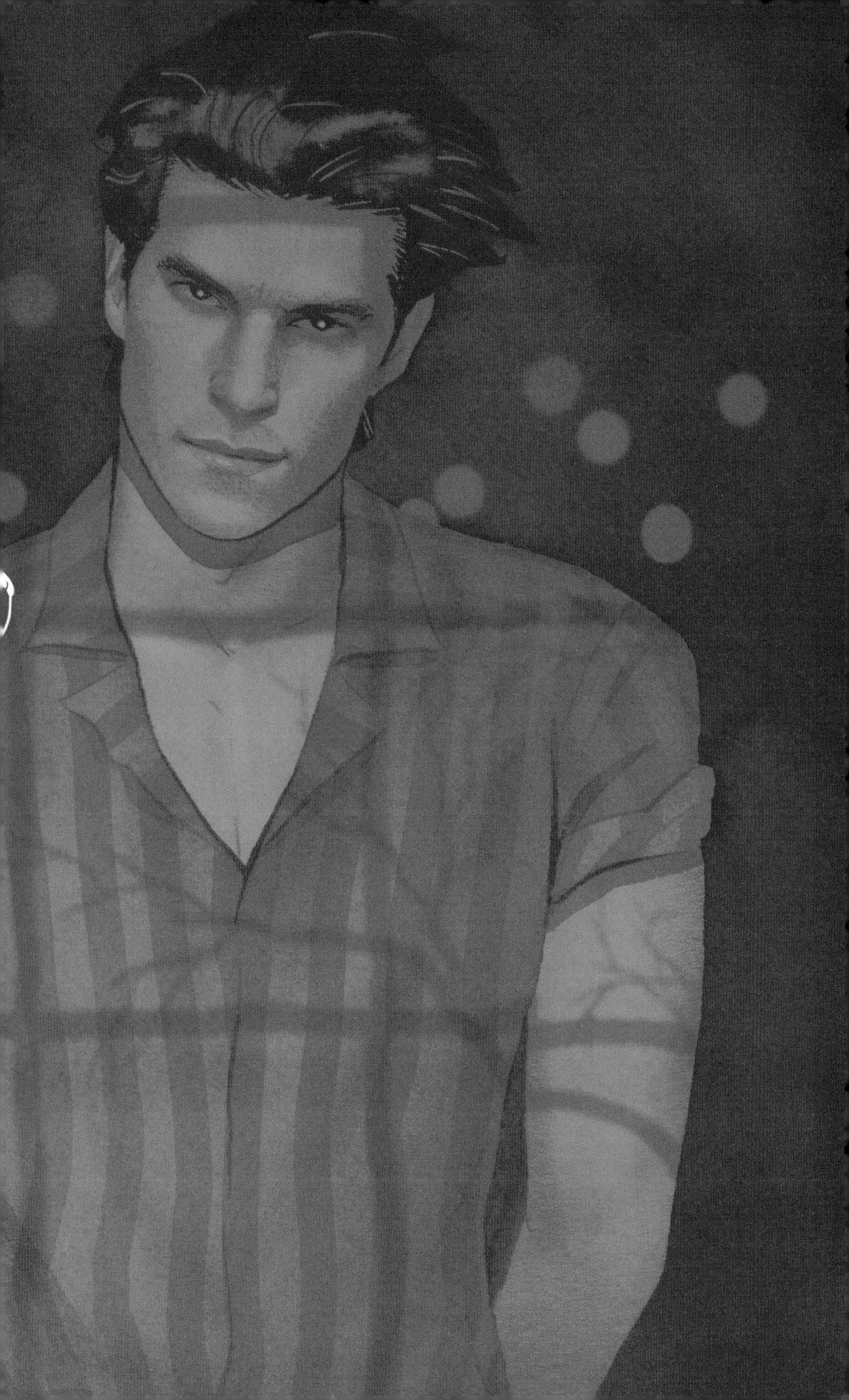

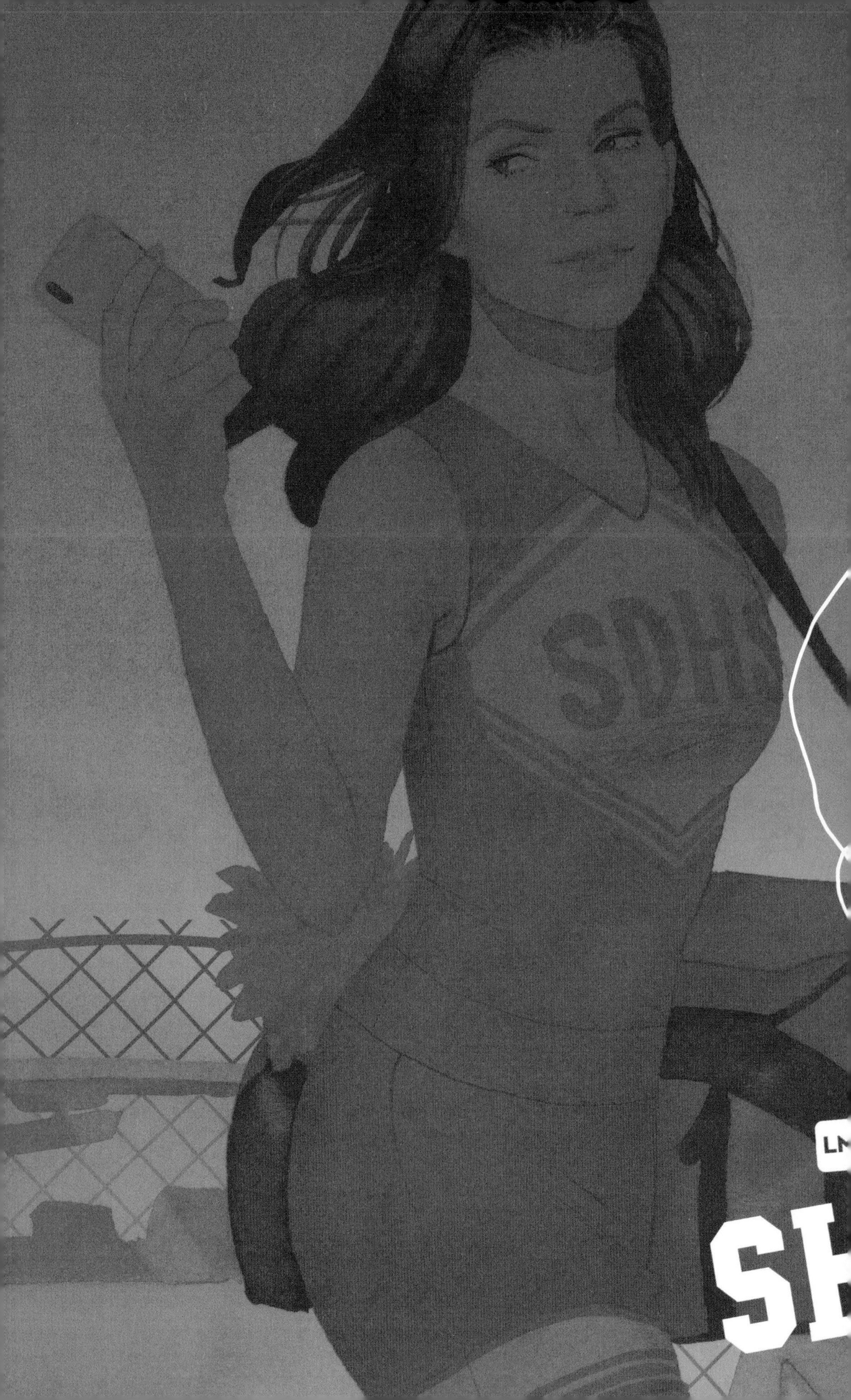

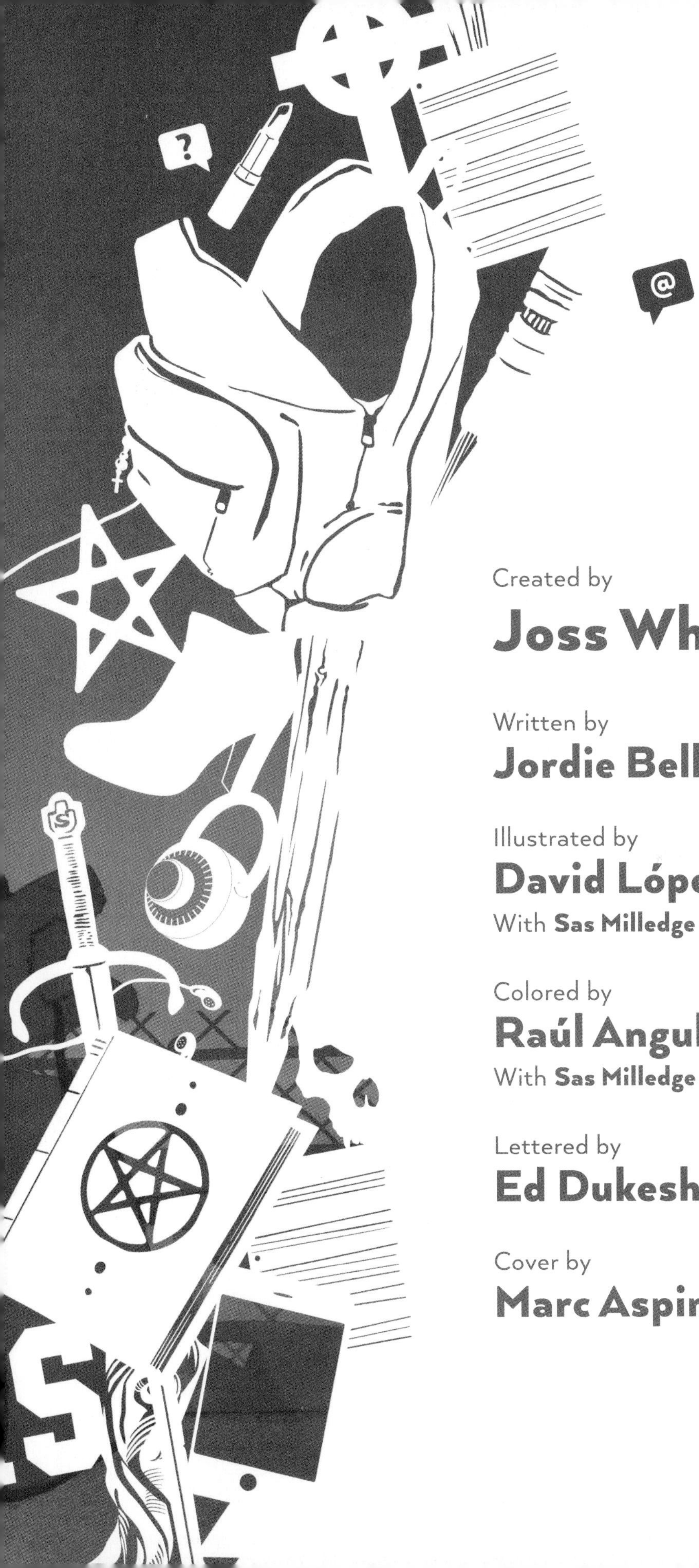

Created by
Joss Whedon

Written by
Jordie Bellaire

Illustrated by
David López
With **Sas Milledge** (Chapter 7)

Colored by
Raúl Angulo
With **Sas Milledge** (Chapter 7)

Lettered by
Ed Dukeshire

Cover by
Marc Aspinall

CHAPTER
FIVE

Issue Five Cover by **Marc Aspinall**

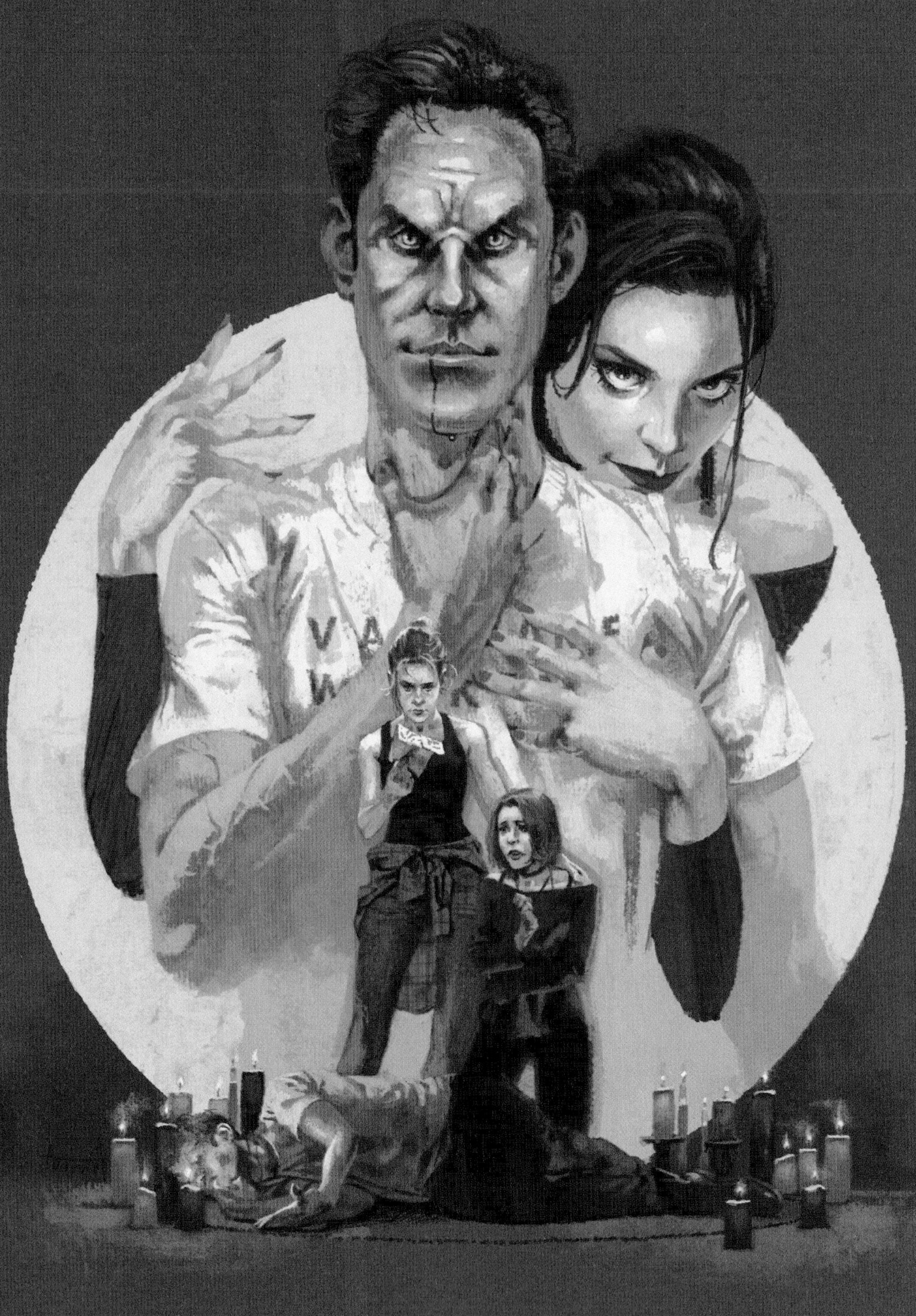

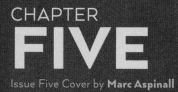

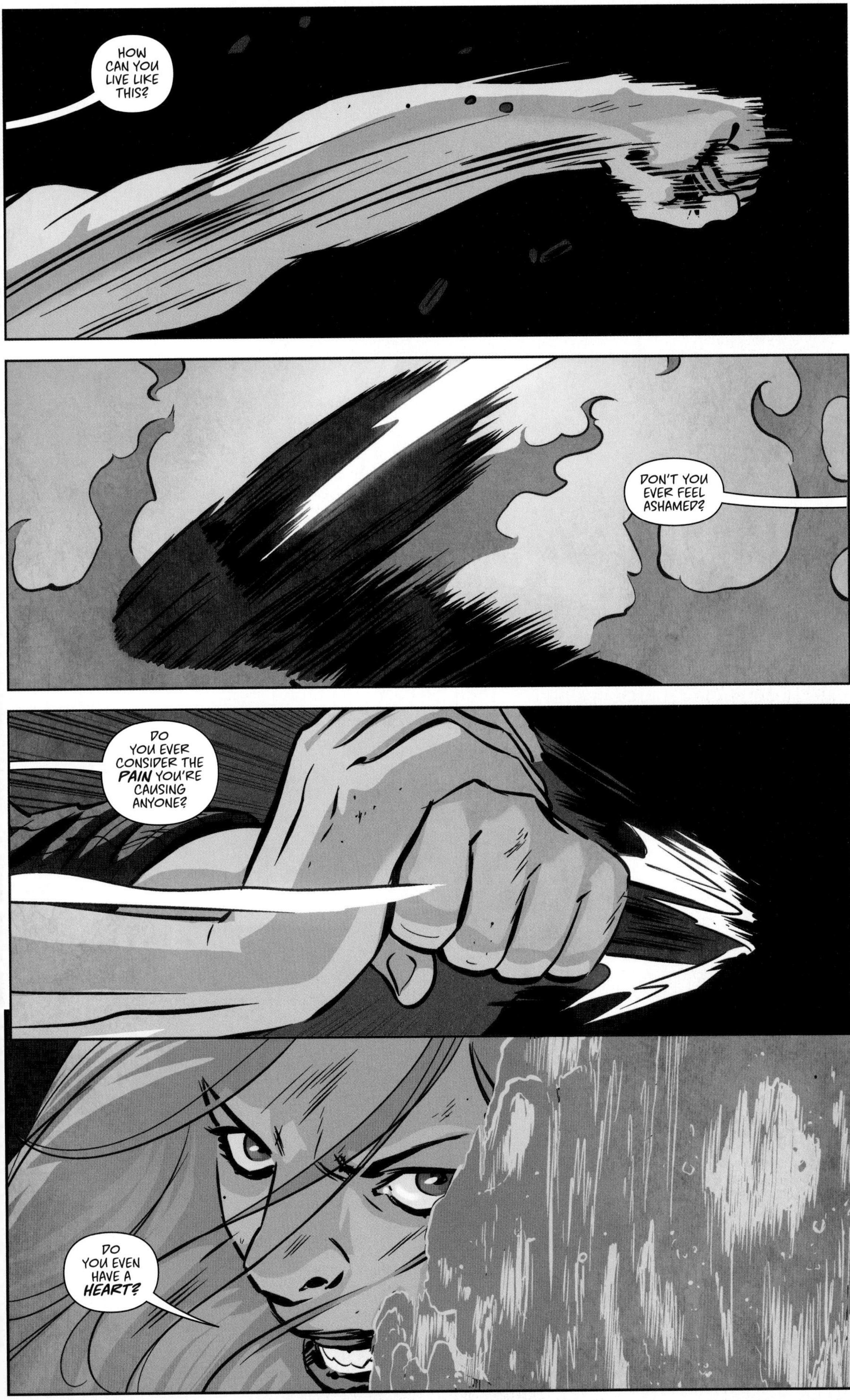
HOW CAN YOU LIVE LIKE THIS?
DON'T YOU EVER FEEL ASHAMED?
DO YOU EVER CONSIDER THE PAIN YOU'RE CAUSING ANYONE?
DO YOU EVEN HAVE A HEART?

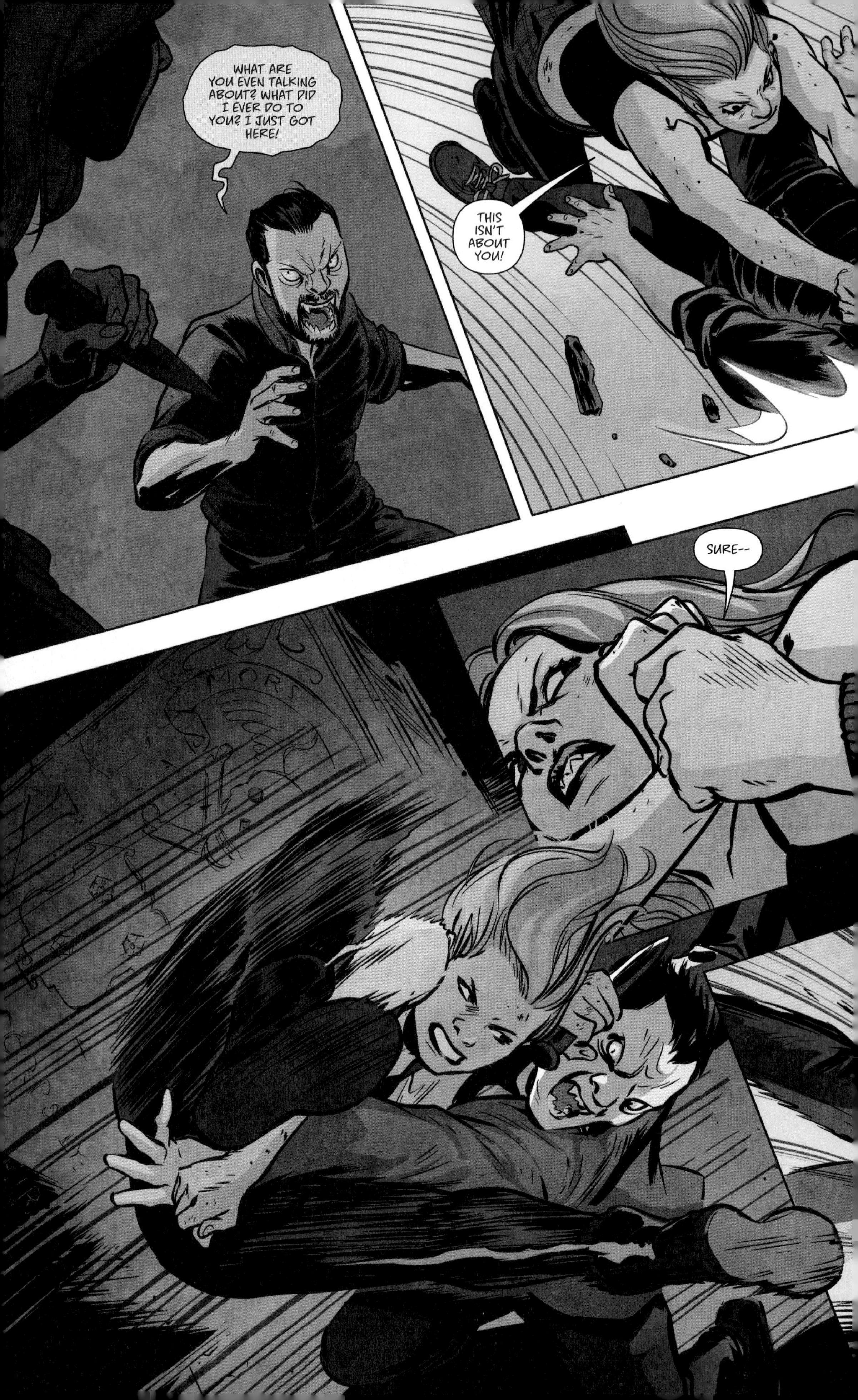
WHAT ARE YOU EVEN TALKING ABOUT? WHAT DID I EVER DO TO YOU? I JUST GOT HERE!
THIS ISN'T ABOUT YOU!
SURE--

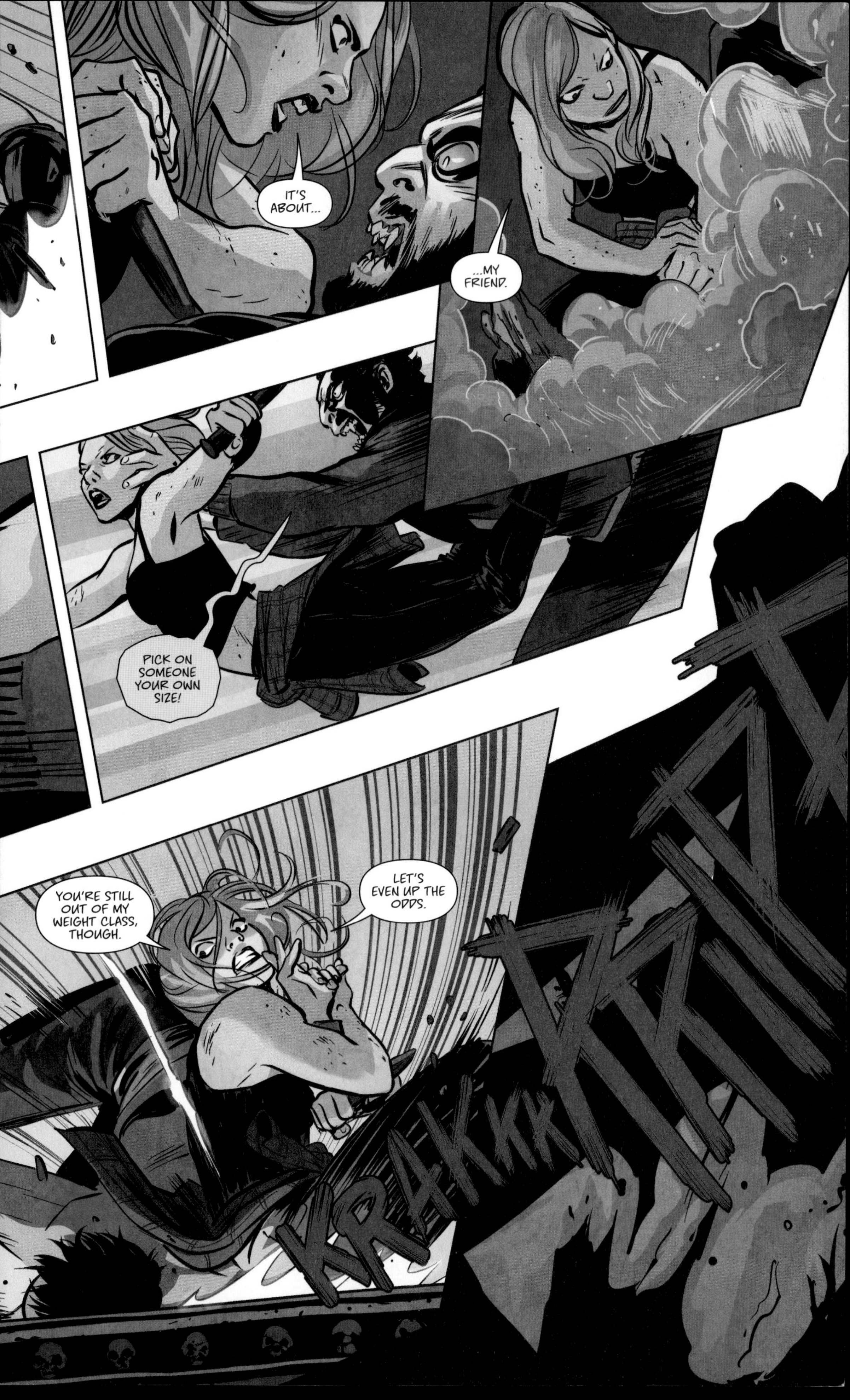
IT'S ABOUT...
...MY FRIEND.
PICK ON SOMEONE YOUR OWN SIZE!
YOU'RE STILL OUT OF MY WEIGHT CLASS, THOUGH.
LET'S EVEN UP THE ODDS.
KRAKKKK

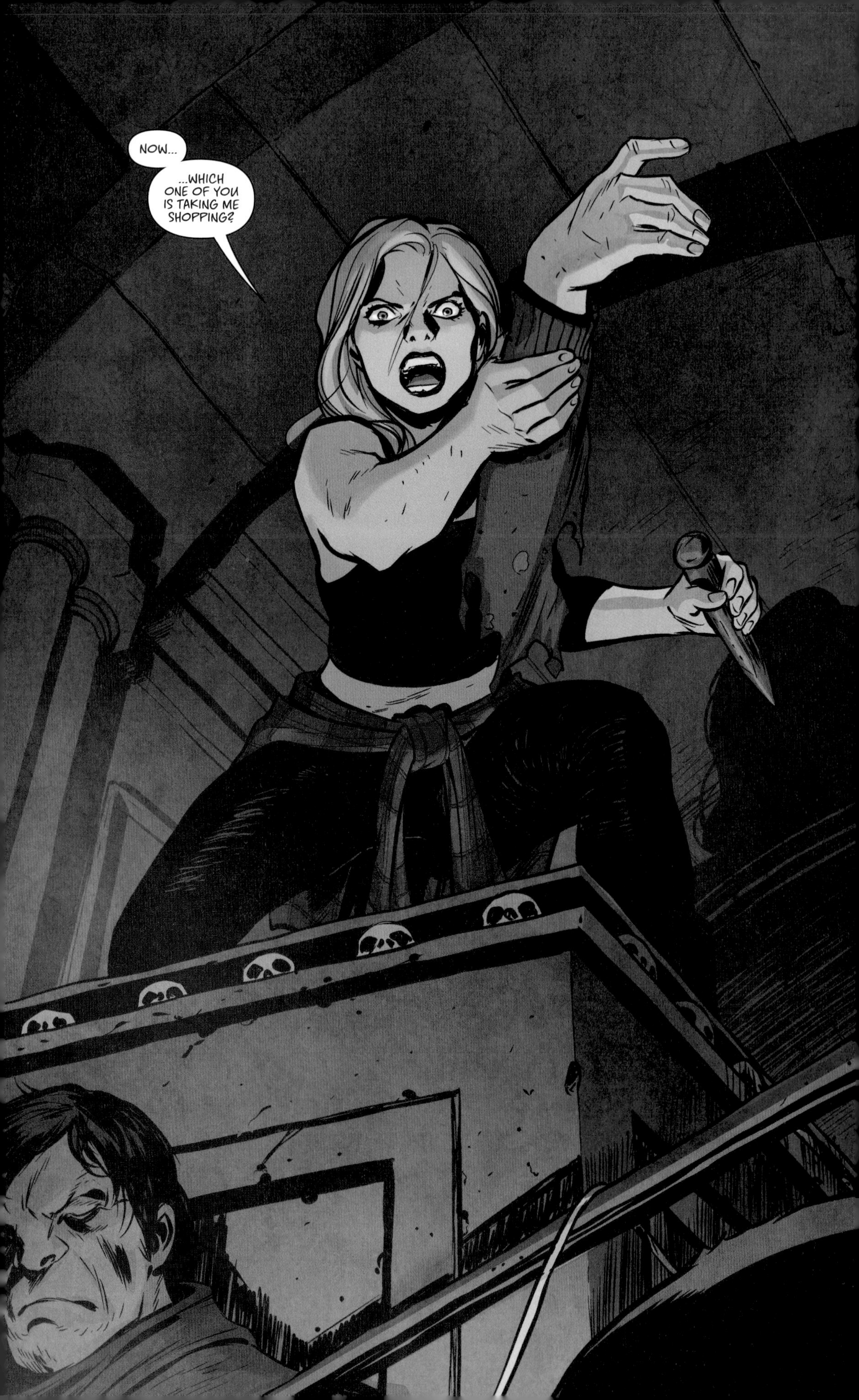
NOW...
...WHICH ONE OF YOU IS TAKING ME SHOPPING?

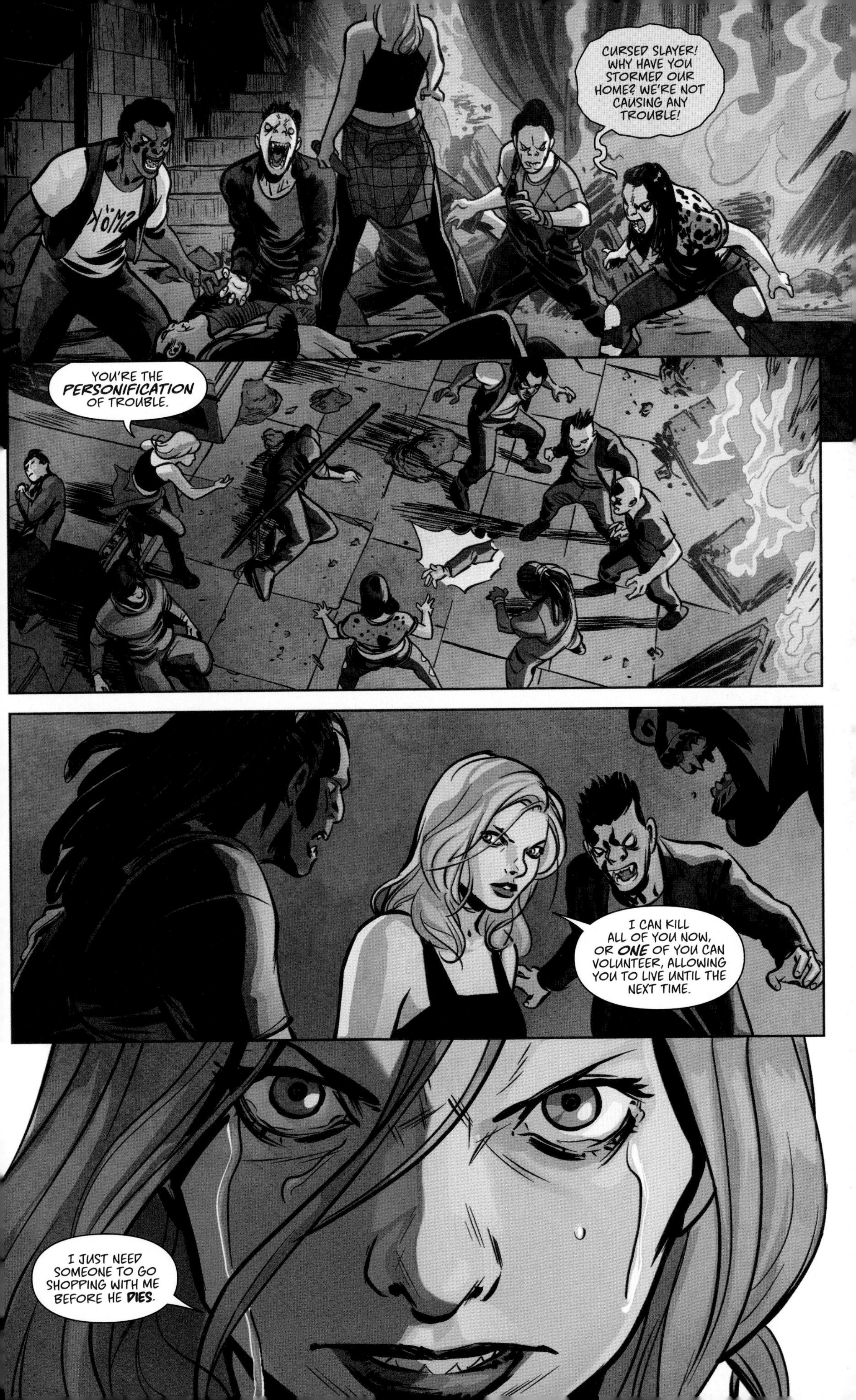

CURSED SLAYER! WHY HAVE YOU STORMED OUR HOME? WE'RE NOT CAUSING ANY TROUBLE!
YOU'RE THE PERSONIFICATION OF TROUBLE.
I CAN KILL ALL OF YOU NOW, OR ONE OF YOU CAN VOLUNTEER, ALLOWING YOU TO LIVE UNTIL THE NEXT TIME.
I JUST NEED SOMEONE TO GO SHOPPING WITH ME BEFORE HE DIES.

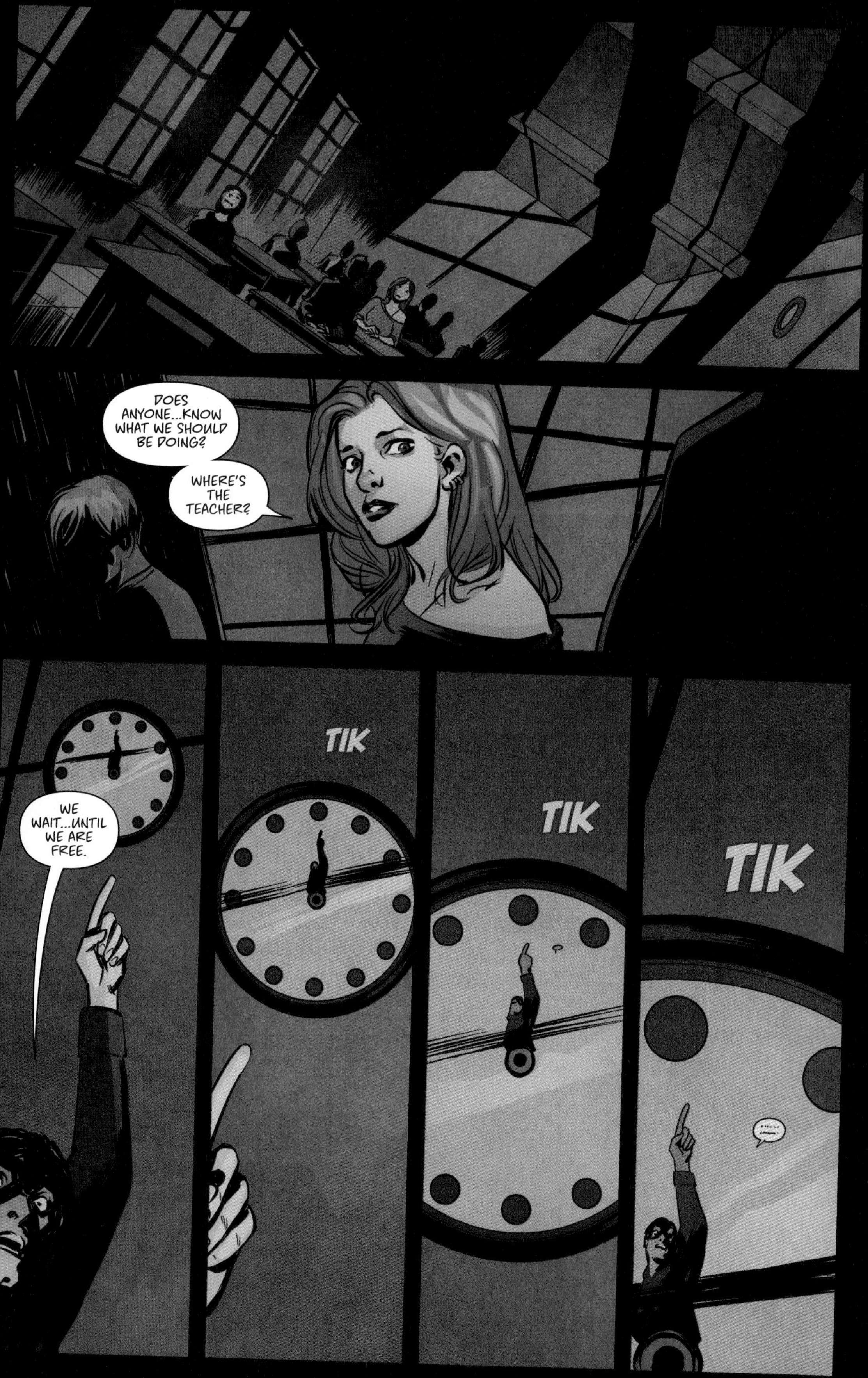
DOES ANYONE...KNOW WHAT WE SHOULD BE DOING?
WHERE'S THE TEACHER?
WE WAIT...UNTIL WE ARE FREE.
TIK
TIK
TIK

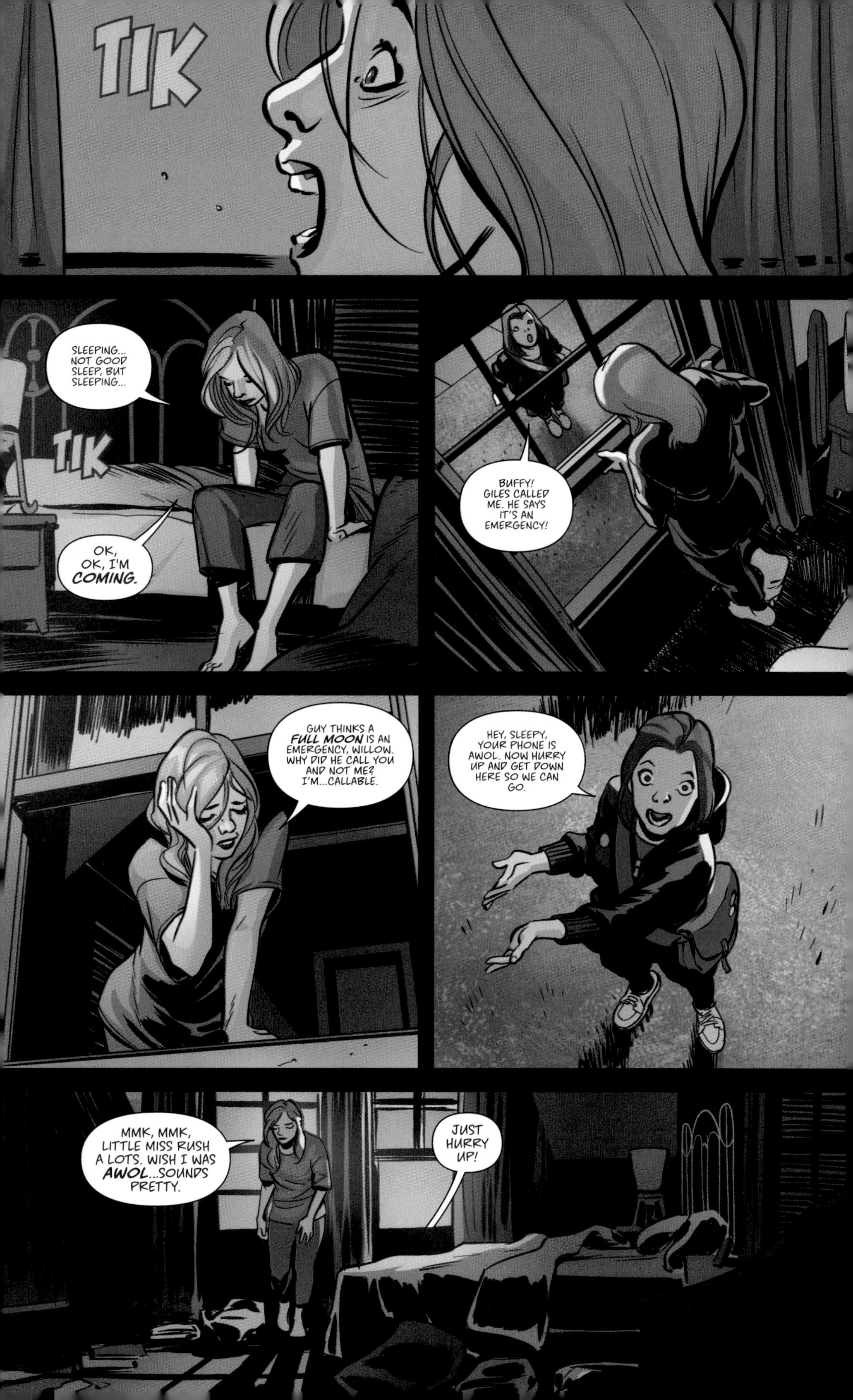

TIK
SLEEPING... NOT GOOD SLEEP, BUT SLEEPING...
TIK
OK, OK, I'M COMING.
BUFFY! GILES CALLED ME. HE SAYS IT'S AN EMERGENCY!
GUY THINKS A FULL MOON IS AN EMERGENCY, WILLOW. WHY DID HE CALL YOU AND NOT ME? I'M...CALLABLE.
HEY, SLEEPY, YOUR PHONE IS AWOL. NOW HURRY UP AND GET DOWN HERE SO WE CAN GO.
MMK, MMK, LITTLE MISS RUSH A LOTS. WISH I WAS AWOL...SOUNDS PRETTY.
JUST HURRY UP!

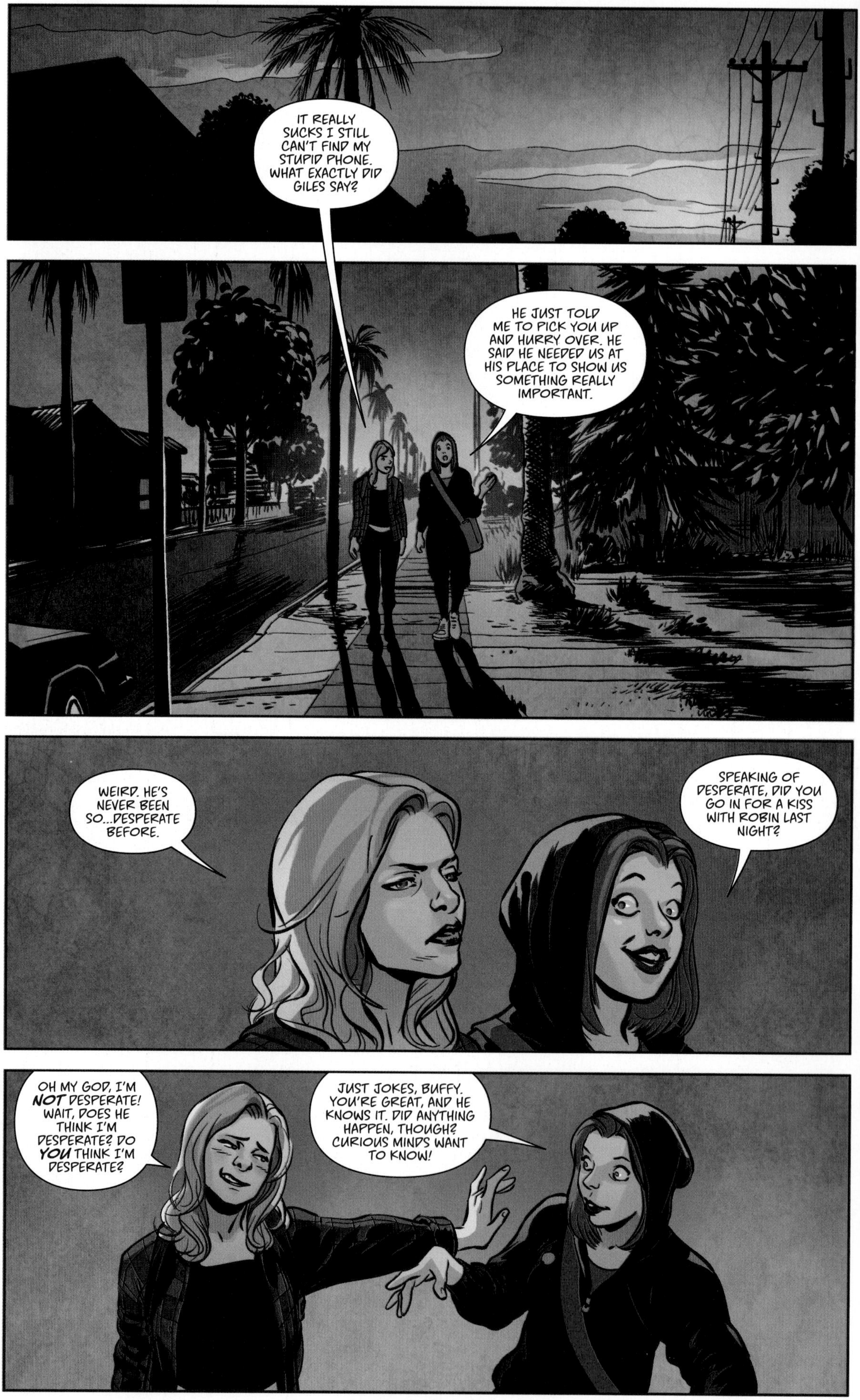
IT REALLY SUCKS I STILL CAN'T FIND MY STUPID PHONE. WHAT EXACTLY DID GILES SAY?
HE JUST TOLD ME TO PICK YOU UP AND HURRY OVER. HE SAID HE NEEDED US AT HIS PLACE TO SHOW US SOMETHING REALLY IMPORTANT.
WEIRD. HE'S NEVER BEEN SO...DESPERATE BEFORE.
SPEAKING OF DESPERATE, DID YOU GO IN FOR A KISS WITH ROBIN LAST NIGHT?
OH MY GOD, I'M **NOT** DESPERATE! WAIT, DOES HE THINK I'M DESPERATE? DO **YOU** THINK I'M DESPERATE?
JUST JOKES, BUFFY. YOU'RE GREAT, AND HE KNOWS IT. DID ANYTHING HAPPEN, THOUGH? CURIOUS MINDS WANT TO KNOW!

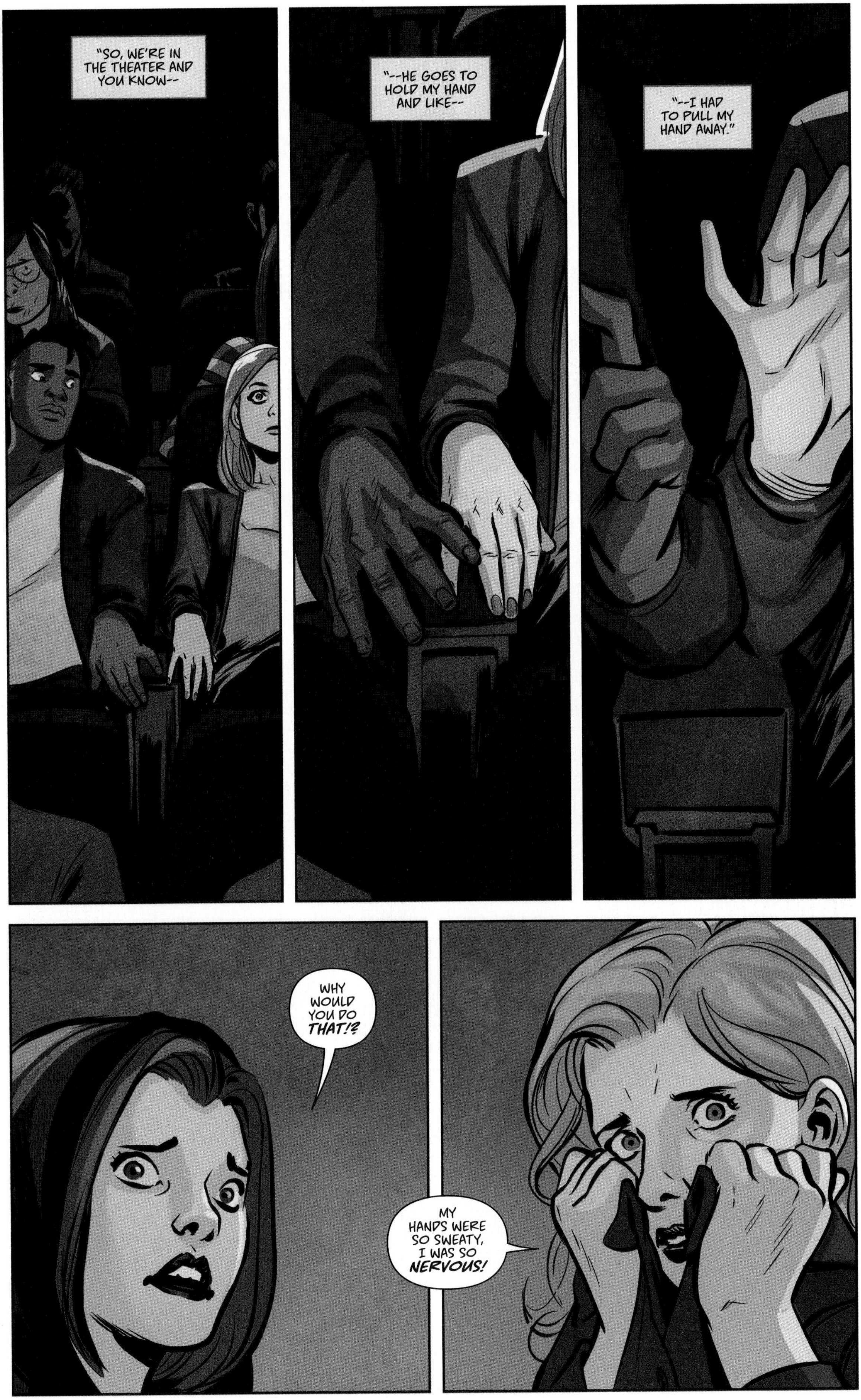
"SO, WE'RE IN THE THEATER AND YOU KNOW--
"--HE GOES TO HOLD MY HAND AND LIKE--
"--I HAD TO PULL MY HAND AWAY."
WHY WOULD YOU DO *THAT!?*
MY HANDS WERE SO SWEATY, I WAS SO *NERVOUS!*

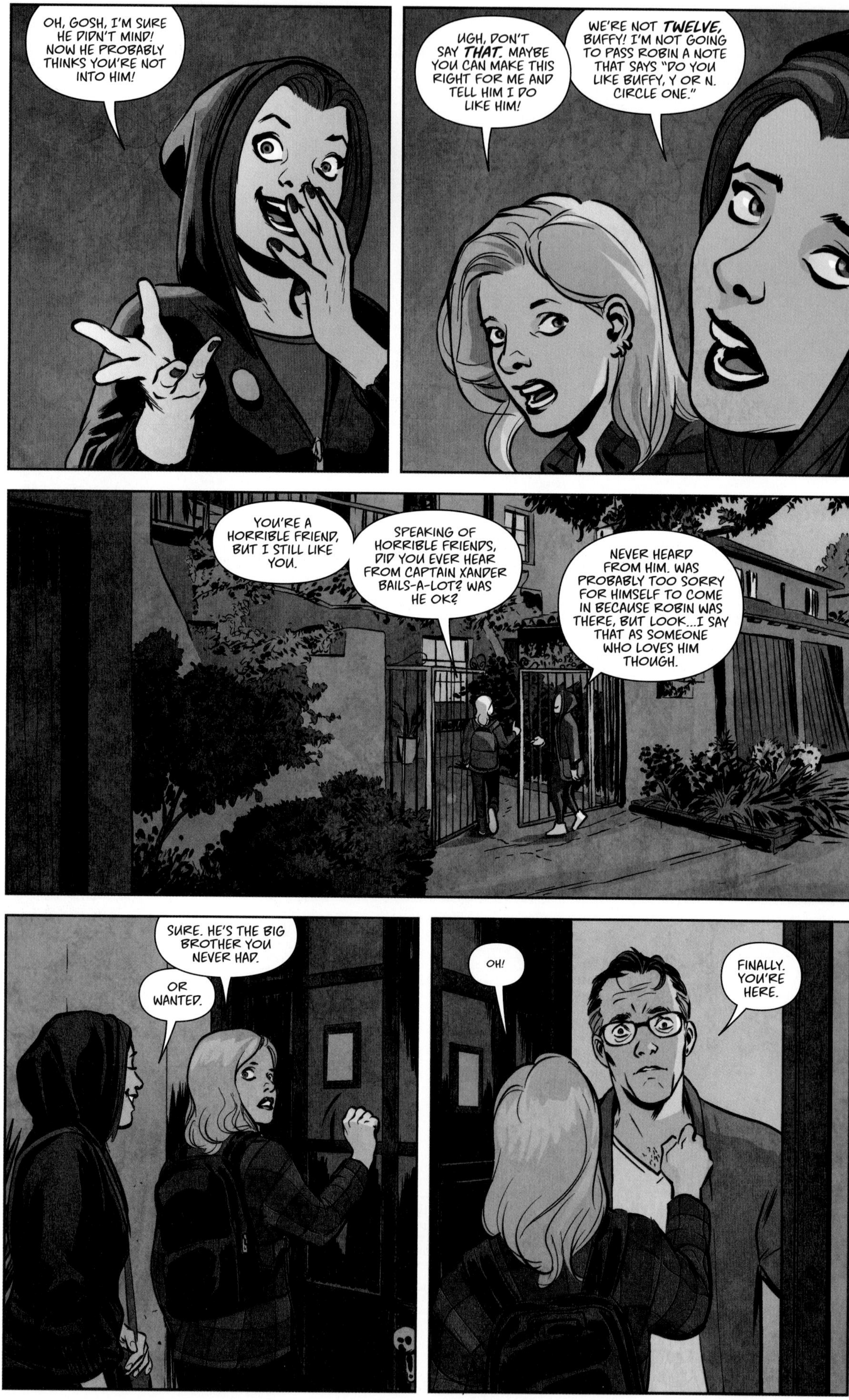
OH, GOSH, I'M SURE HE DIDN'T MIND! NOW HE PROBABLY THINKS YOU'RE NOT INTO HIM!
UGH, DON'T SAY **THAT.** MAYBE YOU CAN MAKE THIS RIGHT FOR ME AND TELL HIM I DO LIKE HIM!
WE'RE NOT ***TWELVE,*** BUFFY! I'M NOT GOING TO PASS ROBIN A NOTE THAT SAYS "DO YOU LIKE BUFFY, Y OR N. CIRCLE ONE."
YOU'RE A HORRIBLE FRIEND, BUT I STILL LIKE YOU.
SPEAKING OF HORRIBLE FRIENDS, DID YOU EVER HEAR FROM CAPTAIN XANDER BAILS-A-LOT? WAS HE OK?
NEVER HEARD FROM HIM. WAS PROBABLY TOO SORRY FOR HIMSELF TO COME IN BECAUSE ROBIN WAS THERE, BUT LOOK...I SAY THAT AS SOMEONE WHO LOVES HIM THOUGH.
SURE. HE'S THE BIG BROTHER YOU NEVER HAD.
OR WANTED.
OH!
FINALLY. YOU'RE HERE.

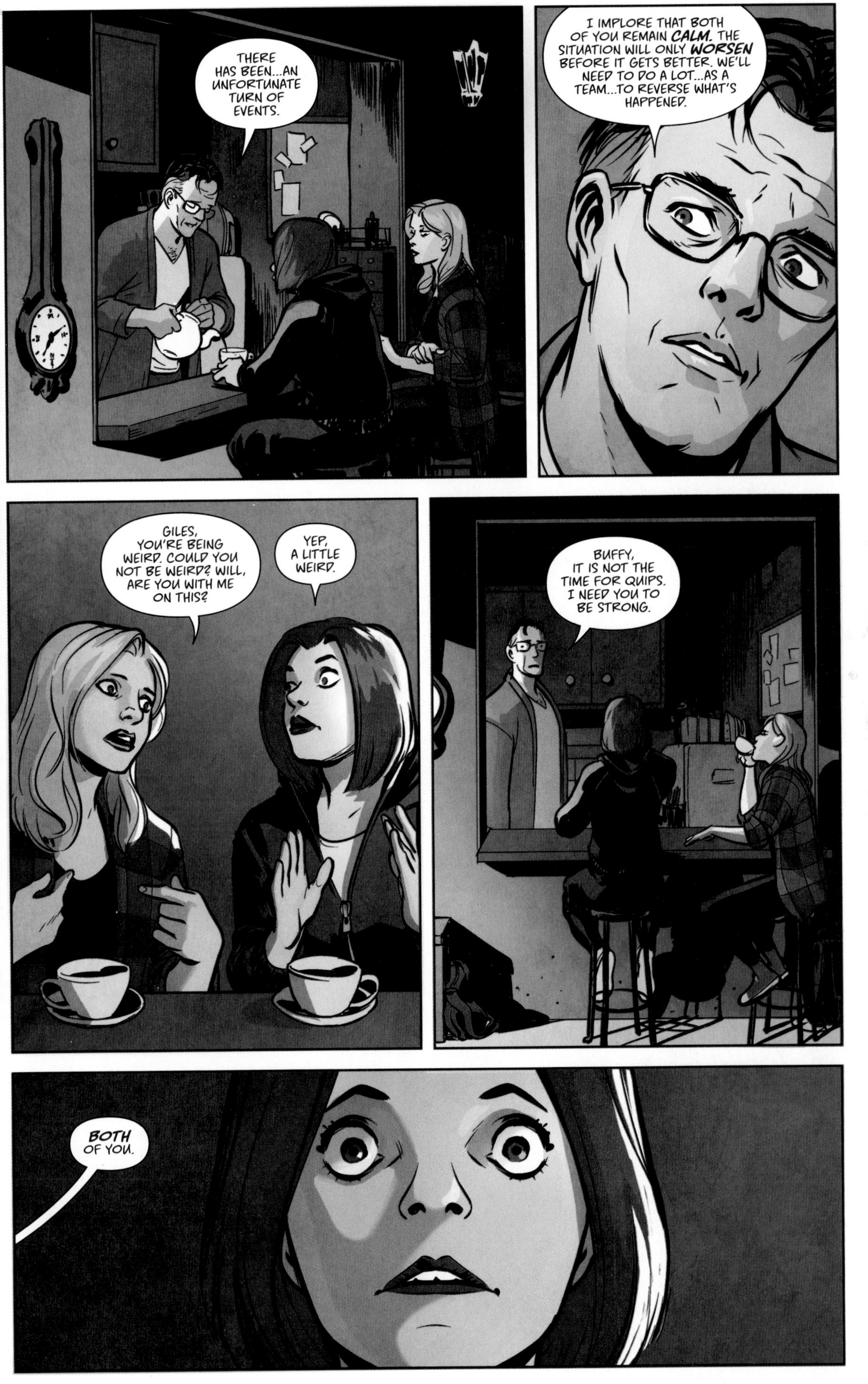
THERE HAS BEEN...AN UNFORTUNATE TURN OF EVENTS.
I IMPLORE THAT BOTH OF YOU REMAIN CALM. THE SITUATION WILL ONLY WORSEN BEFORE IT GETS BETTER. WE'LL NEED TO DO A LOT...AS A TEAM...TO REVERSE WHAT'S HAPPENED.
GILES, YOU'RE BEING WEIRD. COULD YOU NOT BE WEIRD? WILL, ARE YOU WITH ME ON THIS?
YEP, A LITTLE WEIRD.
BUFFY, IT IS NOT THE TIME FOR QUIPS. I NEED YOU TO BE STRONG.
BOTH OF YOU.

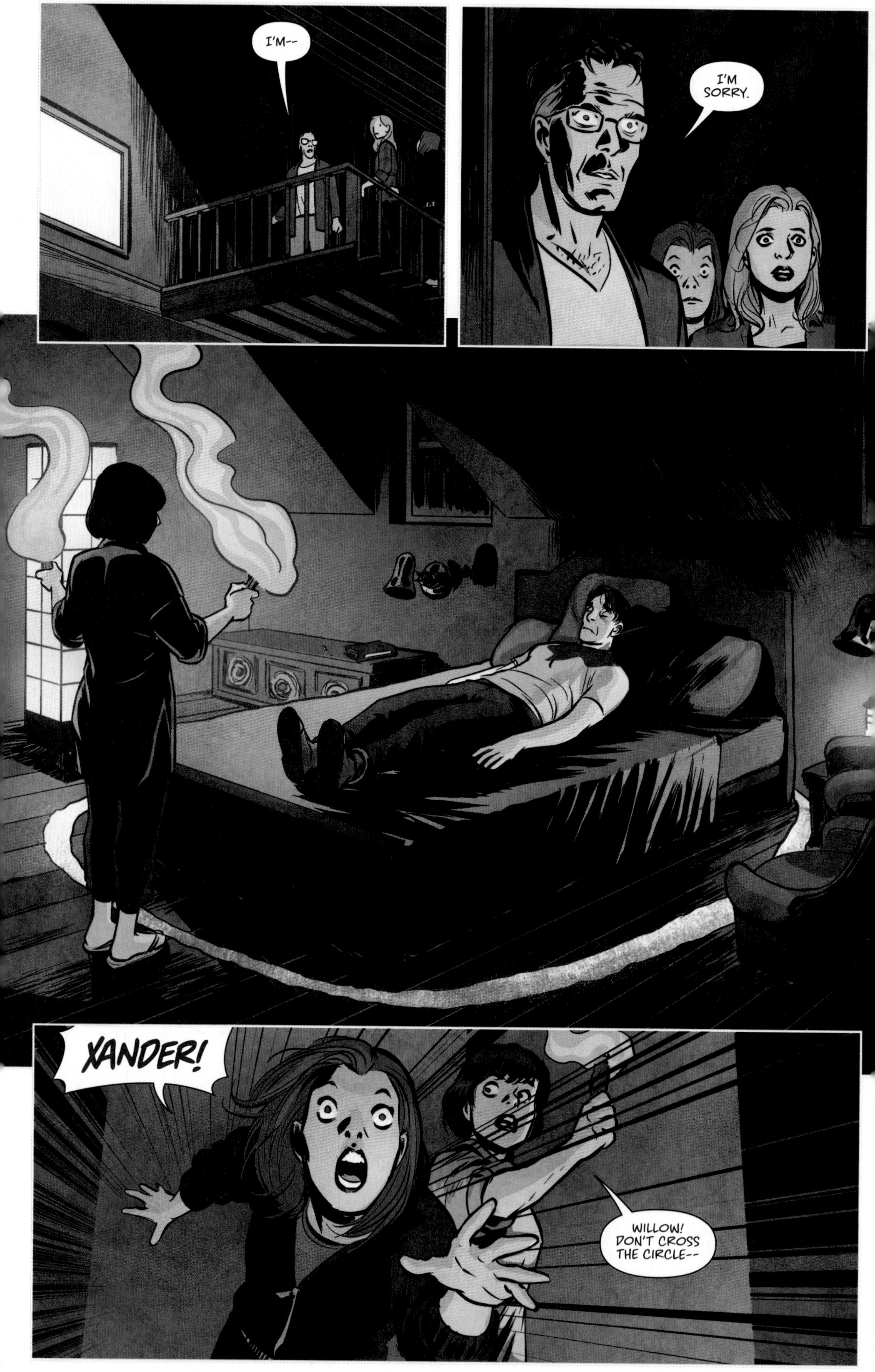
I'M--
I'M SORRY.
XANDER!
WILLOW! DON'T CROSS THE CIRCLE--

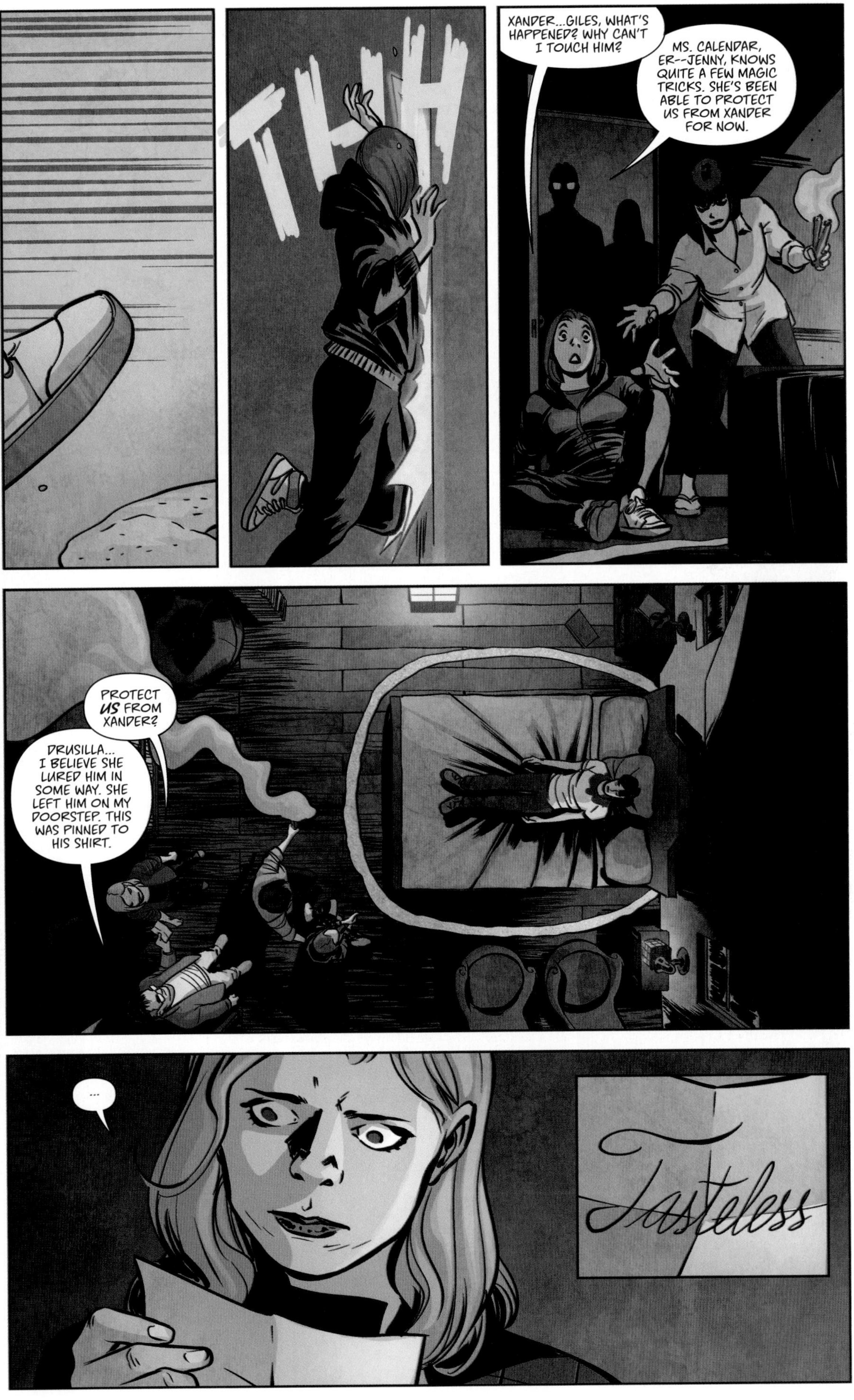
THUH
XANDER...GILES, WHAT'S HAPPENED? WHY CAN'T I TOUCH HIM?
MS. CALENDAR, ER--JENNY, KNOWS QUITE A FEW MAGIC TRICKS. SHE'S BEEN ABLE TO PROTECT US FROM XANDER FOR NOW.
PROTECT US FROM XANDER?
DRUSILLA... I BELIEVE SHE LURED HIM IN SOME WAY. SHE LEFT HIM ON MY DOORSTEP. THIS WAS PINNED TO HIS SHIRT.
...
Tasteless

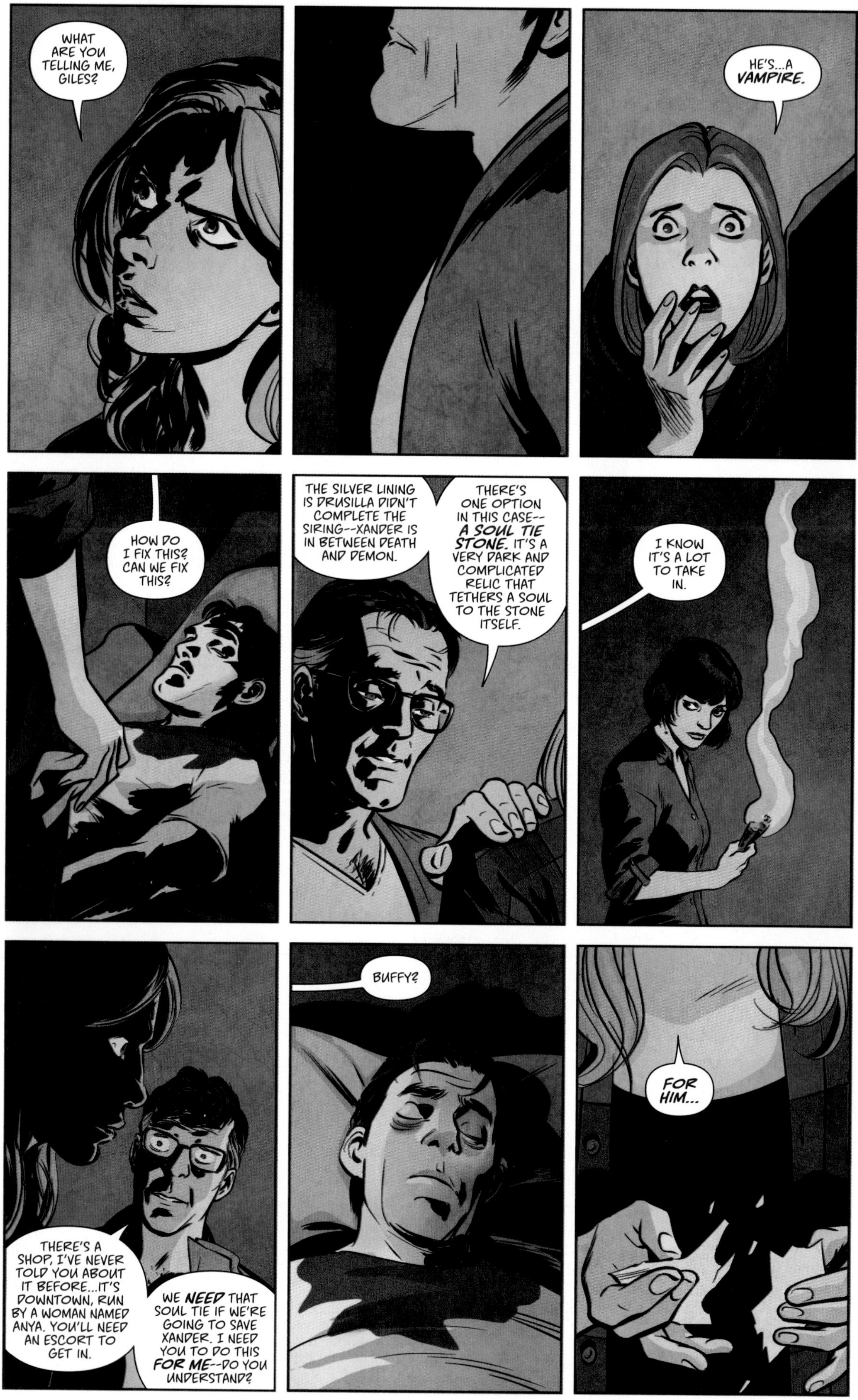
WHAT ARE YOU TELLING ME, GILES?
HE'S...A VAMPIRE.
HOW DO I FIX THIS? CAN WE FIX THIS?
THE SILVER LINING IS DRUSILLA DIDN'T COMPLETE THE SIRING--XANDER IS IN BETWEEN DEATH AND DEMON.
THERE'S ONE OPTION IN THIS CASE--A SOUL TIE STONE. IT'S A VERY DARK AND COMPLICATED RELIC THAT TETHERS A SOUL TO THE STONE ITSELF.
I KNOW IT'S A LOT TO TAKE IN.
THERE'S A SHOP, I'VE NEVER TOLD YOU ABOUT IT BEFORE...IT'S DOWNTOWN, RUN BY A WOMAN NAMED ANYA. YOU'LL NEED AN ESCORT TO GET IN.
WE NEED THAT SOUL TIE IF WE'RE GOING TO SAVE XANDER. I NEED YOU TO DO THIS FOR ME--DO YOU UNDERSTAND?
BUFFY?
FOR HIM...

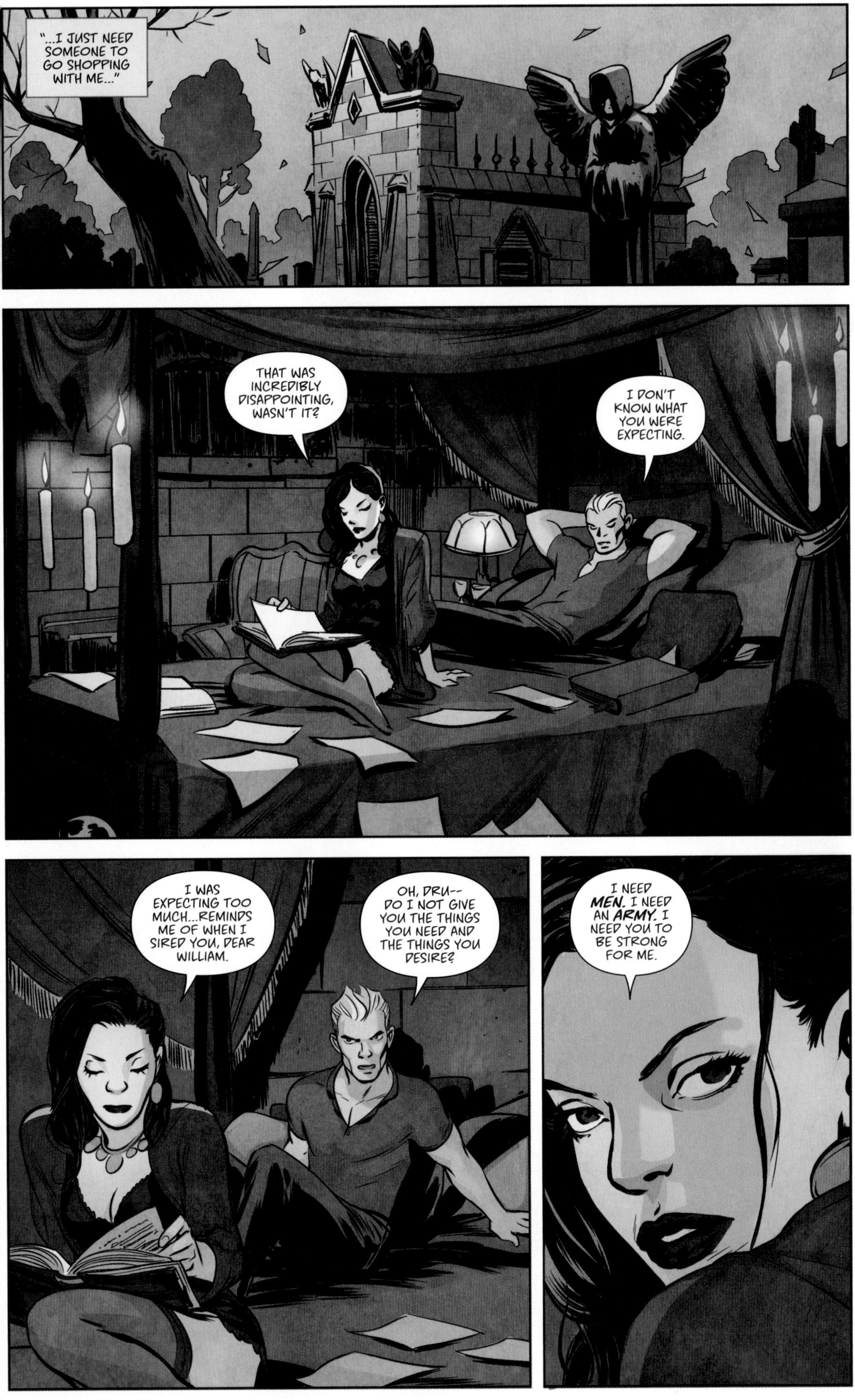
"...I JUST NEED SOMEONE TO GO SHOPPING WITH ME..."
THAT WAS INCREDIBLY DISAPPOINTING, WASN'T IT?
I DON'T KNOW WHAT YOU WERE EXPECTING.
I WAS EXPECTING TOO MUCH...REMINDS ME OF WHEN I SIRED YOU, DEAR WILLIAM.
OH, DRU-- DO I NOT GIVE YOU THE THINGS YOU NEED AND THE THINGS YOU DESIRE?
I NEED MEN. I NEED AN ARMY. I NEED YOU TO BE STRONG FOR ME.

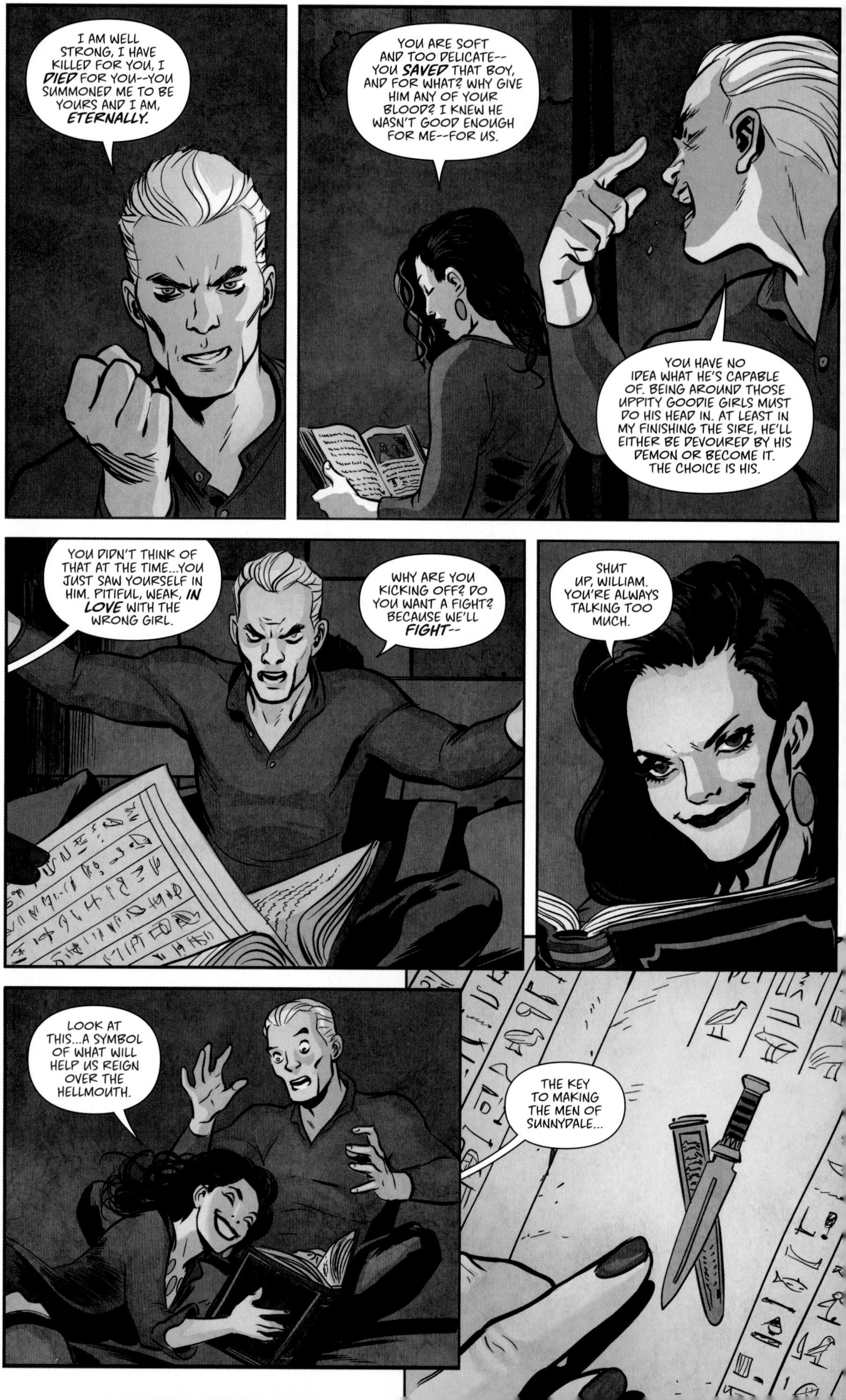
I AM WELL STRONG, I HAVE KILLED FOR YOU, I DIED FOR YOU--YOU SUMMONED ME TO BE YOURS AND I AM, ETERNALLY.
YOU ARE SOFT AND TOO DELICATE--YOU SAVED THAT BOY, AND FOR WHAT? WHY GIVE HIM ANY OF YOUR BLOOD? I KNEW HE WASN'T GOOD ENOUGH FOR ME--FOR US.
YOU HAVE NO IDEA WHAT HE'S CAPABLE OF. BEING AROUND THOSE UPPITY GOODIE GIRLS MUST DO HIS HEAD IN. AT LEAST IN MY FINISHING THE SIRE, HE'LL EITHER BE DEVOURED BY HIS DEMON OR BECOME IT. THE CHOICE IS HIS.
YOU DIDN'T THINK OF THAT AT THE TIME...YOU JUST SAW YOURSELF IN HIM. PITIFUL, WEAK, IN LOVE WITH THE WRONG GIRL.
WHY ARE YOU KICKING OFF? DO YOU WANT A FIGHT? BECAUSE WE'LL FIGHT--
SHUT UP, WILLIAM. YOU'RE ALWAYS TALKING TOO MUCH.
LOOK AT THIS...A SYMBOL OF WHAT WILL HELP US REIGN OVER THE HELLMOUTH.
THE KEY TO MAKING THE MEN OF SUNNYDALE...

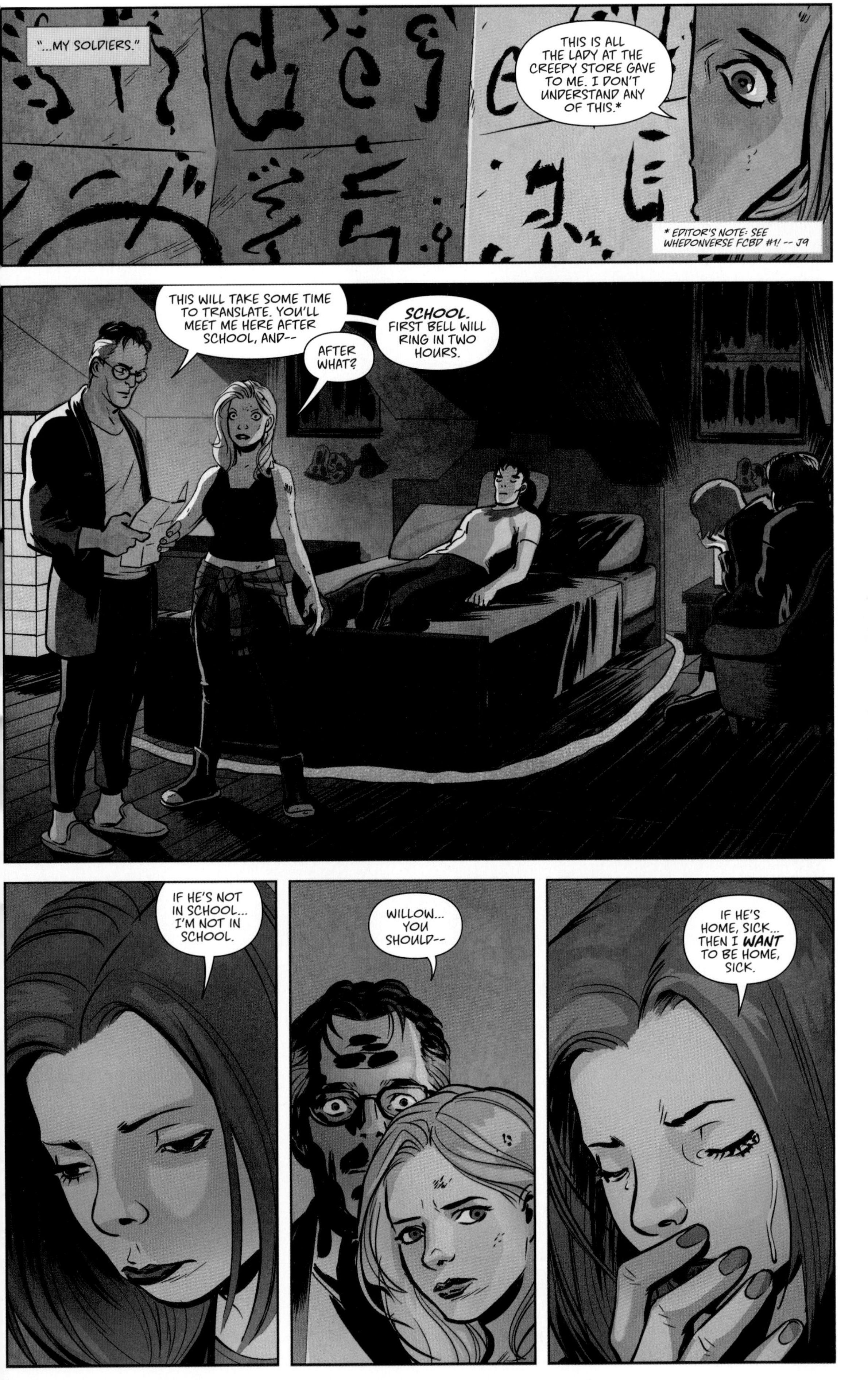
"...MY SOLDIERS."
THIS IS ALL THE LADY AT THE CREEPY STORE GAVE TO ME. I DON'T UNDERSTAND ANY OF THIS.*
* EDITOR'S NOTE: SEE WHEDONVERSE FCBD #1! -- J9
THIS WILL TAKE SOME TIME TO TRANSLATE. YOU'LL MEET ME HERE AFTER SCHOOL, AND--
AFTER WHAT?
SCHOOL. FIRST BELL WILL RING IN TWO HOURS.
IF HE'S NOT IN SCHOOL... I'M NOT IN SCHOOL.
WILLOW... YOU SHOULD--
IF HE'S HOME, SICK... THEN I WANT TO BE HOME, SICK.

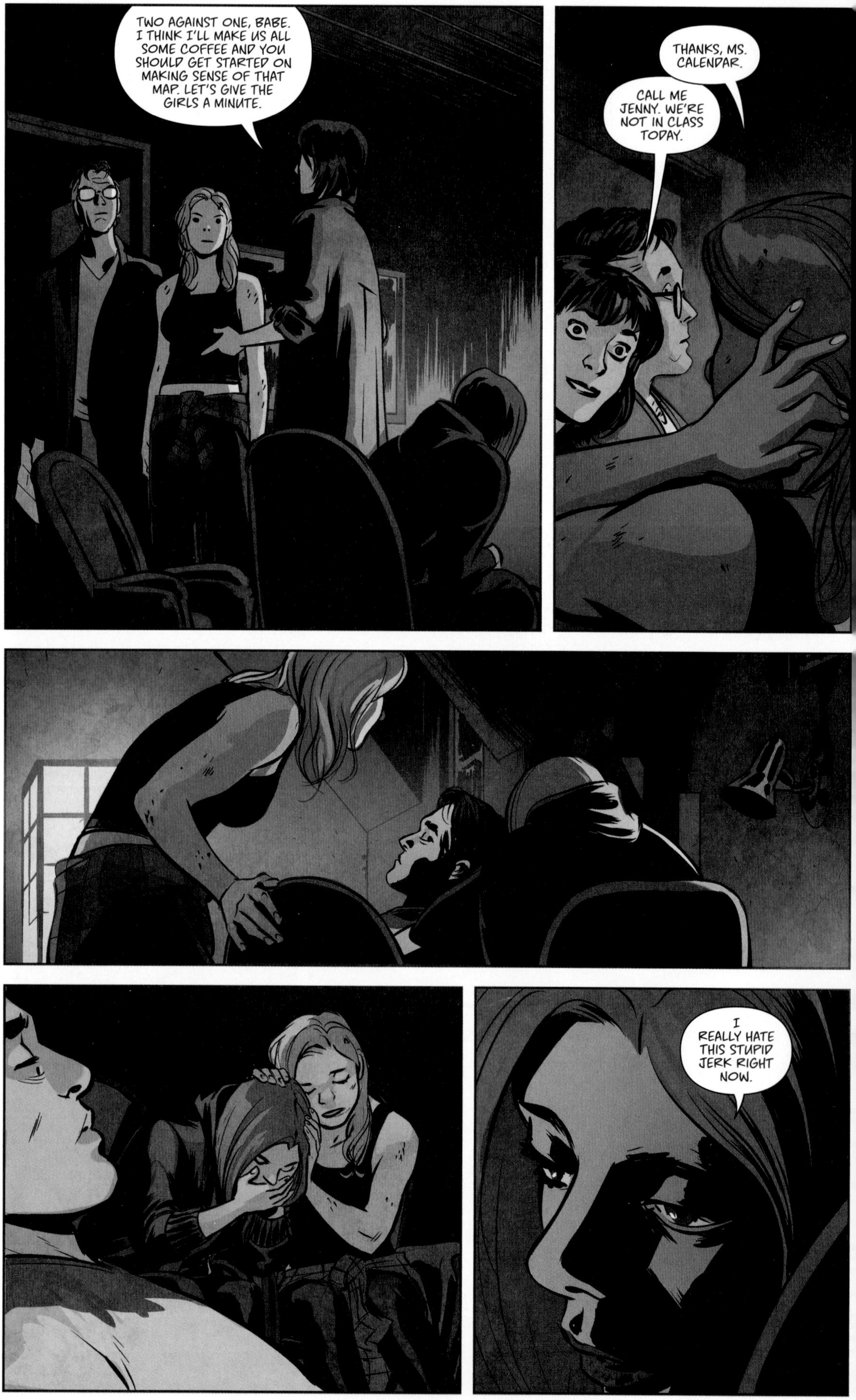
TWO AGAINST ONE, BABE. I THINK I'LL MAKE US ALL SOME COFFEE AND YOU SHOULD GET STARTED ON MAKING SENSE OF THAT MAP. LET'S GIVE THE GIRLS A MINUTE.
THANKS, MS. CALENDAR.
CALL ME JENNY. WE'RE NOT IN CLASS TODAY.
I REALLY HATE THIS STUPID JERK RIGHT NOW.

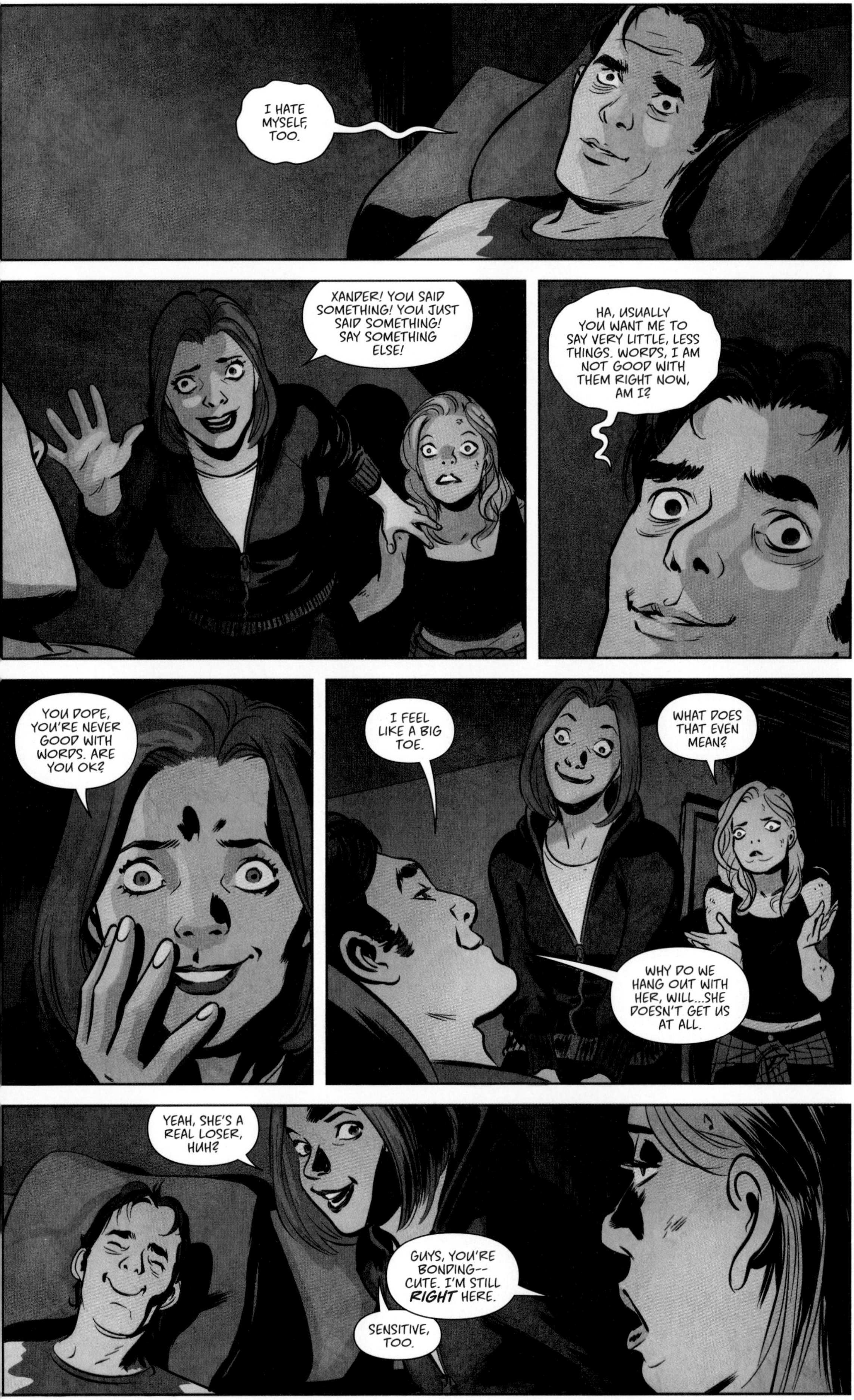
I HATE MYSELF, TOO.
XANDER! YOU SAID SOMETHING! YOU JUST SAID SOMETHING! SAY SOMETHING ELSE!
HA, USUALLY YOU WANT ME TO SAY VERY LITTLE, LESS THINGS. WORDS, I AM NOT GOOD WITH THEM RIGHT NOW, AM I?
YOU DOPE, YOU'RE NEVER GOOD WITH WORDS. ARE YOU OK?
I FEEL LIKE A BIG TOE.
WHAT DOES THAT EVEN MEAN?
WHY DO WE HANG OUT WITH HER, WILL...SHE DOESN'T GET US AT ALL.
YEAH, SHE'S A REAL LOSER, HUH?
GUYS, YOU'RE BONDING-- CUTE. I'M STILL **RIGHT** HERE.
SENSITIVE, TOO.

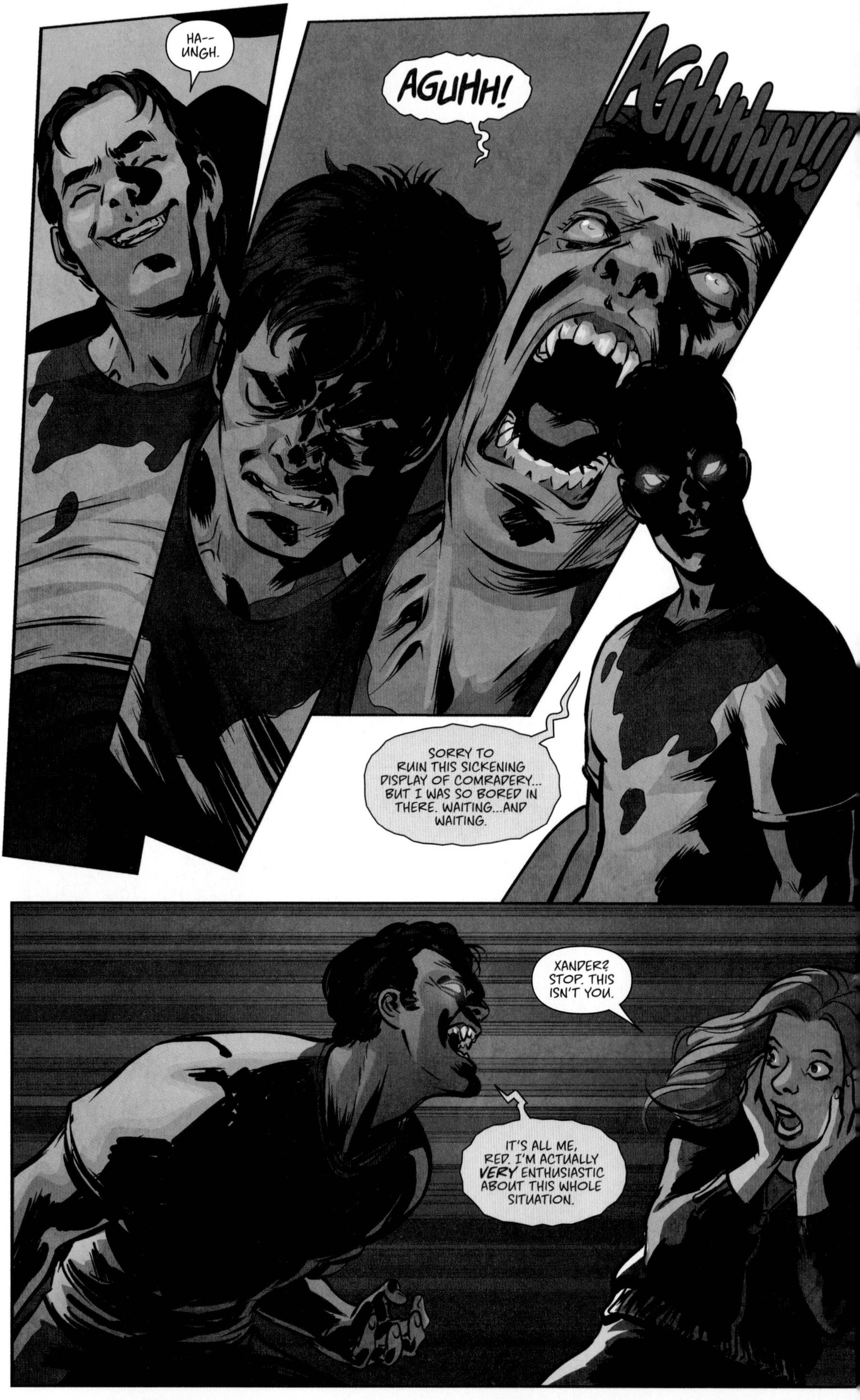
HA-- UNGH.
AGUHH!
AGHHHHHH!!
SORRY TO RUIN THIS SICKENING DISPLAY OF COMRADERY... BUT I WAS SO BORED IN THERE. WAITING...AND WAITING.
XANDER? STOP. THIS ISN'T YOU.
IT'S ALL ME, RED. I'M ACTUALLY VERY ENTHUSIASTIC ABOUT THIS WHOLE SITUATION.

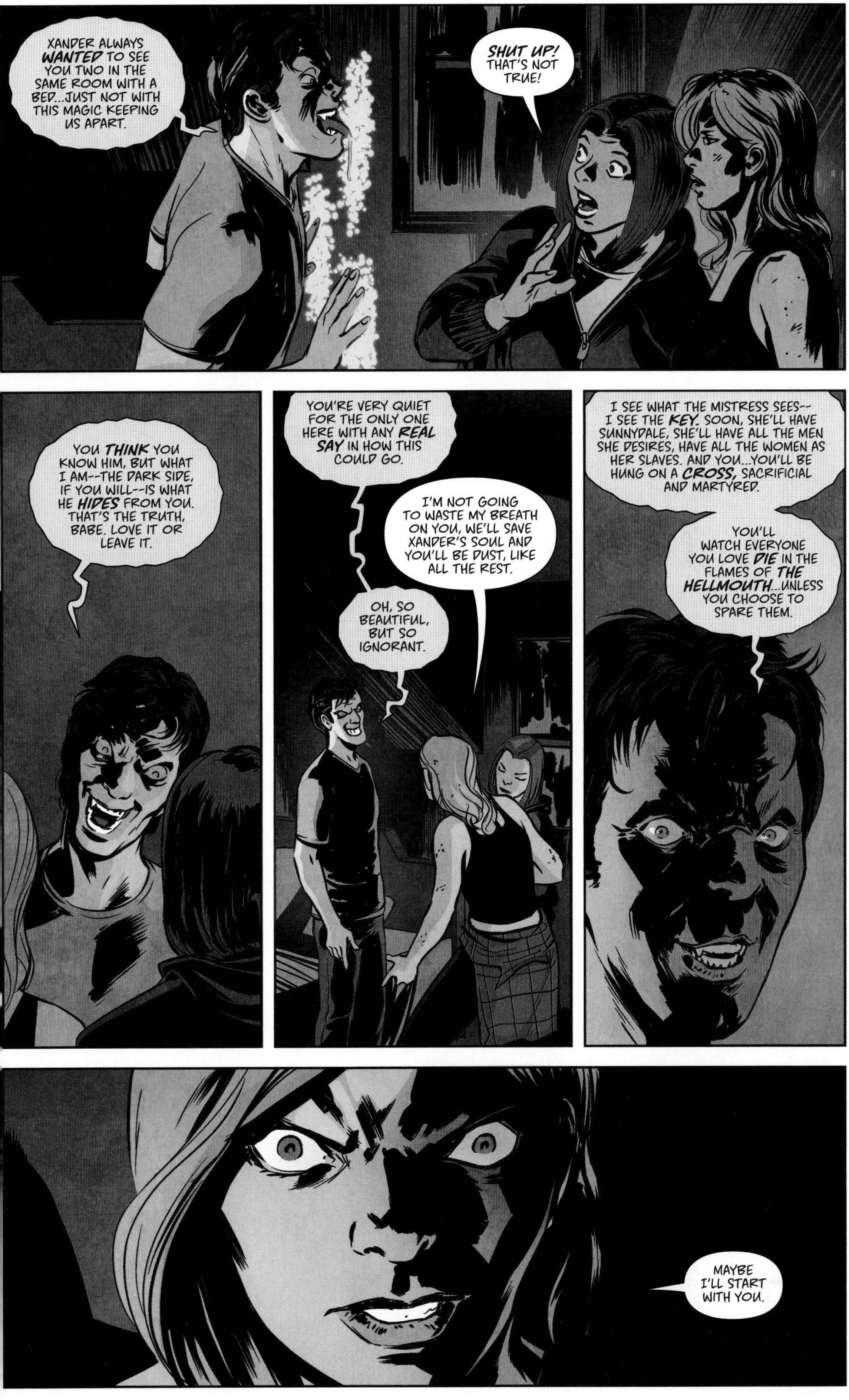
XANDER ALWAYS WANTED TO SEE YOU TWO IN THE SAME ROOM WITH A BED...JUST NOT WITH THIS MAGIC KEEPING US APART.
SHUT UP! THAT'S NOT TRUE!
YOU THINK YOU KNOW HIM, BUT WHAT I AM--THE DARK SIDE, IF YOU WILL--IS WHAT HE HIDES FROM YOU. THAT'S THE TRUTH, BABE. LOVE IT OR LEAVE IT.
YOU'RE VERY QUIET FOR THE ONLY ONE HERE WITH ANY REAL SAY IN HOW THIS COULD GO.
I'M NOT GOING TO WASTE MY BREATH ON YOU, WE'LL SAVE XANDER'S SOUL AND YOU'LL BE DUST, LIKE ALL THE REST.
OH, SO BEAUTIFUL, BUT SO IGNORANT.
I SEE WHAT THE MISTRESS SEES--I SEE THE KEY. SOON, SHE'LL HAVE SUNNYDALE, SHE'LL HAVE ALL THE MEN SHE DESIRES, HAVE ALL THE WOMEN AS HER SLAVES. AND YOU...YOU'LL BE HUNG ON A CROSS, SACRIFICIAL AND MARTYRED.
YOU'LL WATCH EVERYONE YOU LOVE DIE IN THE FLAMES OF THE HELLMOUTH...UNLESS YOU CHOOSE TO SPARE THEM.
MAYBE I'LL START WITH YOU.

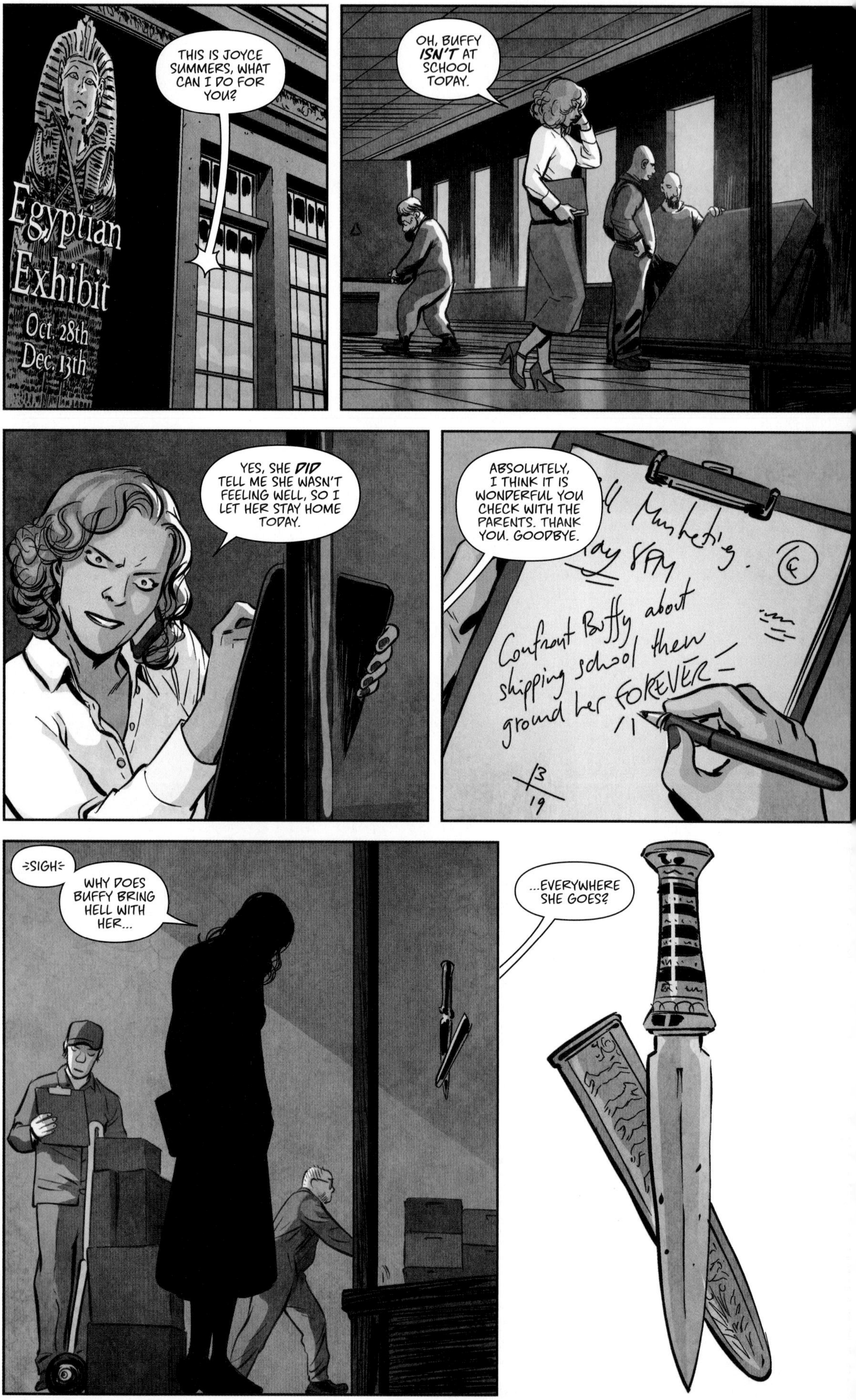
Egyptian Exhibit
Oct. 28th
Dec. 13th
THIS IS JOYCE SUMMERS, WHAT CAN I DO FOR YOU?
OH, BUFFY ISN'T AT SCHOOL TODAY.
YES, SHE DID TELL ME SHE WASN'T FEELING WELL, SO I LET HER STAY HOME TODAY.
ABSOLUTELY, I THINK IT IS WONDERFUL YOU CHECK WITH THE PARENTS. THANK YOU. GOODBYE.
Confront Buffy about skipping school then ground her FOREVER
=SIGH=
WHY DOES BUFFY BRING HELL WITH HER...
...EVERYWHERE SHE GOES?

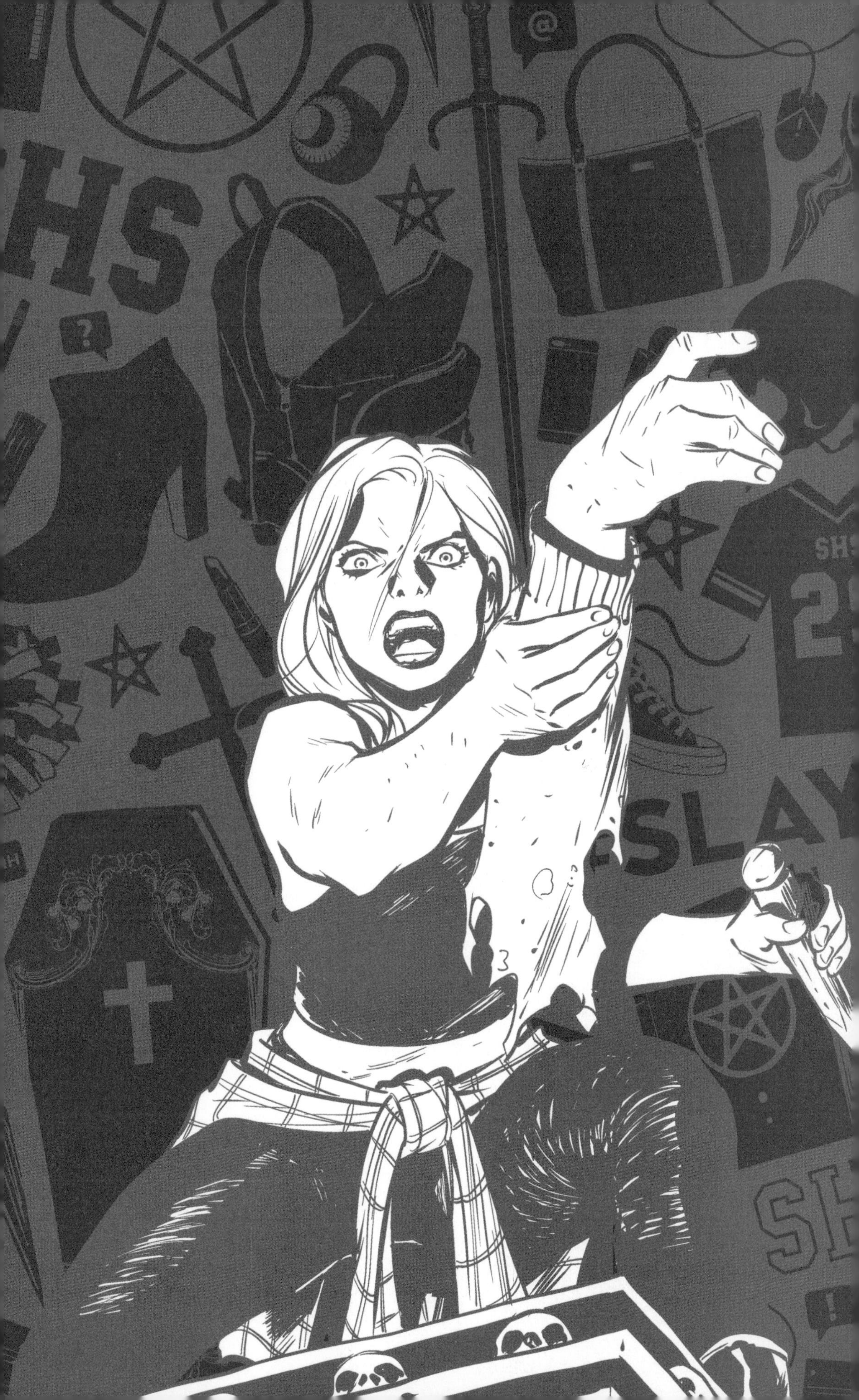
SHS
SLAY

CHAPTER SIX

Issue Six Cover by **Marc Aspinall**

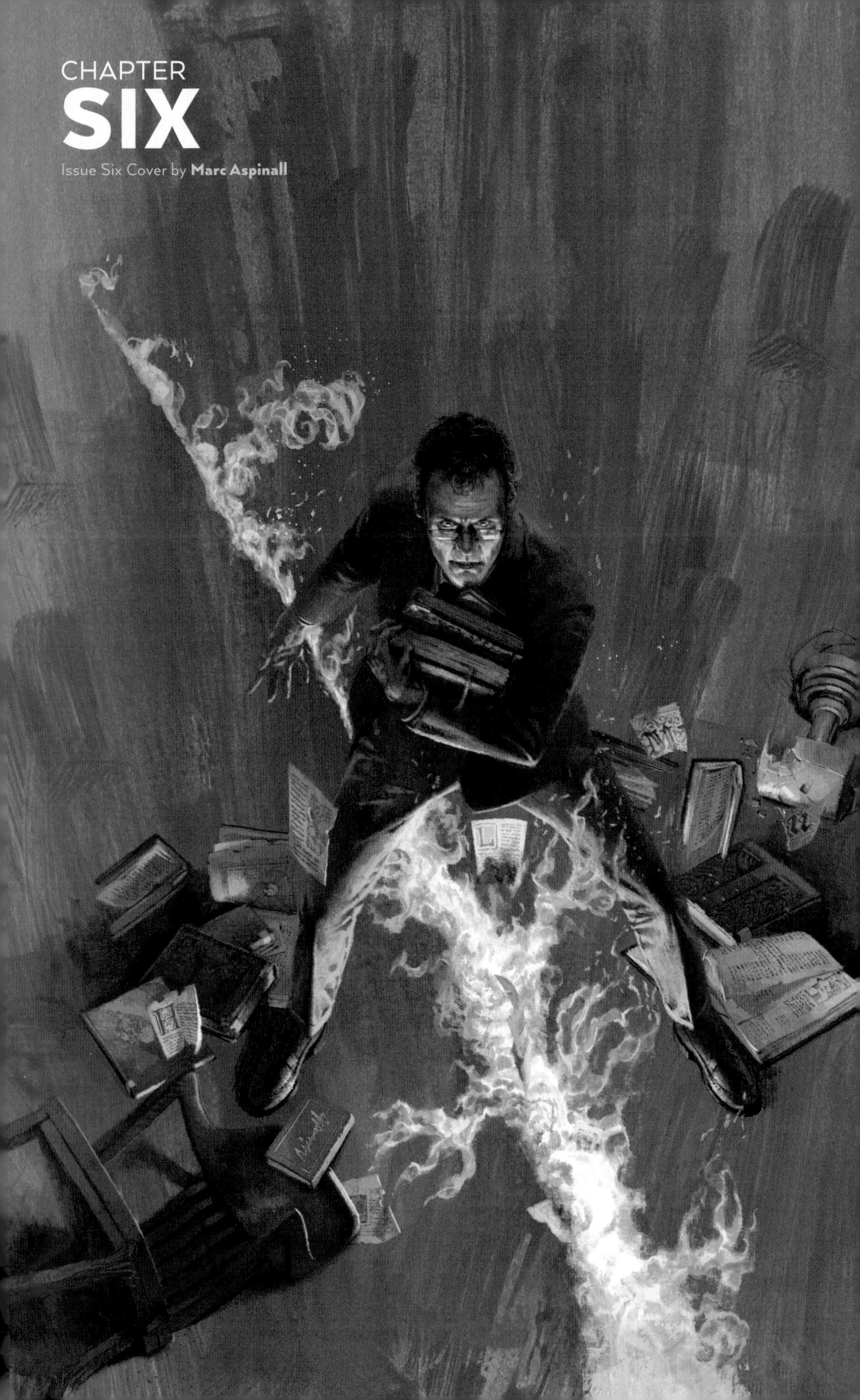

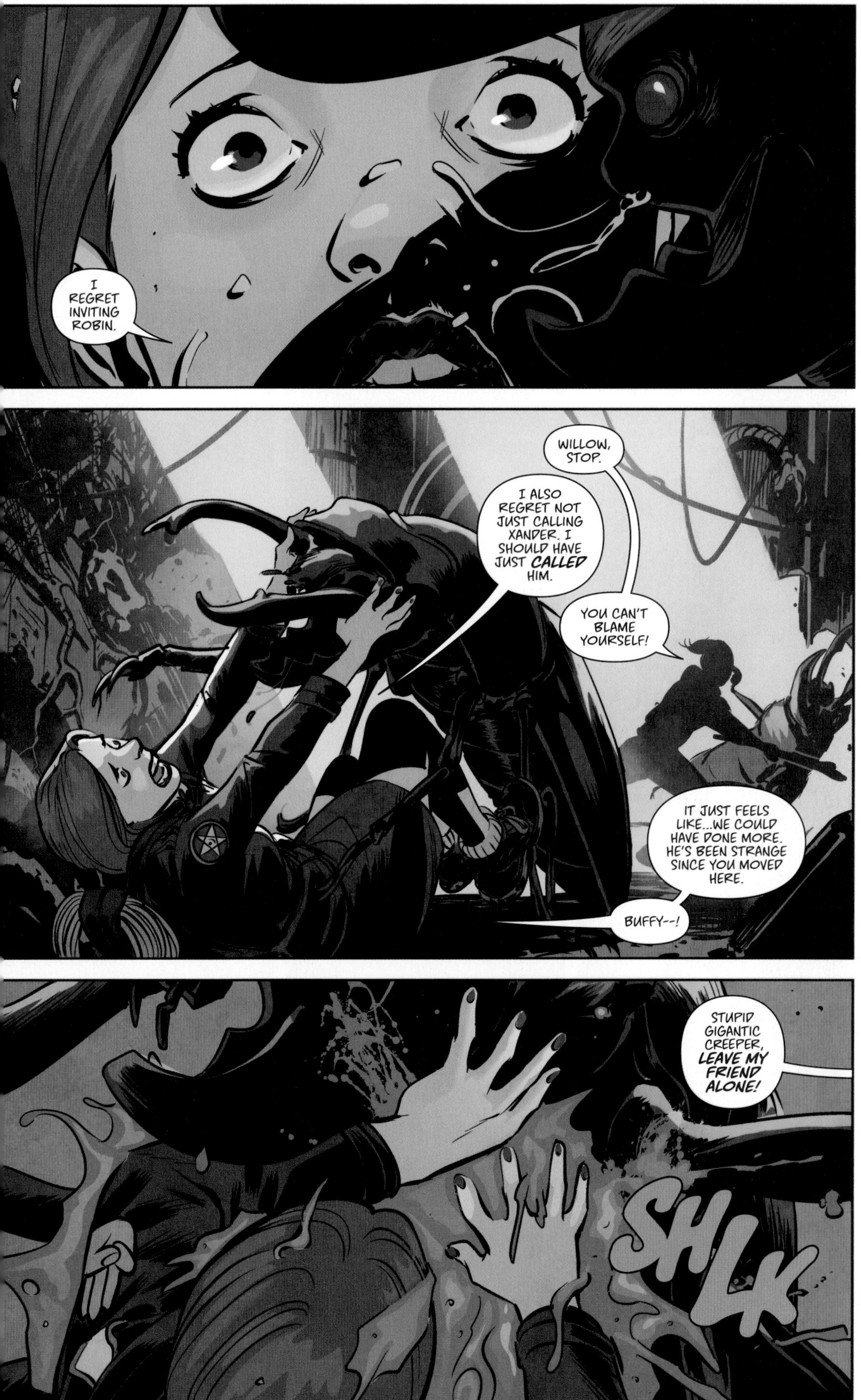
I REGRET INVITING ROBIN.
WILLOW, STOP.
I ALSO REGRET NOT JUST CALLING XANDER. I SHOULD HAVE JUST CALLED HIM.
YOU CAN'T BLAME YOURSELF!
IT JUST FEELS LIKE...WE COULD HAVE DONE MORE. HE'S BEEN STRANGE SINCE YOU MOVED HERE.
BUFFY--!
STUPID GIGANTIC CREEPER, LEAVE MY FRIEND ALONE!
SHLK

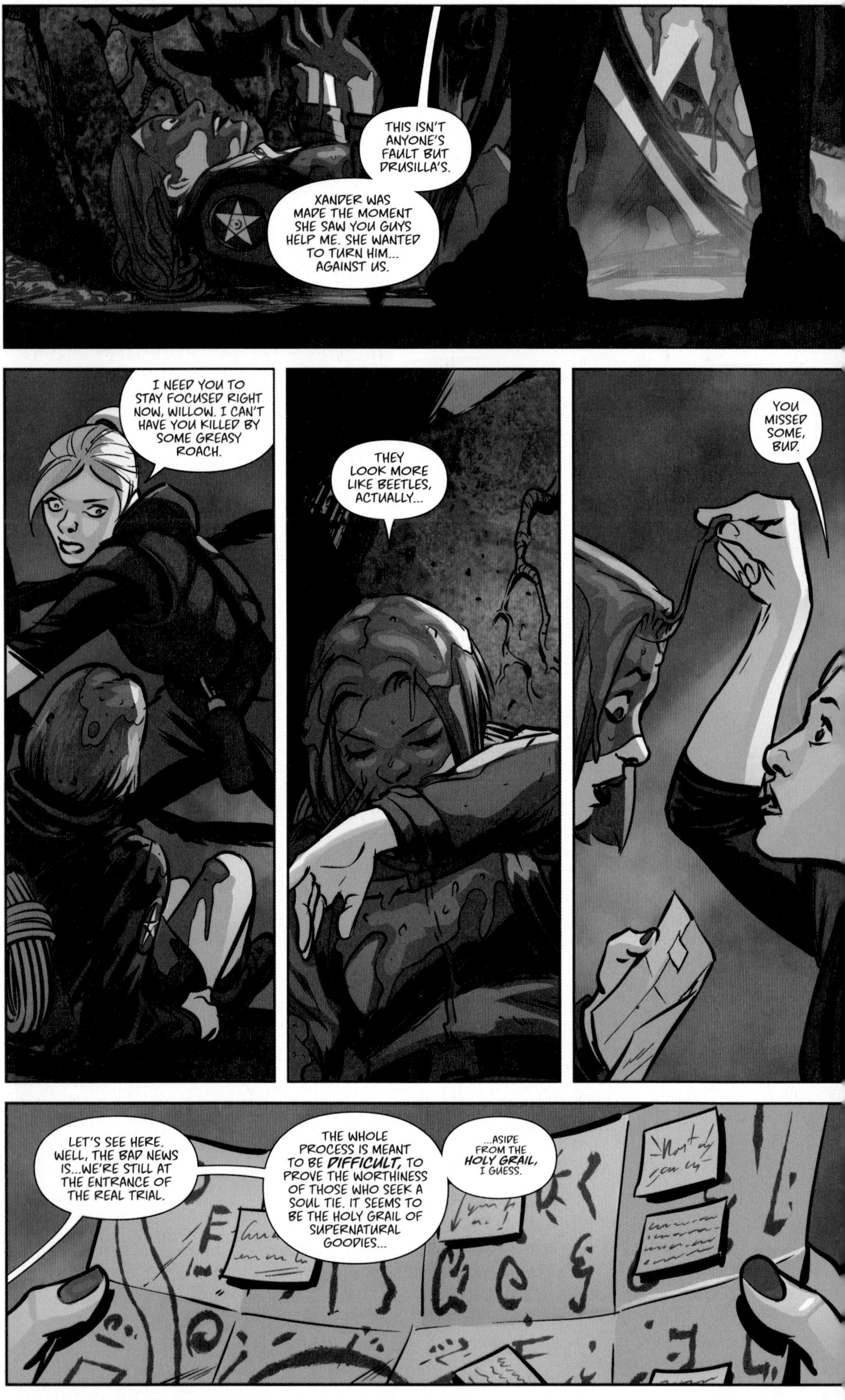
THIS ISN'T ANYONE'S FAULT BUT DRUSILLA'S.
XANDER WAS MADE THE MOMENT SHE SAW YOU GUYS HELP ME. SHE WANTED TO TURN HIM... AGAINST US.
I NEED YOU TO STAY FOCUSED RIGHT NOW, WILLOW. I CAN'T HAVE YOU KILLED BY SOME GREASY ROACH.
THEY LOOK MORE LIKE BEETLES, ACTUALLY...
YOU MISSED SOME, BUD.
LET'S SEE HERE. WELL, THE BAD NEWS IS...WE'RE STILL AT THE ENTRANCE OF THE REAL TRIAL.
THE WHOLE PROCESS IS MEANT TO BE DIFFICULT, TO PROVE THE WORTHINESS OF THOSE WHO SEEK A SOUL TIE. IT SEEMS TO BE THE HOLY GRAIL OF SUPERNATURAL GOODIES...
...ASIDE FROM THE HOLY GRAIL, I GUESS.

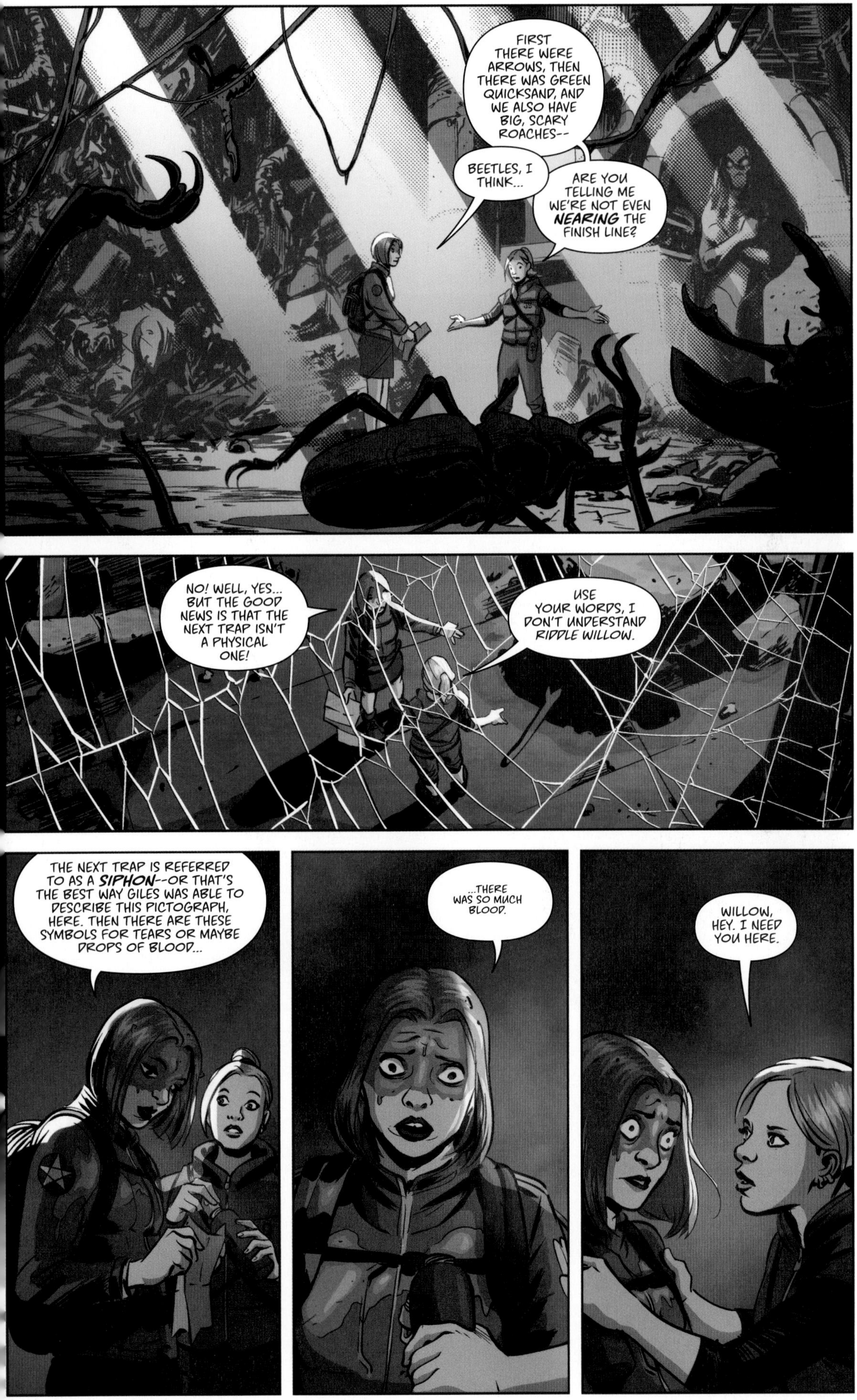
FIRST THERE WERE ARROWS, THEN THERE WAS GREEN QUICKSAND, AND WE ALSO HAVE BIG, SCARY ROACHES--
BEETLES, I THINK...
ARE YOU TELLING ME WE'RE NOT EVEN NEARING THE FINISH LINE?
NO! WELL, YES... BUT THE GOOD NEWS IS THAT THE NEXT TRAP ISN'T A PHYSICAL ONE!
USE YOUR WORDS, I DON'T UNDERSTAND RIDDLE WILLOW.
THE NEXT TRAP IS REFERRED TO AS A SIPHON--OR THAT'S THE BEST WAY GILES WAS ABLE TO DESCRIBE THIS PICTOGRAPH, HERE. THEN THERE ARE THESE SYMBOLS FOR TEARS OR MAYBE DROPS OF BLOOD...
...THERE WAS SO MUCH BLOOD.
WILLOW, HEY. I NEED YOU HERE.

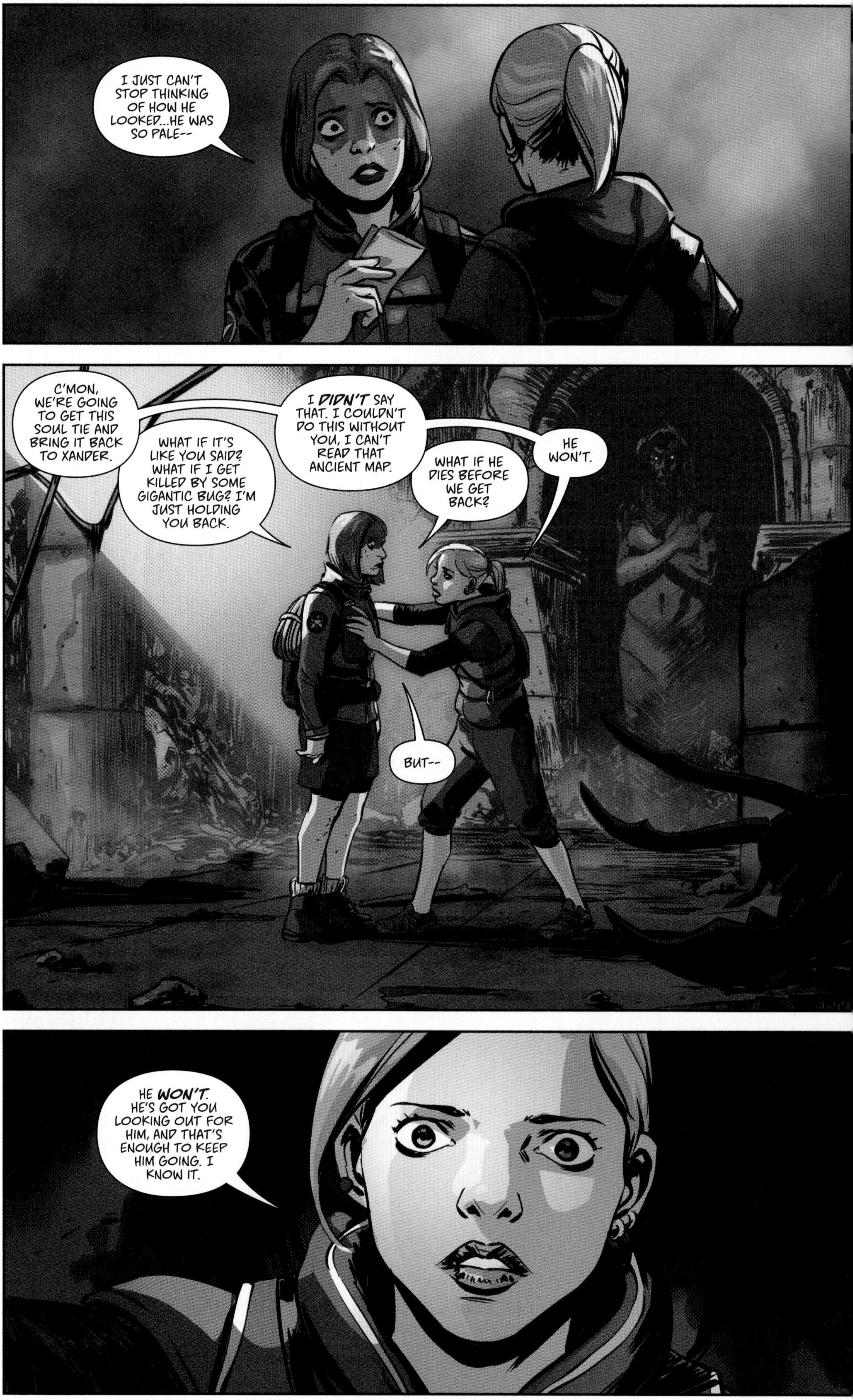
I JUST CAN'T STOP THINKING OF HOW HE LOOKED...HE WAS SO PALE--
C'MON, WE'RE GOING TO GET THIS SOUL TIE AND BRING IT BACK TO XANDER.
WHAT IF IT'S LIKE YOU SAID? WHAT IF I GET KILLED BY SOME GIGANTIC BUG? I'M JUST HOLDING YOU BACK.
I DIDN'T SAY THAT. I COULDN'T DO THIS WITHOUT YOU, I CAN'T READ THAT ANCIENT MAP.
WHAT IF HE DIES BEFORE WE GET BACK?
HE WON'T.
BUT--
HE WON'T. HE'S GOT YOU LOOKING OUT FOR HIM, AND THAT'S ENOUGH TO KEEP HIM GOING. I KNOW IT.

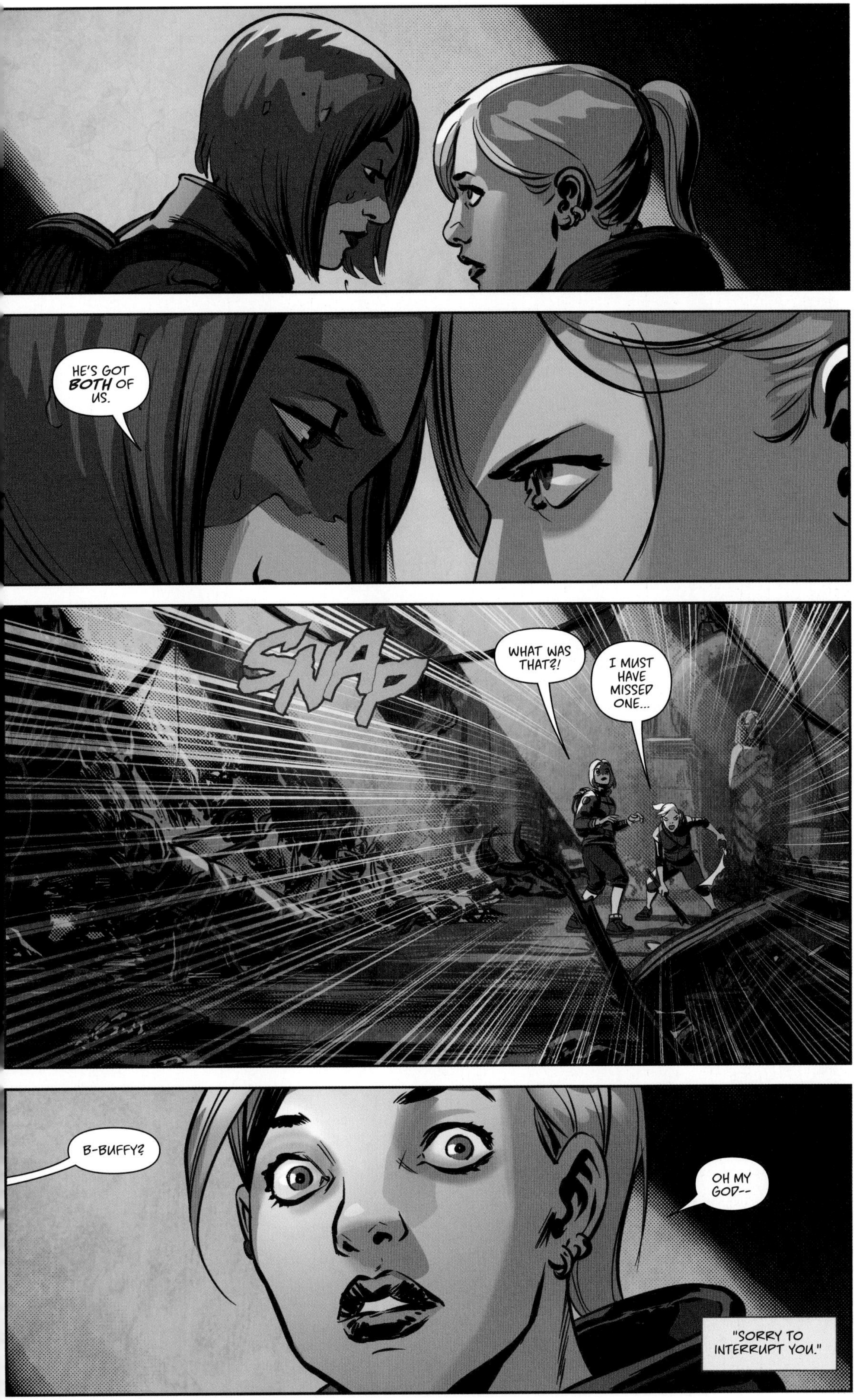
HE'S GOT BOTH OF US.
SNAP
WHAT WAS THAT?!
I MUST HAVE MISSED ONE...
B-BUFFY?
OH MY GOD--
"SORRY TO INTERRUPT YOU."

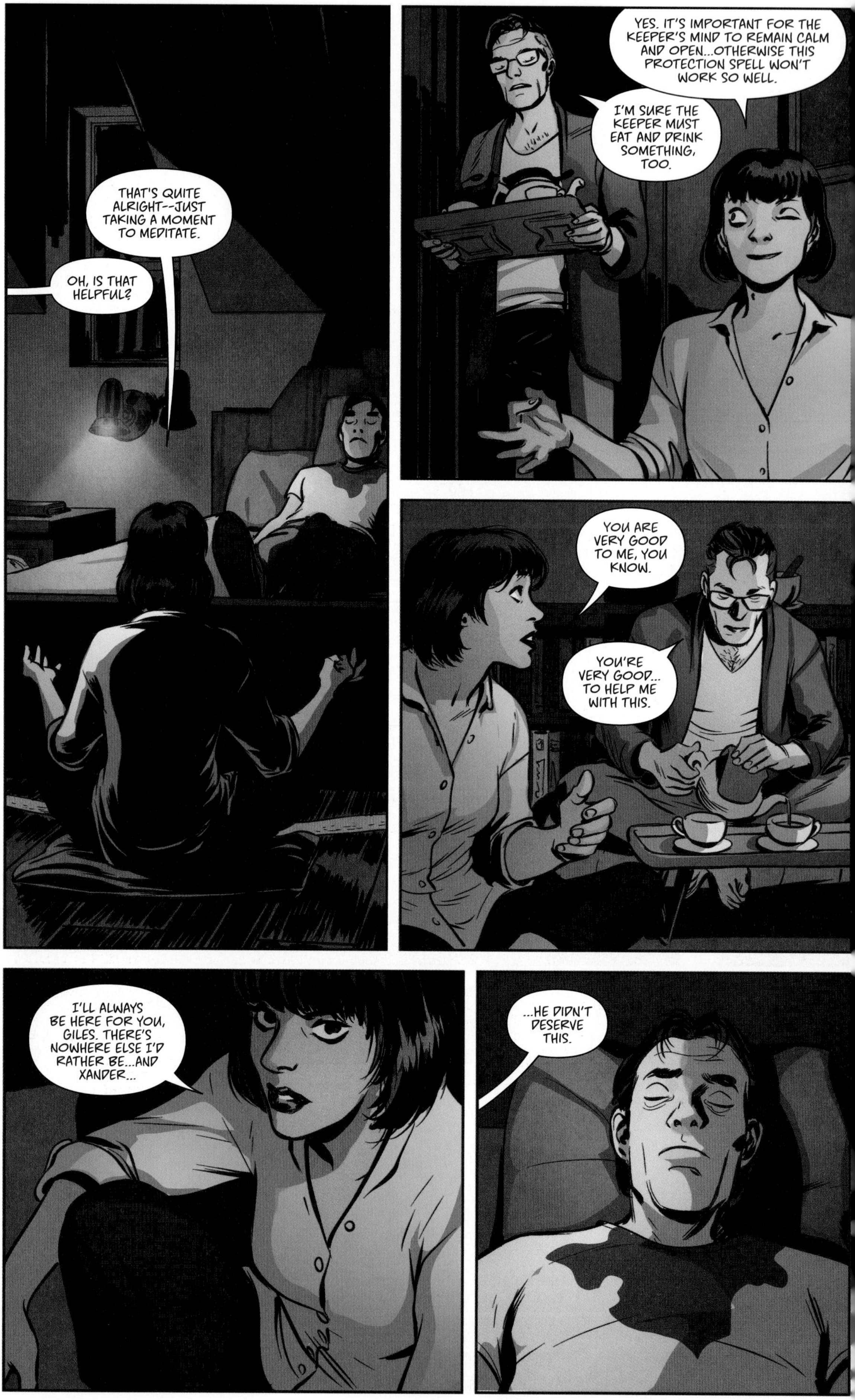
THAT'S QUITE ALRIGHT--JUST TAKING A MOMENT TO MEDITATE.
OH, IS THAT HELPFUL?
YES. IT'S IMPORTANT FOR THE KEEPER'S MIND TO REMAIN CALM AND OPEN...OTHERWISE THIS PROTECTION SPELL WON'T WORK SO WELL.
I'M SURE THE KEEPER MUST EAT AND DRINK SOMETHING, TOO.
YOU ARE VERY GOOD TO ME, YOU KNOW.
YOU'RE VERY GOOD... TO HELP ME WITH THIS.
I'LL ALWAYS BE HERE FOR YOU, GILES. THERE'S NOWHERE ELSE I'D RATHER BE...AND XANDER...
...HE DIDN'T DESERVE THIS.

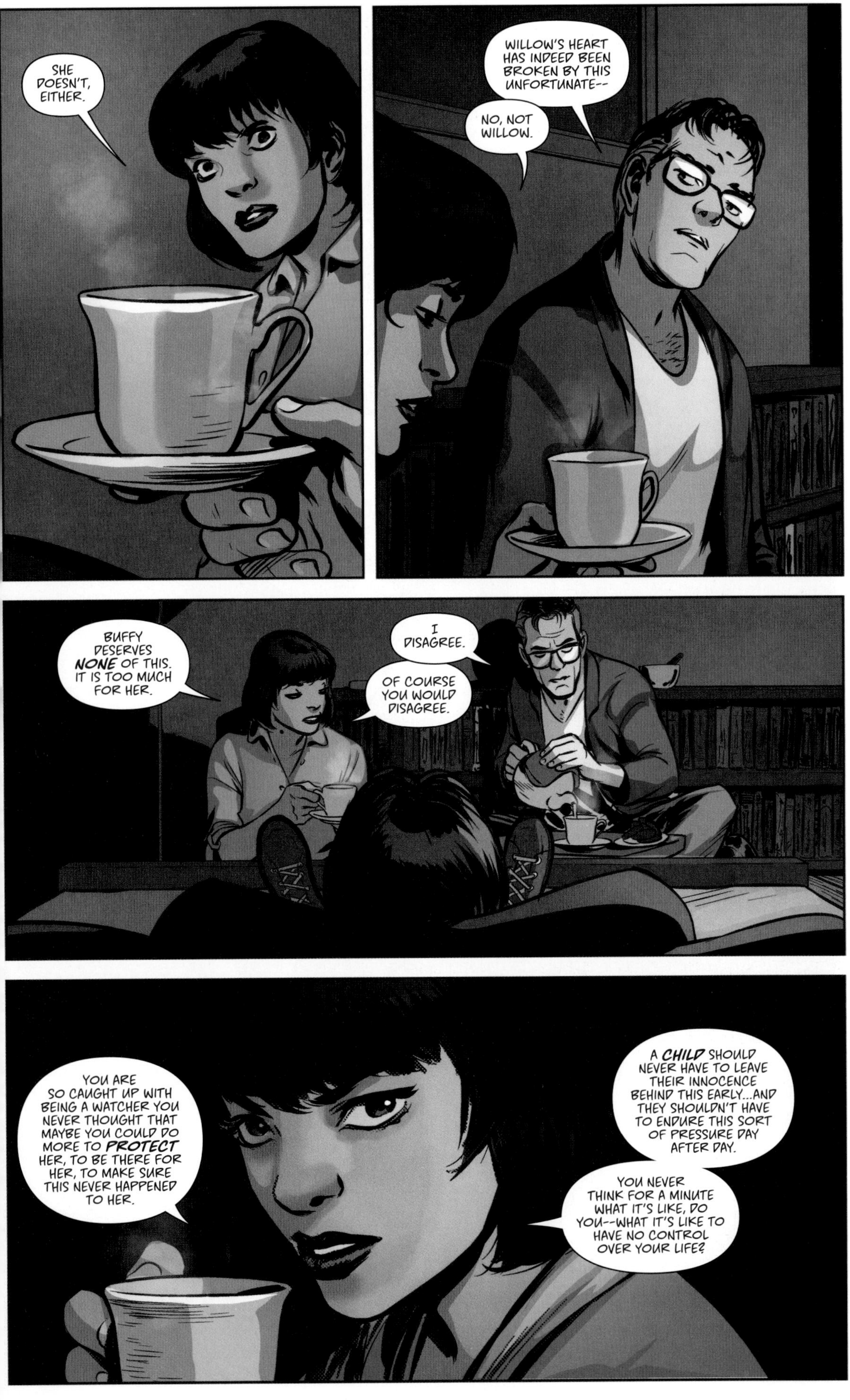
SHE DOESN'T, EITHER.
WILLOW'S HEART HAS INDEED BEEN BROKEN BY THIS UNFORTUNATE--
NO, NOT WILLOW.
BUFFY DESERVES NONE OF THIS. IT IS TOO MUCH FOR HER.
I DISAGREE.
OF COURSE YOU WOULD DISAGREE.
YOU ARE SO CAUGHT UP WITH BEING A WATCHER YOU NEVER THOUGHT THAT MAYBE YOU COULD DO MORE TO PROTECT HER, TO BE THERE FOR HER, TO MAKE SURE THIS NEVER HAPPENED TO HER.
A CHILD SHOULD NEVER HAVE TO LEAVE THEIR INNOCENCE BEHIND THIS EARLY...AND THEY SHOULDN'T HAVE TO ENDURE THIS SORT OF PRESSURE DAY AFTER DAY.
YOU NEVER THINK FOR A MINUTE WHAT IT'S LIKE, DO YOU--WHAT IT'S LIKE TO HAVE NO CONTROL OVER YOUR LIFE?

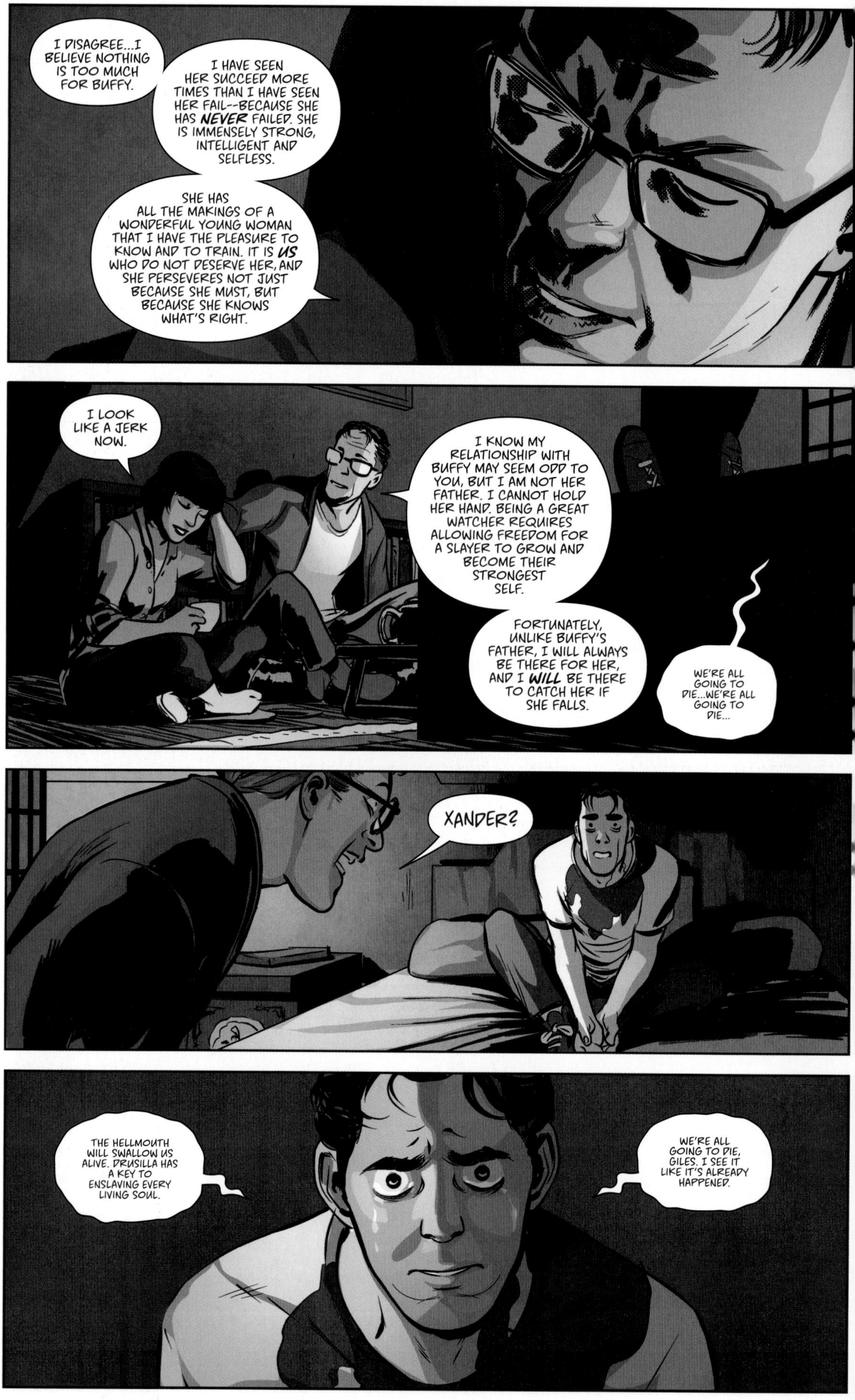
I DISAGREE...I BELIEVE NOTHING IS TOO MUCH FOR BUFFY.
I HAVE SEEN HER SUCCEED MORE TIMES THAN I HAVE SEEN HER FAIL--BECAUSE SHE HAS NEVER FAILED. SHE IS IMMENSELY STRONG, INTELLIGENT AND SELFLESS.
SHE HAS ALL THE MAKINGS OF A WONDERFUL YOUNG WOMAN THAT I HAVE THE PLEASURE TO KNOW AND TO TRAIN. IT IS US WHO DO NOT DESERVE HER, AND SHE PERSEVERES NOT JUST BECAUSE SHE MUST, BUT BECAUSE SHE KNOWS WHAT'S RIGHT.
I LOOK LIKE A JERK NOW.
I KNOW MY RELATIONSHIP WITH BUFFY MAY SEEM ODD TO YOU, BUT I AM NOT HER FATHER. I CANNOT HOLD HER HAND. BEING A GREAT WATCHER REQUIRES ALLOWING FREEDOM FOR A SLAYER TO GROW AND BECOME THEIR STRONGEST SELF.
FORTUNATELY, UNLIKE BUFFY'S FATHER, I WILL ALWAYS BE THERE FOR HER, AND I WILL BE THERE TO CATCH HER IF SHE FALLS.
WE'RE ALL GOING TO DIE...WE'RE ALL GOING TO DIE...
XANDER?
THE HELLMOUTH WILL SWALLOW US ALIVE. DRUSILLA HAS A KEY TO ENSLAVING EVERY LIVING SOUL.
WE'RE ALL GOING TO DIE, GILES. I SEE IT LIKE IT'S ALREADY HAPPENED.

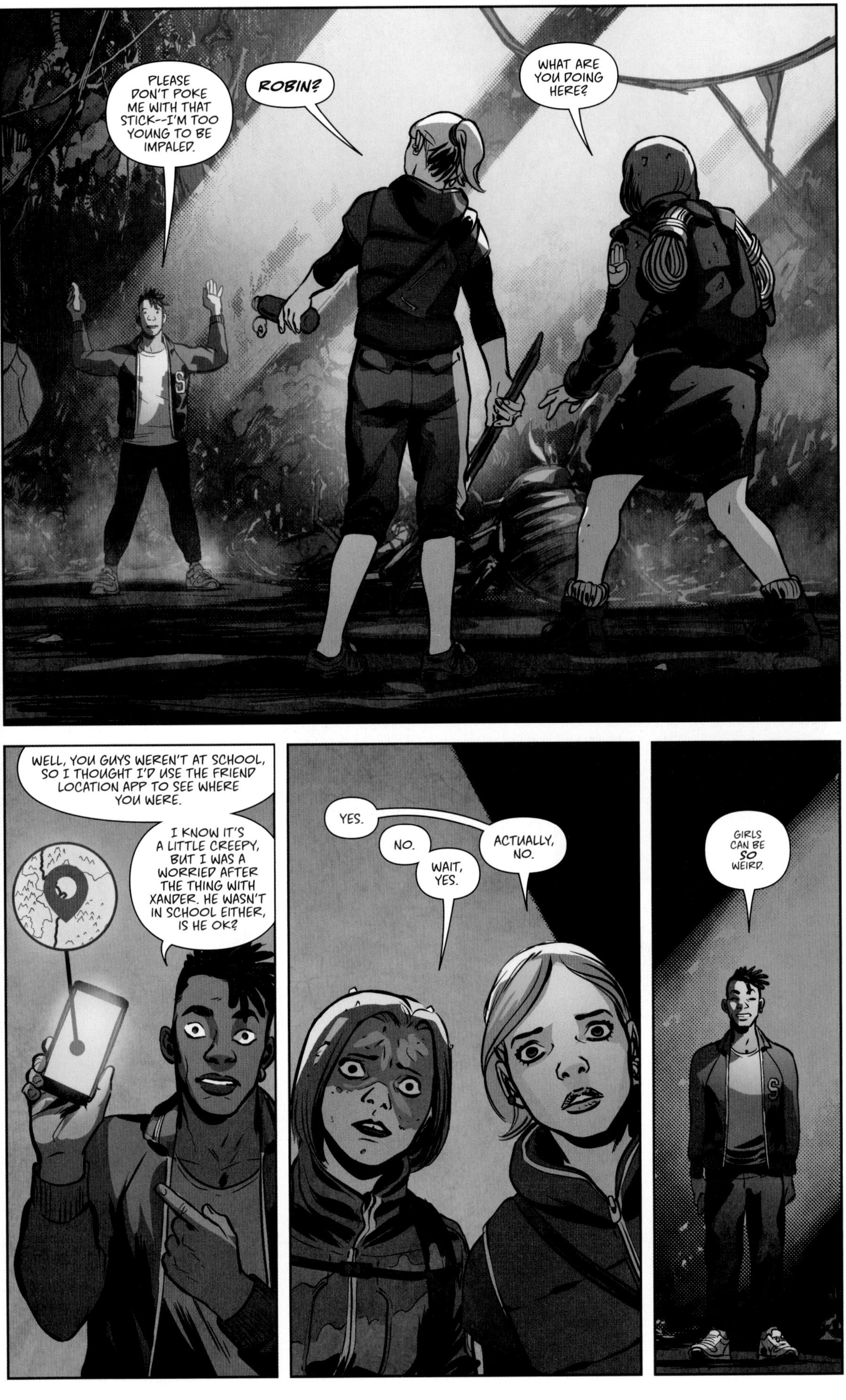
PLEASE DON'T POKE ME WITH THAT STICK--I'M TOO YOUNG TO BE IMPALED.
ROBIN?
WHAT ARE YOU DOING HERE?
WELL, YOU GUYS WEREN'T AT SCHOOL, SO I THOUGHT I'D USE THE FRIEND LOCATION APP TO SEE WHERE YOU WERE.
I KNOW IT'S A LITTLE CREEPY, BUT I WAS A WORRIED AFTER THE THING WITH XANDER. HE WASN'T IN SCHOOL EITHER, IS HE OK?
YES.
NO.
WAIT, YES.
ACTUALLY, NO.
GIRLS CAN BE SO WEIRD.

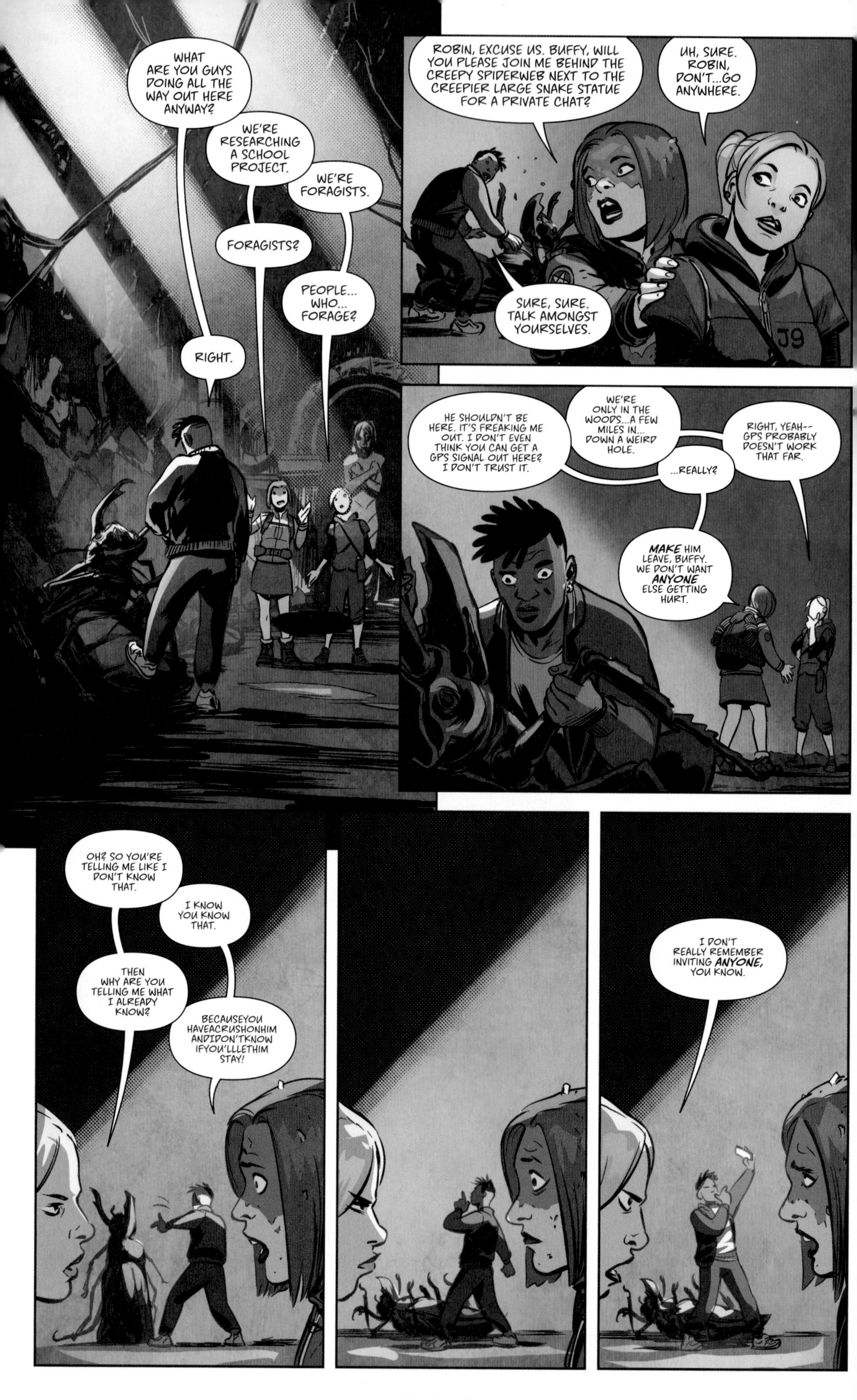

WHAT ARE YOU GUYS DOING ALL THE WAY OUT HERE ANYWAY?
WE'RE RESEARCHING A SCHOOL PROJECT.
WE'RE FORAGISTS.
FORAGISTS?
PEOPLE... WHO... FORAGE?
RIGHT.
ROBIN, EXCUSE US. BUFFY, WILL YOU PLEASE JOIN ME BEHIND THE CREEPY SPIDERWEB NEXT TO THE CREEPIER LARGE SNAKE STATUE FOR A PRIVATE CHAT?
UH, SURE. ROBIN, DON'T...GO ANYWHERE.
SURE, SURE. TALK AMONGST YOURSELVES.
J9
HE SHOULDN'T BE HERE. IT'S FREAKING ME OUT. I DON'T EVEN THINK YOU CAN GET A GPS SIGNAL OUT HERE? I DON'T TRUST IT.
WE'RE ONLY IN THE WOODS...A FEW MILES IN... DOWN A WEIRD HOLE.
...REALLY?
RIGHT, YEAH-- GPS PROBABLY DOESN'T WORK THAT FAR.
MAKE HIM LEAVE, BUFFY. WE DON'T WANT ANYONE ELSE GETTING HURT.
OH? SO YOU'RE TELLING ME LIKE I DON'T KNOW THAT.
I KNOW YOU KNOW THAT.
THEN WHY ARE YOU TELLING ME WHAT I ALREADY KNOW?
BECAUSEYOU HAVEACRUSHONHIM ANDIDON'TKNOW IFYOU'LLLETHIM STAY!
I DON'T REALLY REMEMBER INVITING ANYONE, YOU KNOW.

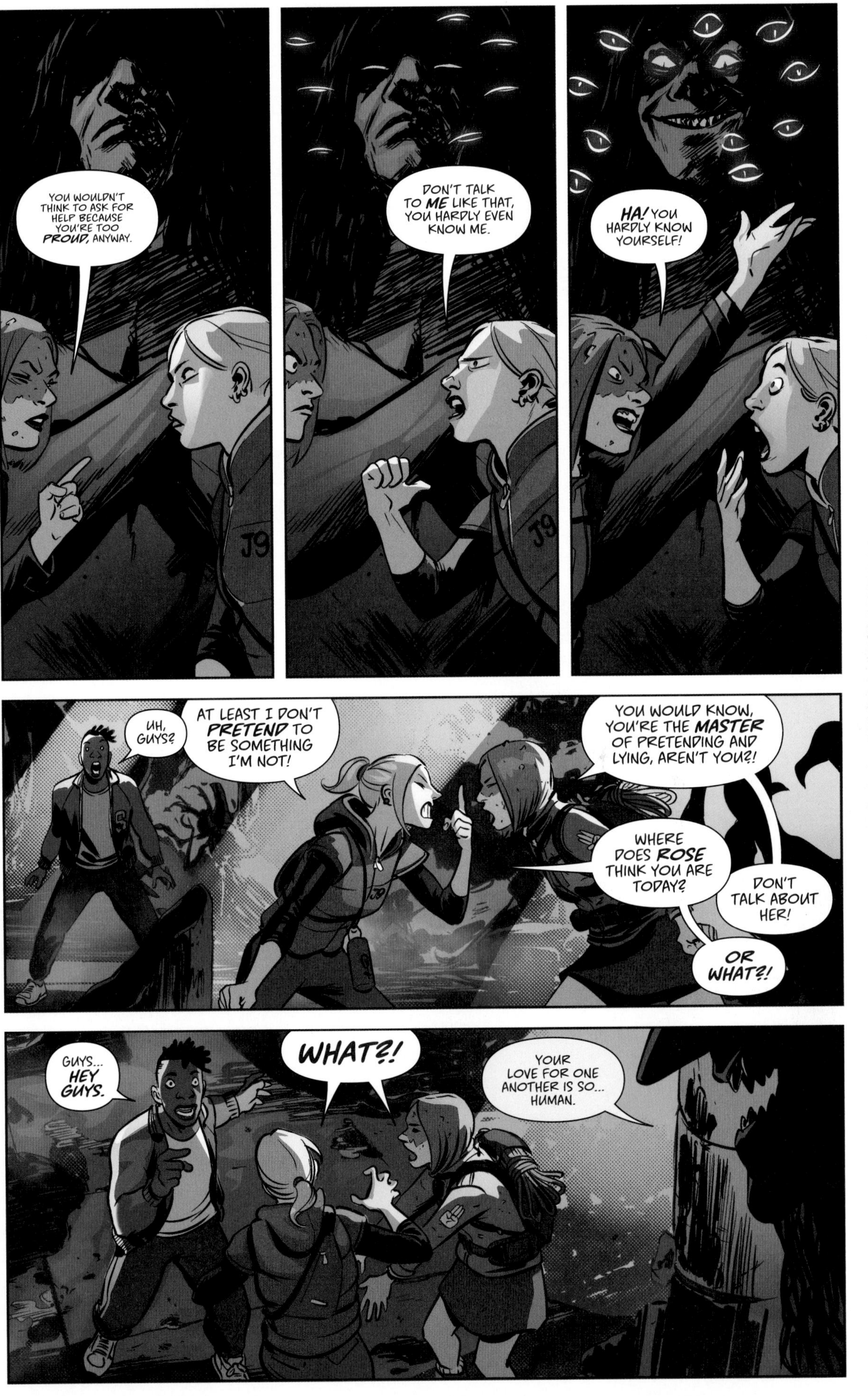
YOU WOULDN'T THINK TO ASK FOR HELP BECAUSE YOU'RE TOO PROUD, ANYWAY.
DON'T TALK TO ME LIKE THAT, YOU HARDLY EVEN KNOW ME.
HA! YOU HARDLY KNOW YOURSELF!
UH, GUYS?
AT LEAST I DON'T PRETEND TO BE SOMETHING I'M NOT!
YOU WOULD KNOW, YOU'RE THE MASTER OF PRETENDING AND LYING, AREN'T YOU?!
WHERE DOES ROSE THINK YOU ARE TODAY?
DON'T TALK ABOUT HER!
OR WHAT?!
GUYS... HEY GUYS.
WHAT?!
YOUR LOVE FOR ONE ANOTHER IS SO... HUMAN.

AND LOVE IS EVER SO MIRED IN RESENTMENT, RESPECT, RAGE...A REAL PLEASURE TO WITNESS. ONLY MEN DARE TO VENTURE THROUGH THESE CAVES...AND THEY CAN BE SO DULL, SO SIMPLE.
BUT YOU TWO ARE SO... COMPLICATED!

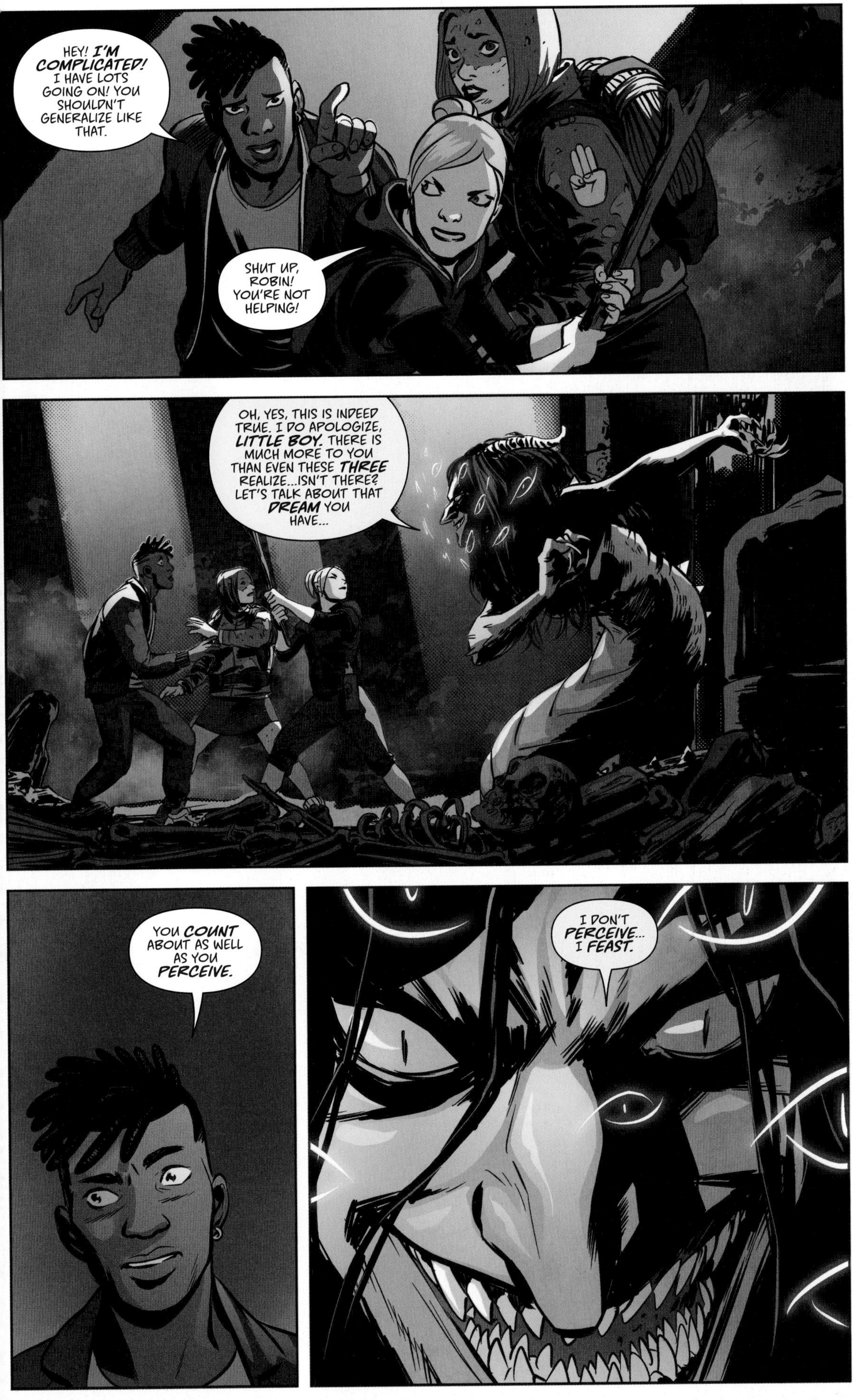
HEY! I'M COMPLICATED! I HAVE LOTS GOING ON! YOU SHOULDN'T GENERALIZE LIKE THAT.
SHUT UP, ROBIN! YOU'RE NOT HELPING!
OH, YES, THIS IS INDEED TRUE. I DO APOLOGIZE, LITTLE BOY. THERE IS MUCH MORE TO YOU THAN EVEN THESE THREE REALIZE...ISN'T THERE? LET'S TALK ABOUT THAT DREAM YOU HAVE...
YOU COUNT ABOUT AS WELL AS YOU PERCEIVE.
I DON'T PERCEIVE... I FEAST.

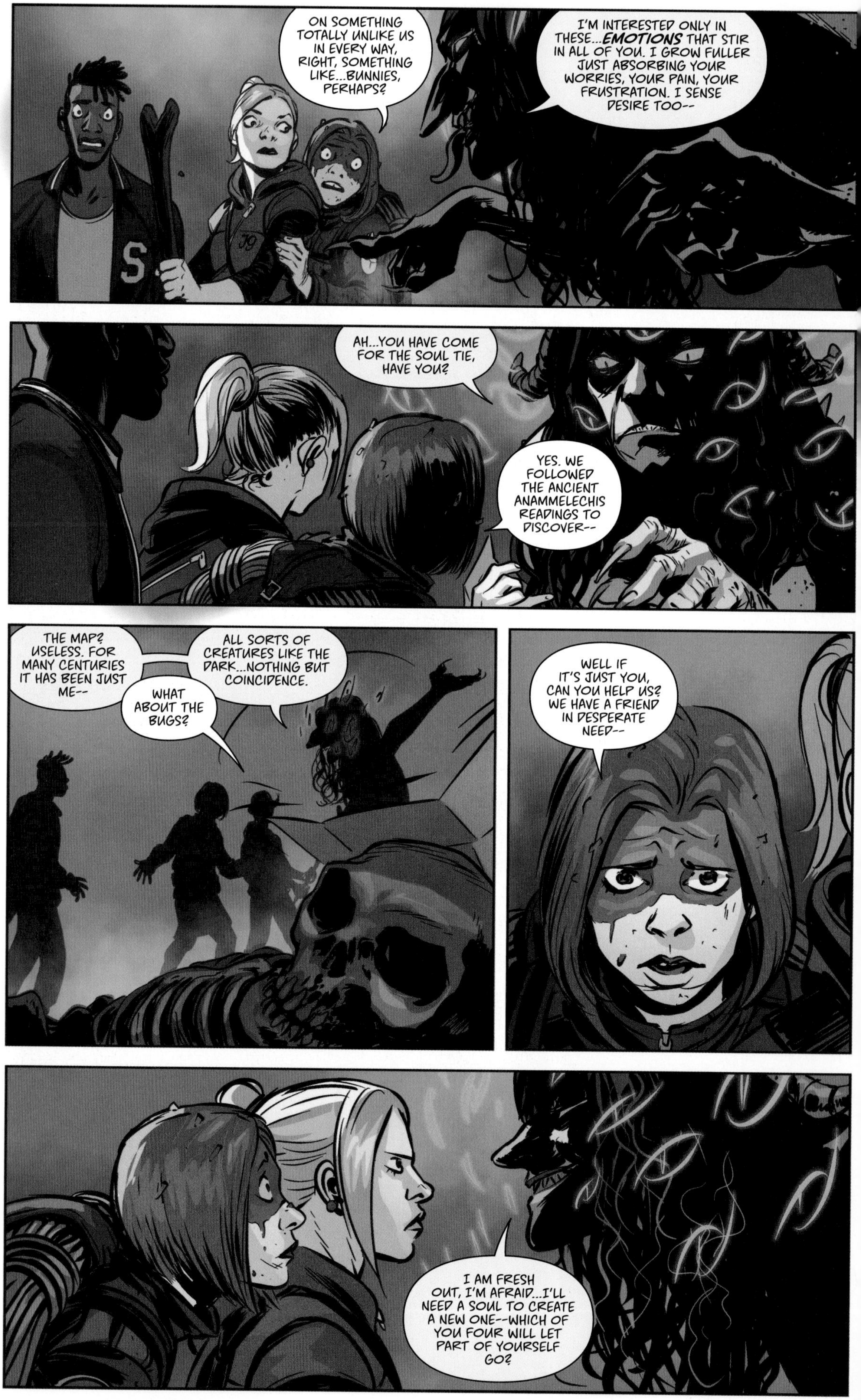
ON SOMETHING TOTALLY UNLIKE US IN EVERY WAY, RIGHT, SOMETHING LIKE...BUNNIES, PERHAPS?
I'M INTERESTED ONLY IN THESE...EMOTIONS THAT STIR IN ALL OF YOU. I GROW FULLER JUST ABSORBING YOUR WORRIES, YOUR PAIN, YOUR FRUSTRATION. I SENSE DESIRE TOO--
AH...YOU HAVE COME FOR THE SOUL TIE, HAVE YOU?
YES. WE FOLLOWED THE ANCIENT ANAMMELECHIS READINGS TO DISCOVER--
THE MAP? USELESS. FOR MANY CENTURIES IT HAS BEEN JUST ME--
WHAT ABOUT THE BUGS?
ALL SORTS OF CREATURES LIKE THE DARK...NOTHING BUT COINCIDENCE.
WELL IF IT'S JUST YOU, CAN YOU HELP US? WE HAVE A FRIEND IN DESPERATE NEED--
I AM FRESH OUT, I'M AFRAID...I'LL NEED A SOUL TO CREATE A NEW ONE--WHICH OF YOU FOUR WILL LET PART OF YOURSELF GO?

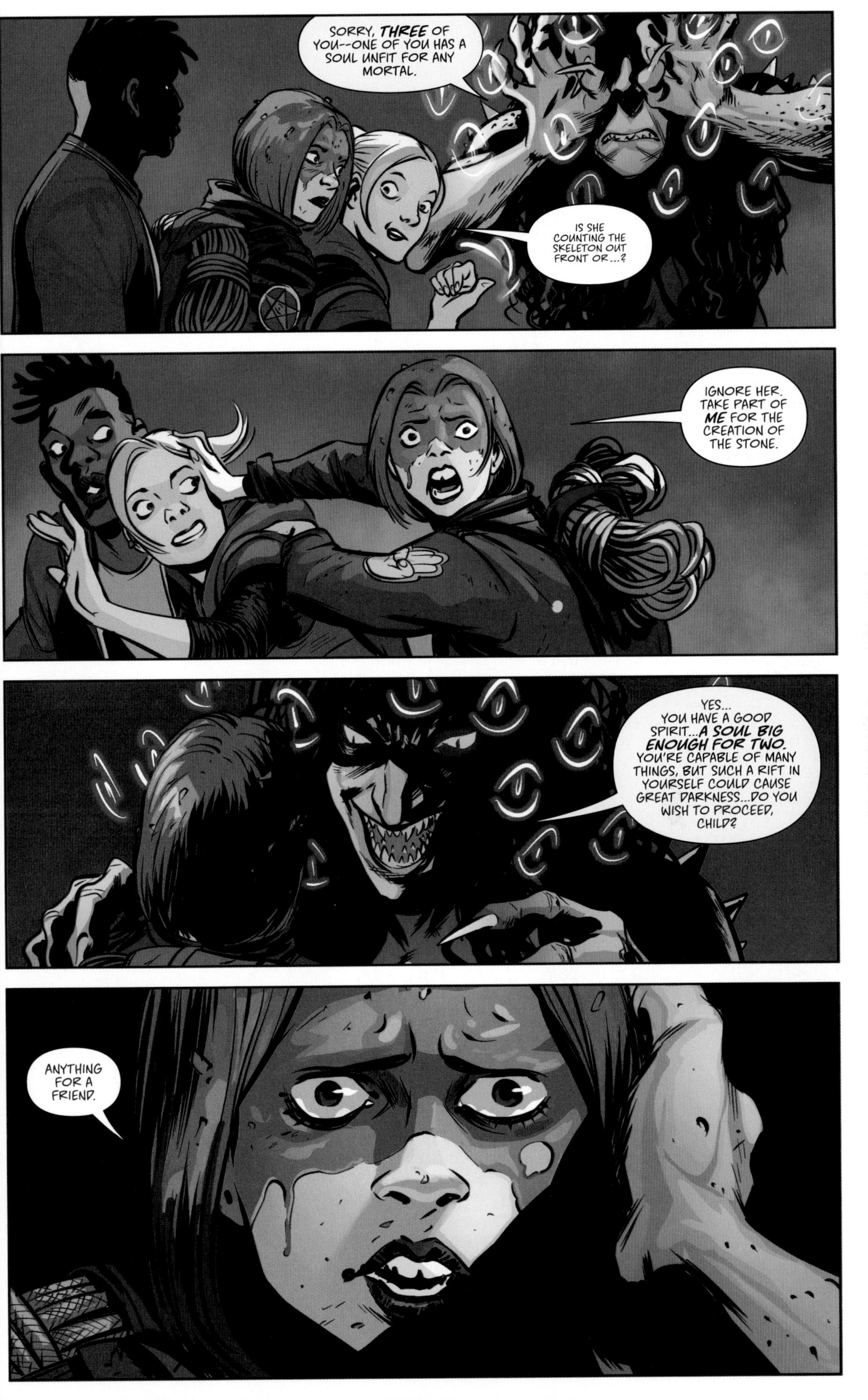
SORRY, THREE OF YOU--ONE OF YOU HAS A SOUL UNFIT FOR ANY MORTAL.
IS SHE COUNTING THE SKELETON OUT FRONT OR...?
IGNORE HER. TAKE PART OF ME FOR THE CREATION OF THE STONE.
YES... YOU HAVE A GOOD SPIRIT...A SOUL BIG ENOUGH FOR TWO. YOU'RE CAPABLE OF MANY THINGS, BUT SUCH A RIFT IN YOURSELF COULD CAUSE GREAT DARKNESS...DO YOU WISH TO PROCEED, CHILD?
ANYTHING FOR A FRIEND.

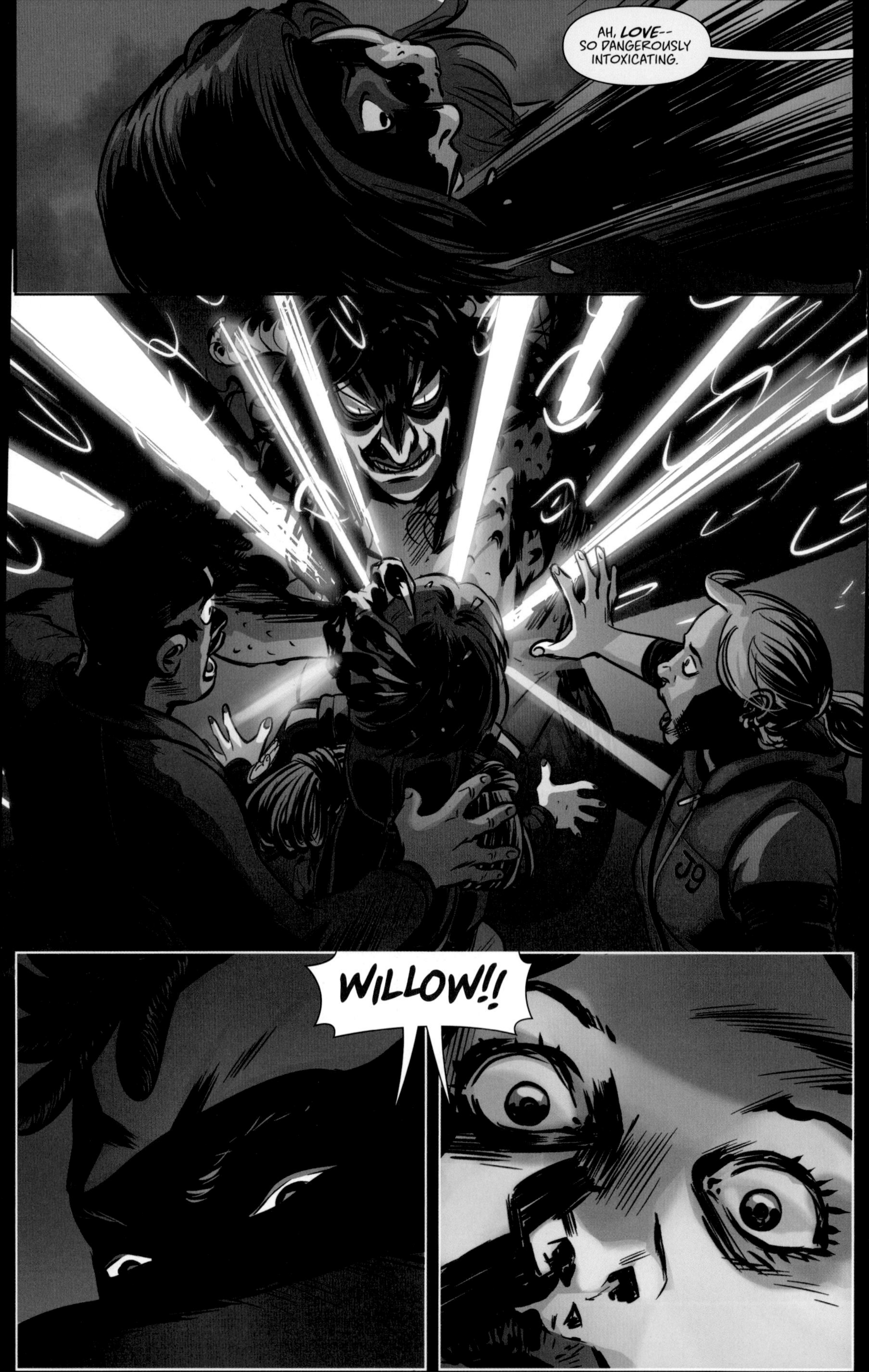
AH, LOVE--
SO DANGEROUSLY
INTOXICATING.
J9
WILLOW!!

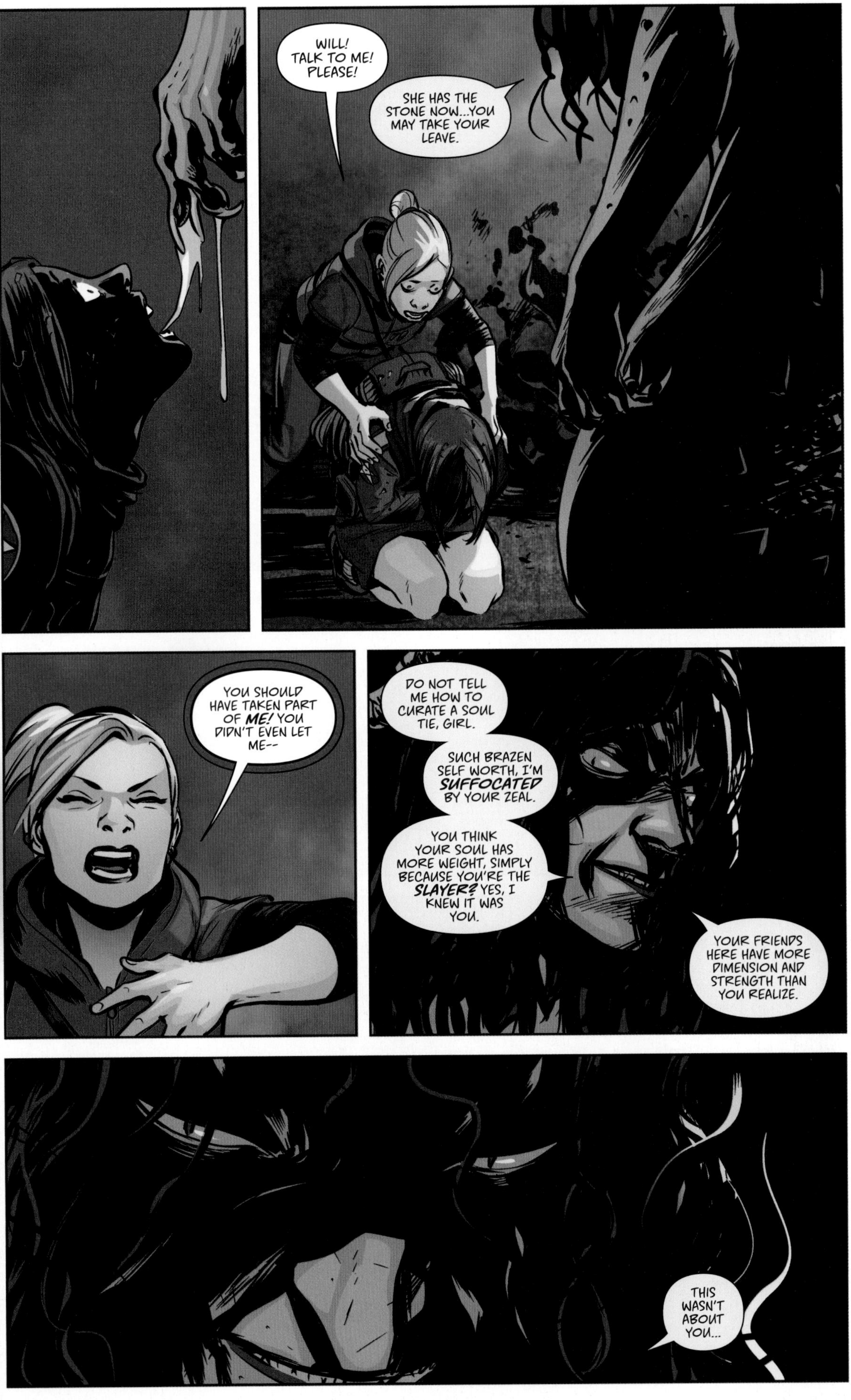
WILL! TALK TO ME! PLEASE!
SHE HAS THE STONE NOW...YOU MAY TAKE YOUR LEAVE.
YOU SHOULD HAVE TAKEN PART OF ME! YOU DIDN'T EVEN LET ME--
DO NOT TELL ME HOW TO CURATE A SOUL TIE, GIRL.
SUCH BRAZEN SELF WORTH, I'M SUFFOCATED BY YOUR ZEAL.
YOU THINK YOUR SOUL HAS MORE WEIGHT, SIMPLY BECAUSE YOU'RE THE SLAYER? YES, I KNEW IT WAS YOU.
YOUR FRIENDS HERE HAVE MORE DIMENSION AND STRENGTH THAN YOU REALIZE.
THIS WASN'T ABOUT YOU...

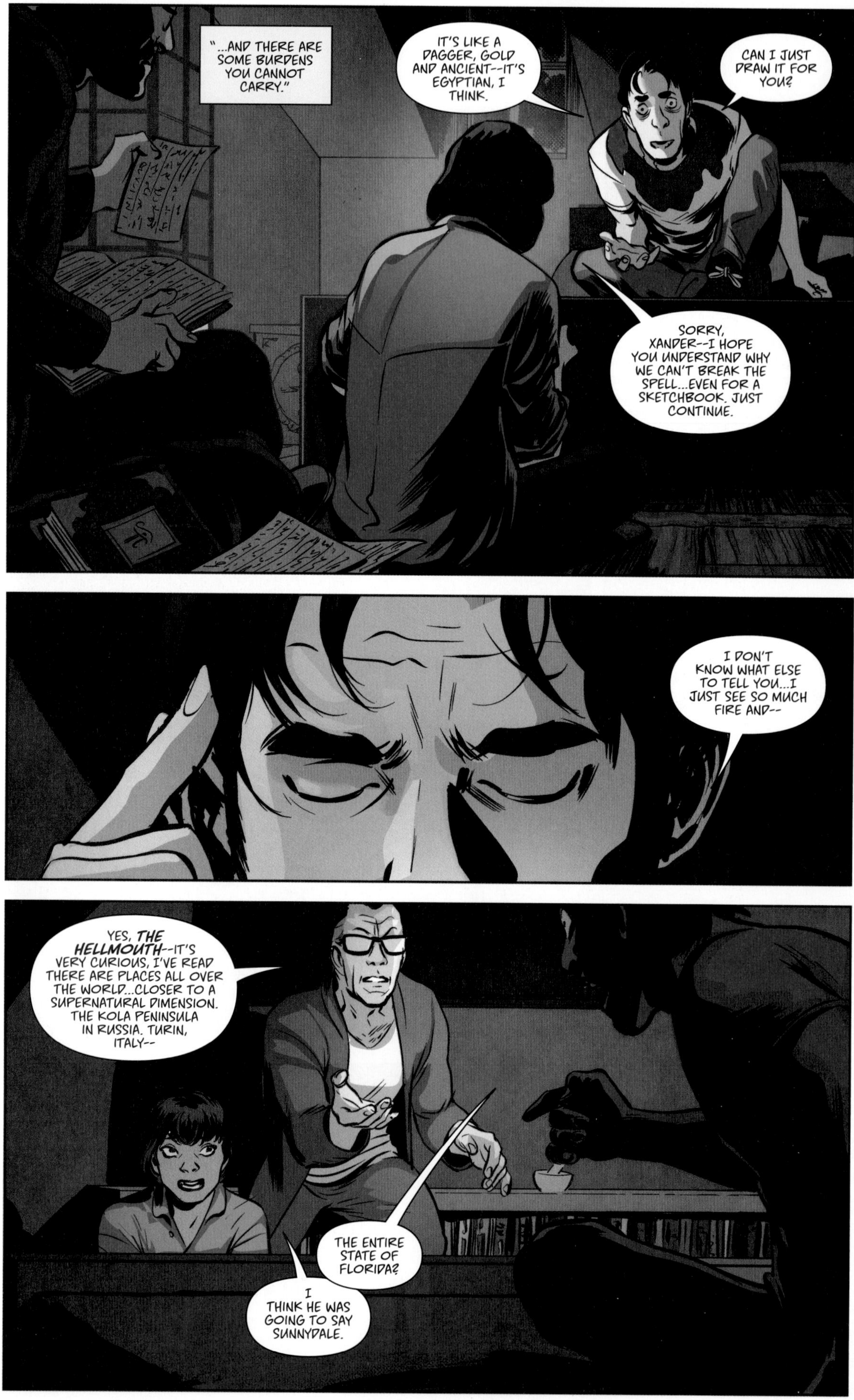
"...AND THERE ARE SOME BURDENS YOU CANNOT CARRY."
IT'S LIKE A DAGGER, GOLD AND ANCIENT--IT'S EGYPTIAN, I THINK.
CAN I JUST DRAW IT FOR YOU?
SORRY, XANDER--I HOPE YOU UNDERSTAND WHY WE CAN'T BREAK THE SPELL...EVEN FOR A SKETCHBOOK. JUST CONTINUE.
I DON'T KNOW WHAT ELSE TO TELL YOU...I JUST SEE SO MUCH FIRE AND--
YES, THE HELLMOUTH--IT'S VERY CURIOUS, I'VE READ THERE ARE PLACES ALL OVER THE WORLD...CLOSER TO A SUPERNATURAL DIMENSION. THE KOLA PENINSULA IN RUSSIA. TURIN, ITALY--
THE ENTIRE STATE OF FLORIDA?
I THINK HE WAS GOING TO SAY SUNNYDALE.

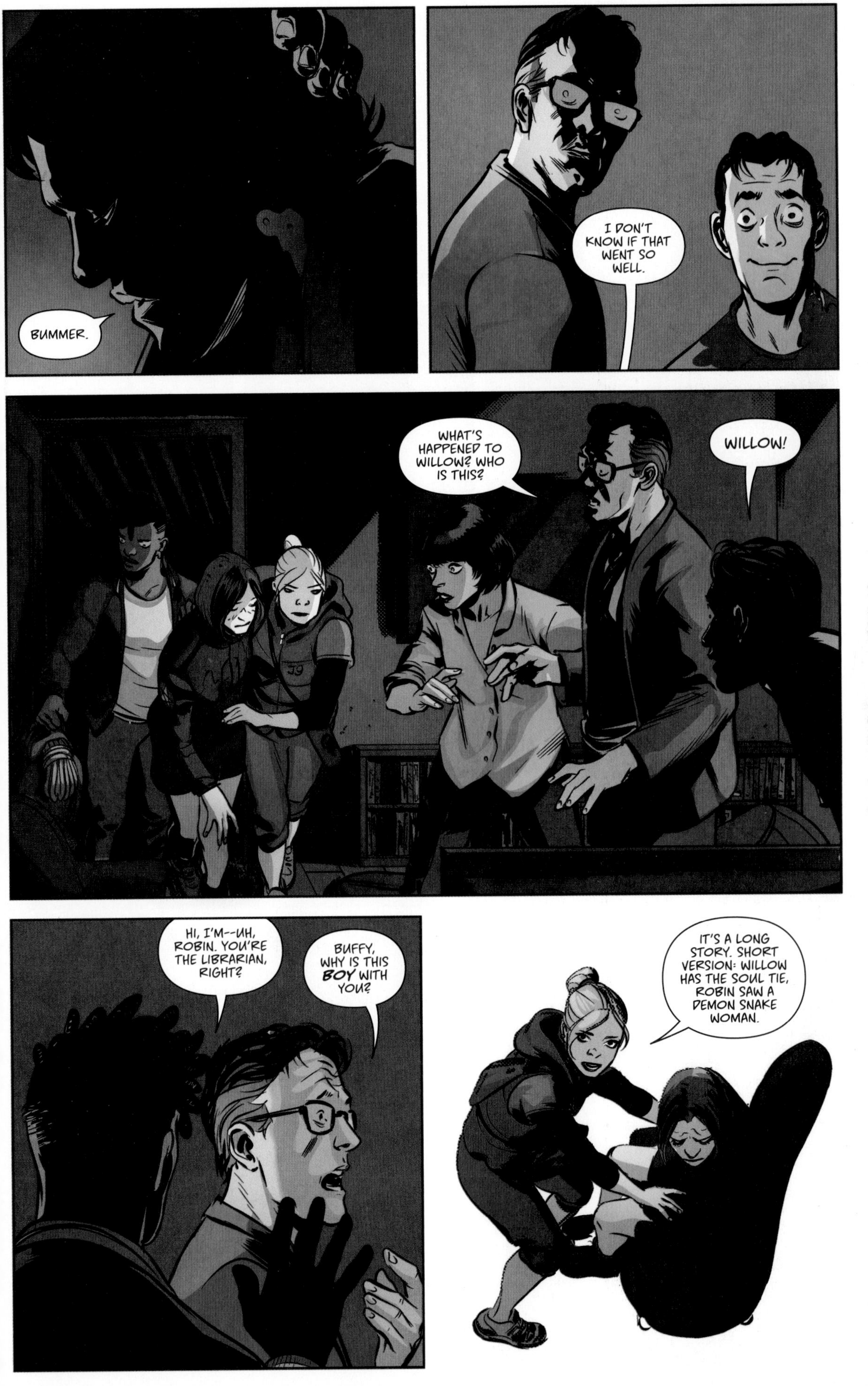
BUMMER.
I DON'T KNOW IF THAT WENT SO WELL.
WHAT'S HAPPENED TO WILLOW? WHO IS THIS?
WILLOW!
HI, I'M--UH, ROBIN. YOU'RE THE LIBRARIAN, RIGHT?
BUFFY, WHY IS THIS BOY WITH YOU?
IT'S A LONG STORY. SHORT VERSION: WILLOW HAS THE SOUL TIE, ROBIN SAW A DEMON SNAKE WOMAN.

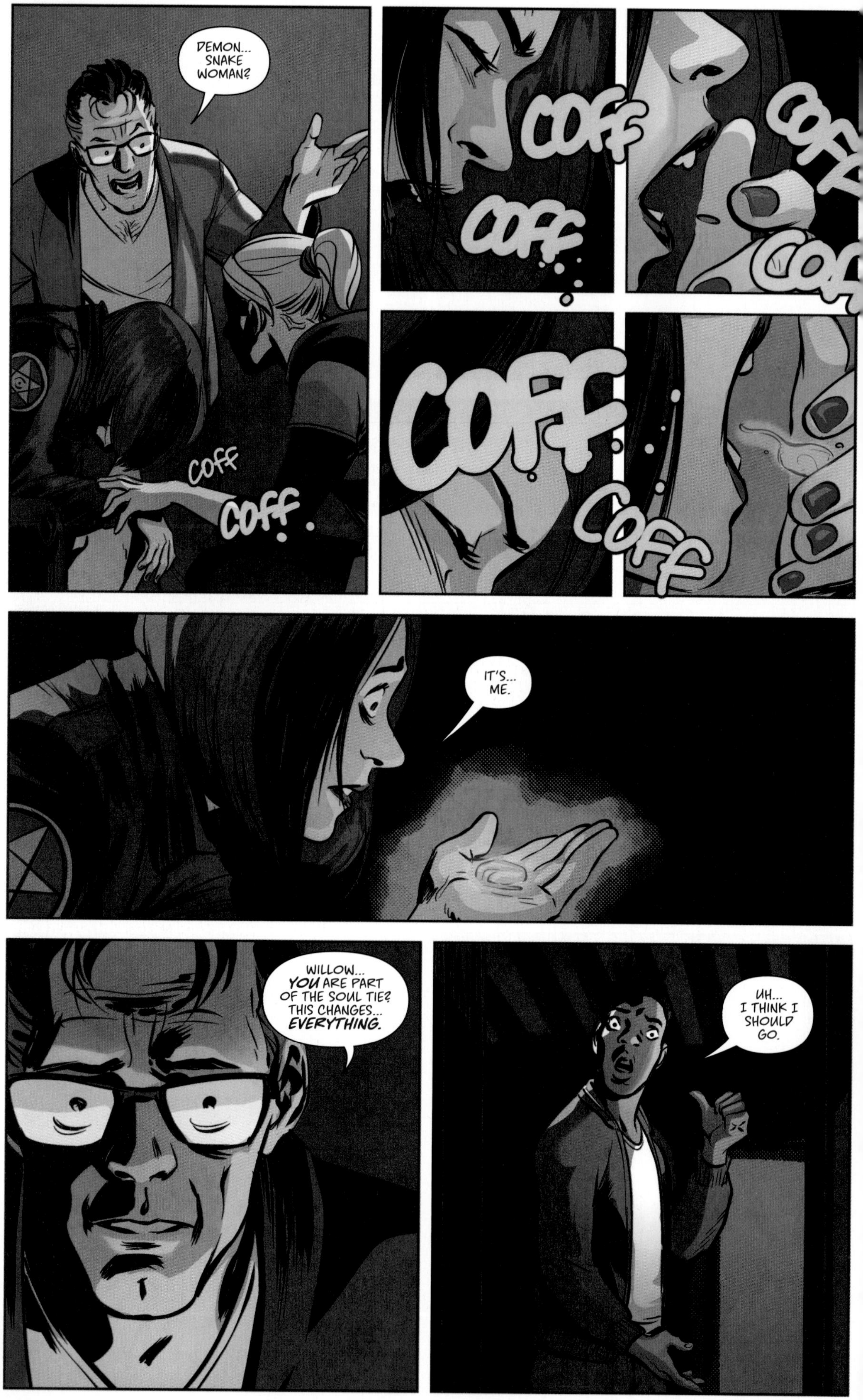
DEMON... SNAKE WOMAN?
COFF
COFF
COFF
COFF
COFF
COFF
COFF
COFF
COFF
IT'S... ME.
WILLOW... *YOU* ARE PART OF THE SOUL TIE? THIS CHANGES... *EVERYTHING.*
UH... I THINK I SHOULD GO.

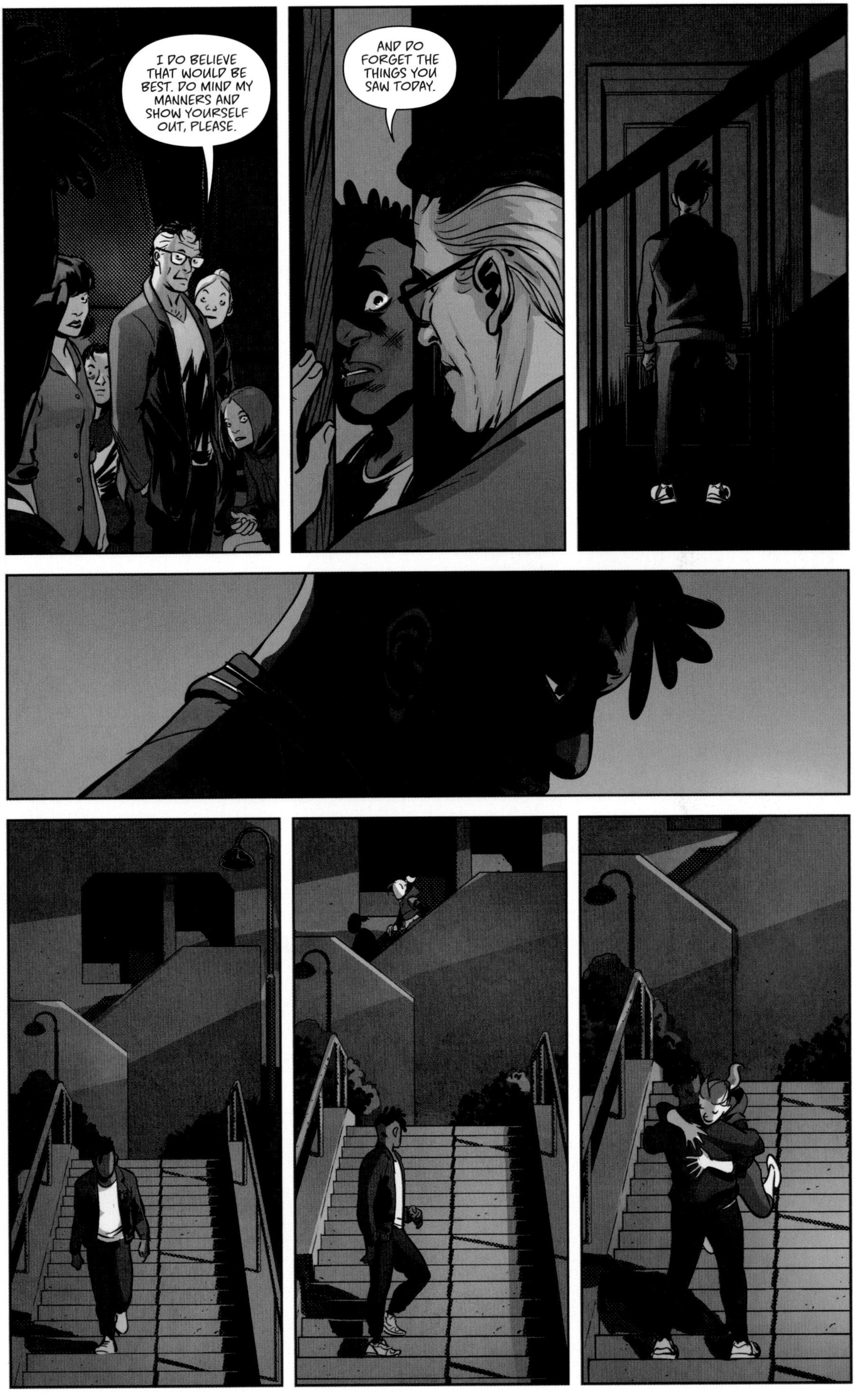
I DO BELIEVE THAT WOULD BE BEST. DO MIND MY MANNERS AND SHOW YOURSELF OUT, PLEASE.
AND DO FORGET THE THINGS YOU SAW TODAY.

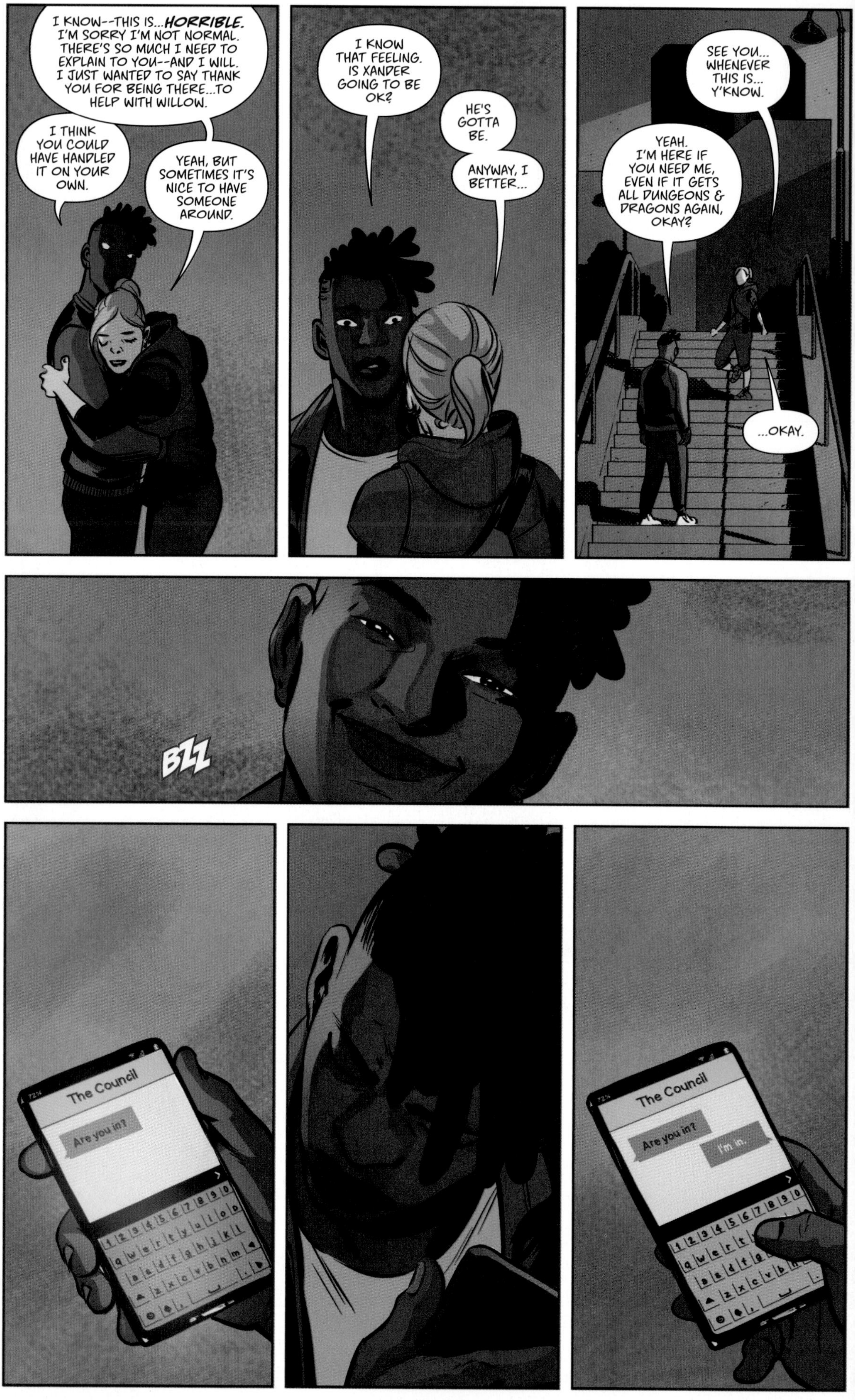
I KNOW--THIS IS...HORRIBLE. I'M SORRY I'M NOT NORMAL. THERE'S SO MUCH I NEED TO EXPLAIN TO YOU--AND I WILL. I JUST WANTED TO SAY THANK YOU FOR BEING THERE...TO HELP WITH WILLOW.
I THINK YOU COULD HAVE HANDLED IT ON YOUR OWN.
YEAH, BUT SOMETIMES IT'S NICE TO HAVE SOMEONE AROUND.
I KNOW THAT FEELING. IS XANDER GOING TO BE OK?
HE'S GOTTA BE.
ANYWAY, I BETTER...
SEE YOU... WHENEVER THIS IS... Y'KNOW.
YEAH. I'M HERE IF YOU NEED ME, EVEN IF IT GETS ALL DUNGEONS & DRAGONS AGAIN, OKAY?
...OKAY.
BZZ
The Council
Are you in?
The Council
Are you in?
I'm in.

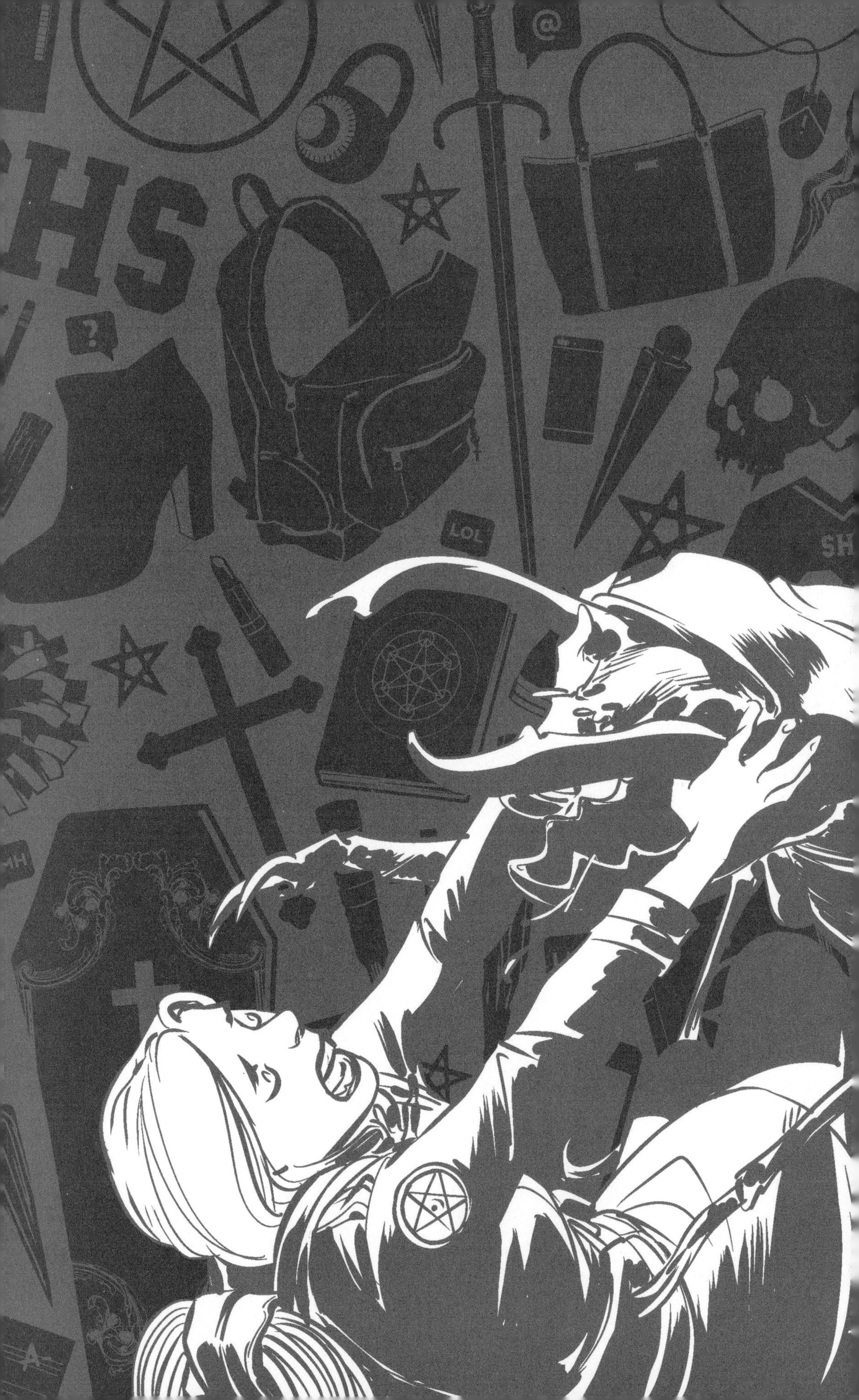
HS
LOL
SH

CHAPTER
SEVEN

Issue Seven Cover by **Marc Aspinall**

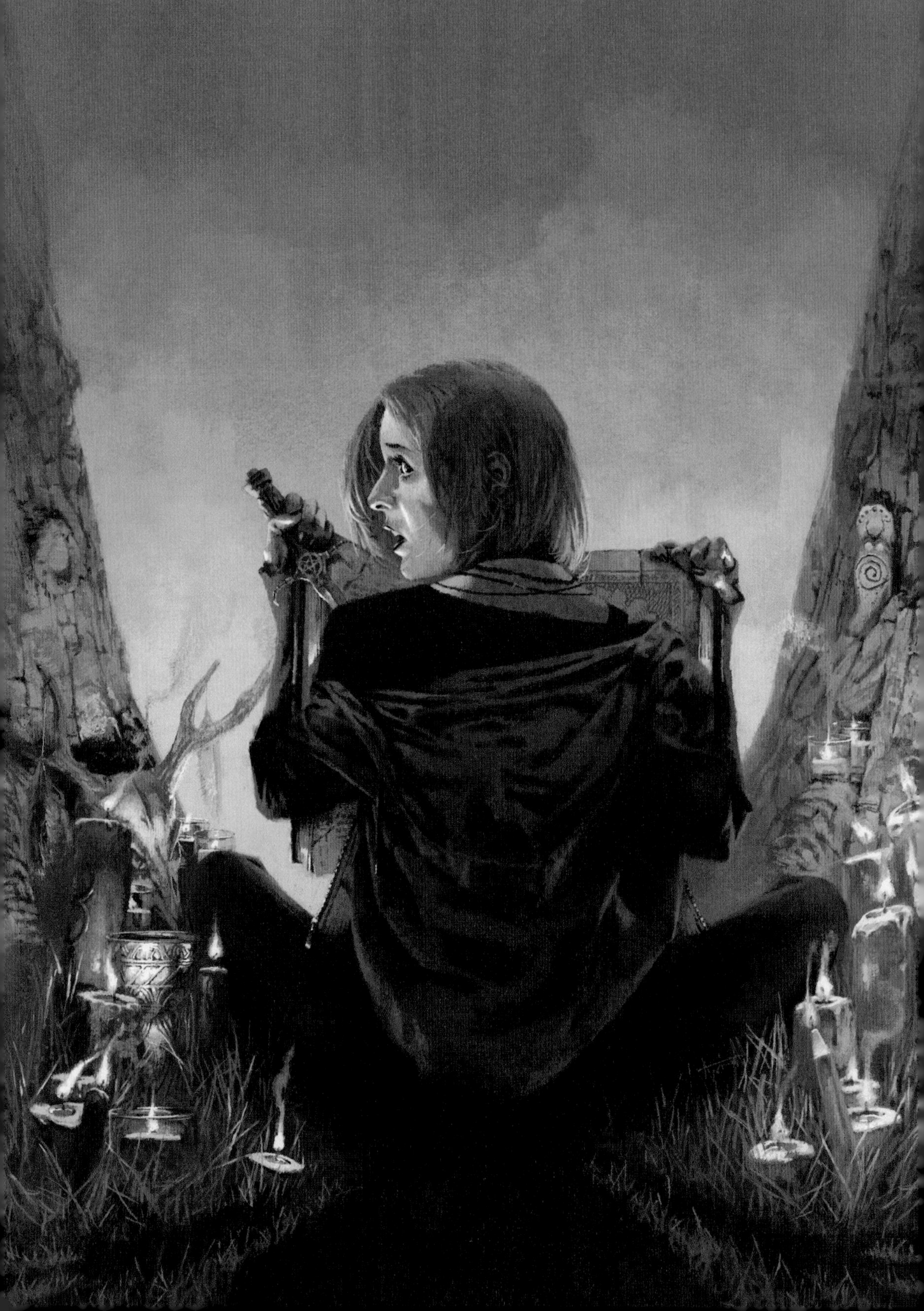

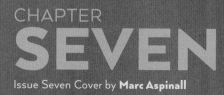

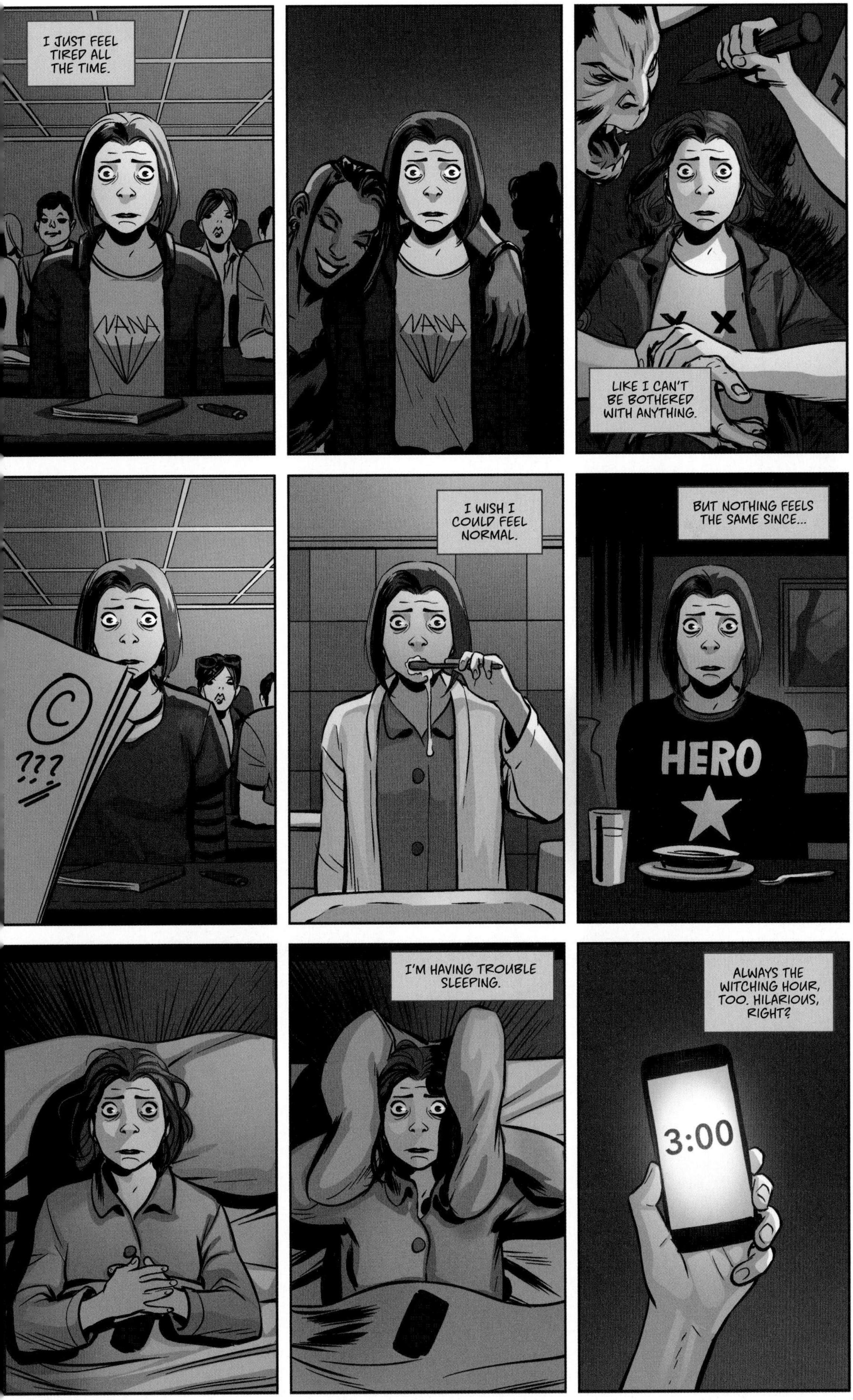
I JUST FEEL TIRED ALL THE TIME.
LIKE I CAN'T BE BOTHERED WITH ANYTHING.
I WISH I COULD FEEL NORMAL.
BUT NOTHING FEELS THE SAME SINCE...
HERO
I'M HAVING TROUBLE SLEEPING.
ALWAYS THE WITCHING HOUR, TOO. HILARIOUS, RIGHT?
3:00

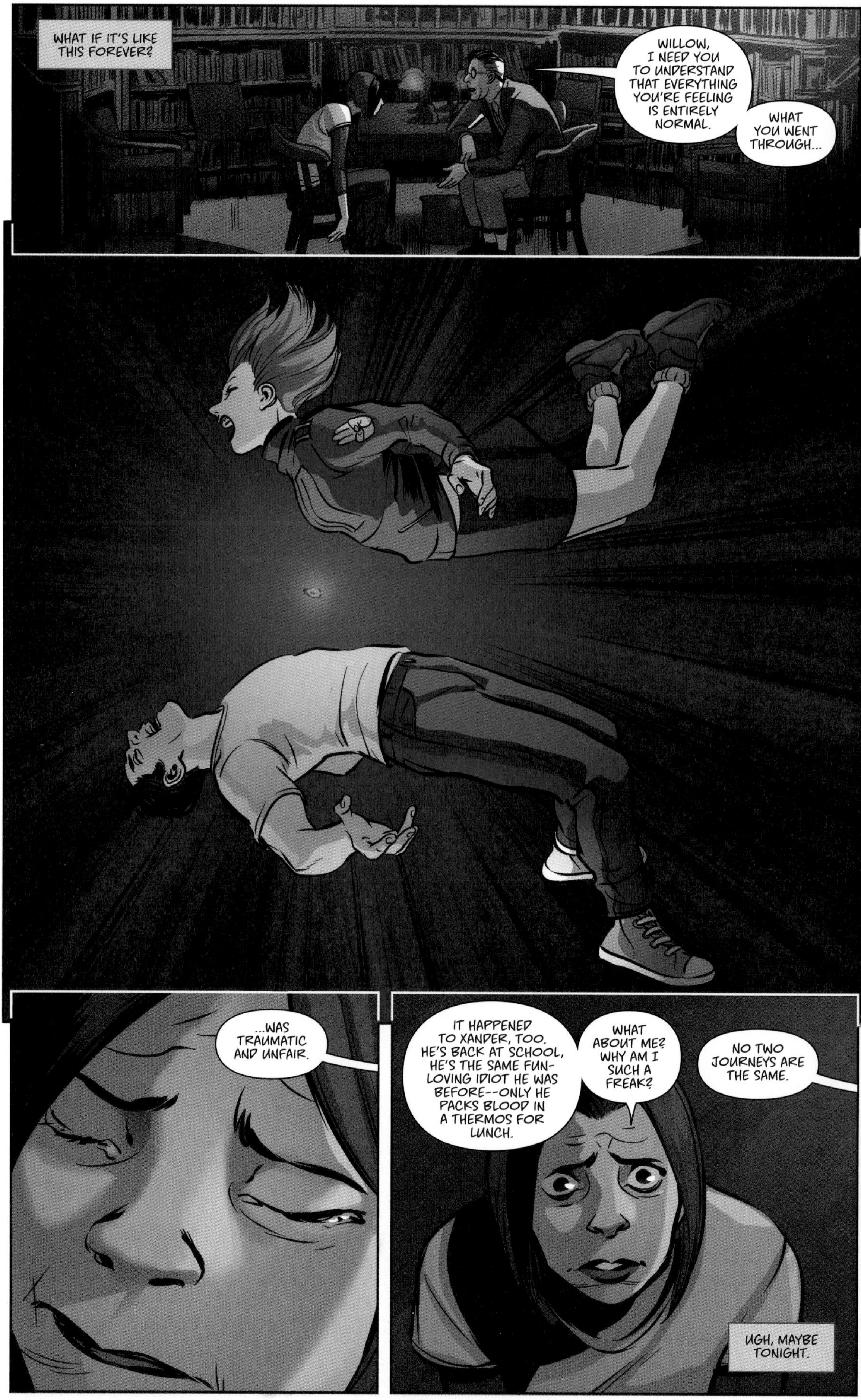
WHAT IF IT'S LIKE THIS FOREVER?
WILLOW, I NEED YOU TO UNDERSTAND THAT EVERYTHING YOU'RE FEELING IS ENTIRELY NORMAL.
WHAT YOU WENT THROUGH...
...WAS TRAUMATIC AND UNFAIR.
IT HAPPENED TO XANDER, TOO. HE'S BACK AT SCHOOL, HE'S THE SAME FUN-LOVING IDIOT HE WAS BEFORE--ONLY HE PACKS BLOOD IN A THERMOS FOR LUNCH.
WHAT ABOUT ME? WHY AM I SUCH A FREAK?
NO TWO JOURNEYS ARE THE SAME.
UGH, MAYBE TONIGHT.

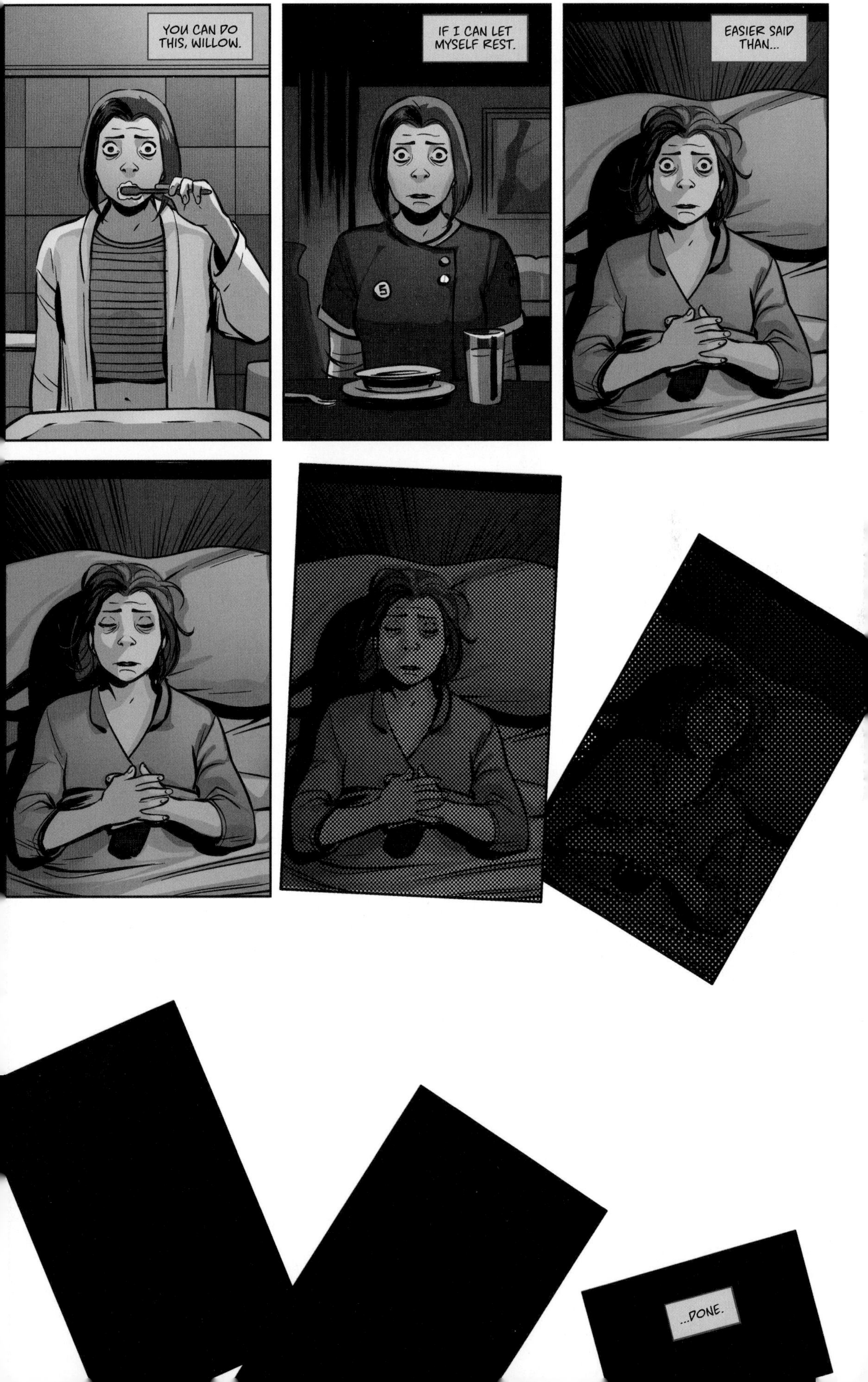
YOU CAN DO THIS, WILLOW.
IF I CAN LET MYSELF REST.
EASIER SAID THAN...
...DONE.

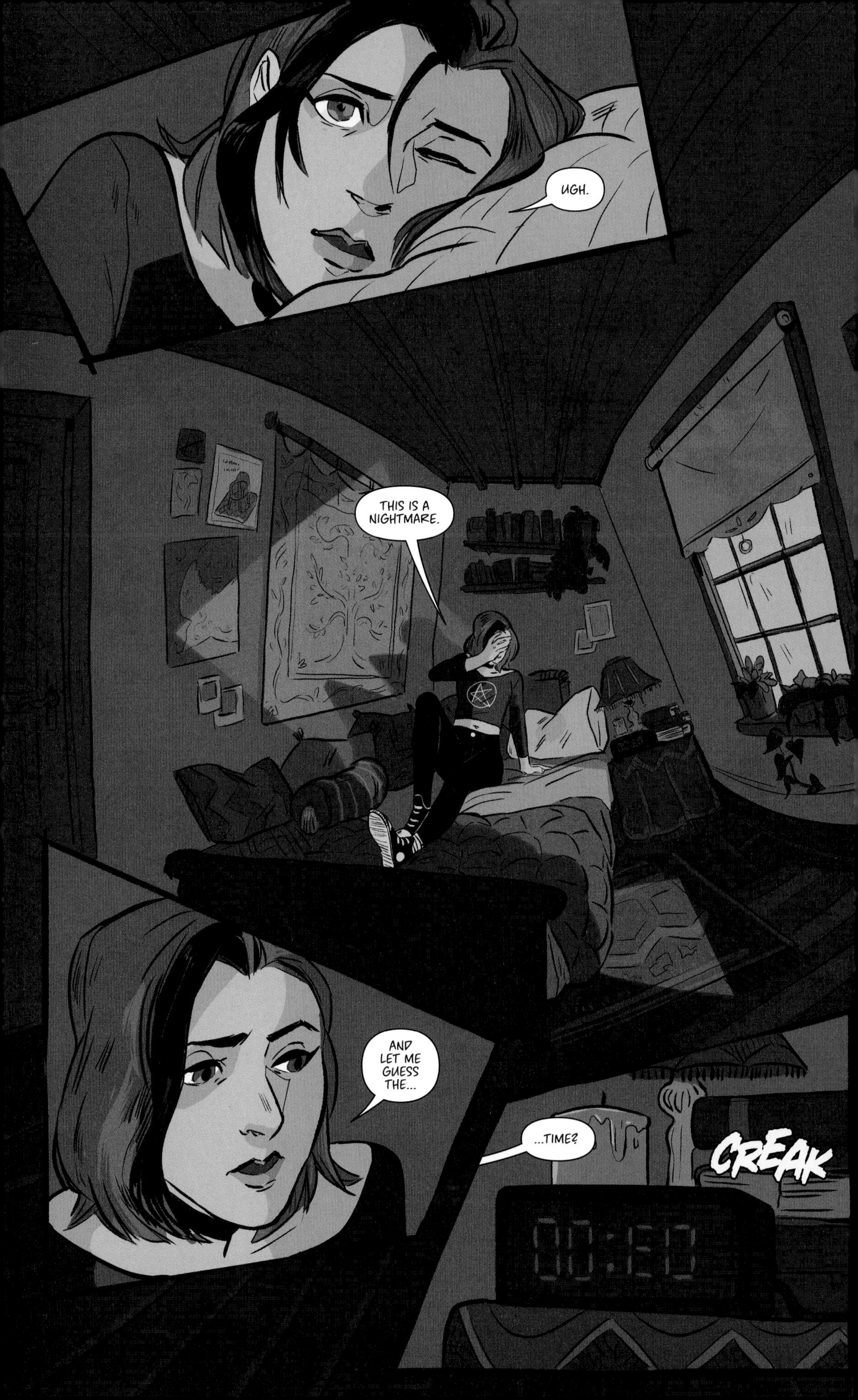
UGH.
THIS IS A NIGHTMARE.
AND LET ME GUESS THE...
...TIME?
CREAK

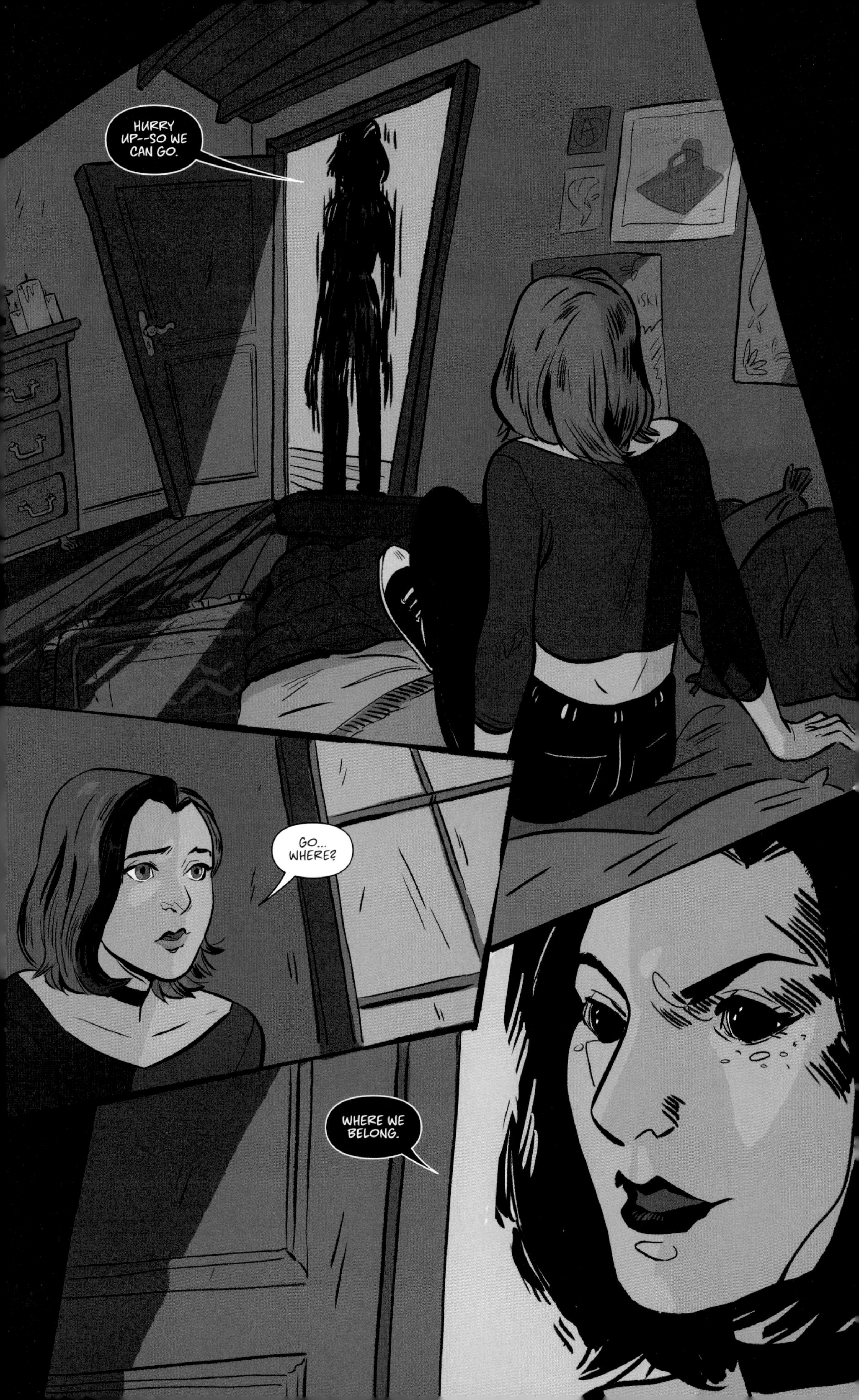
HURRY UP--SO WE CAN GO.
GO... WHERE?
WHERE WE BELONG.

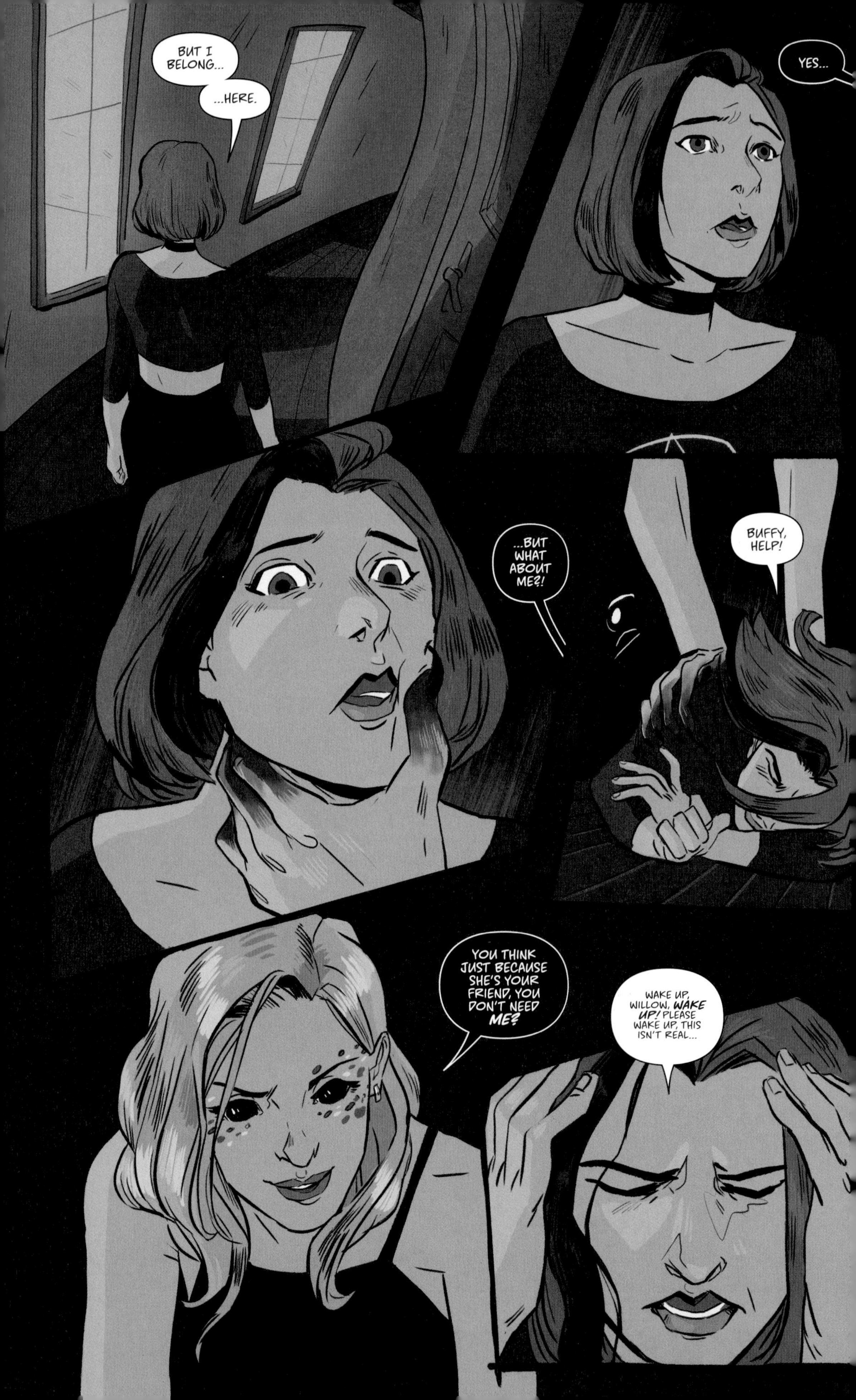
BUT I BELONG...
...HERE.
YES...
...BUT WHAT ABOUT ME?!
BUFFY, HELP!
YOU THINK JUST BECAUSE SHE'S YOUR FRIEND, YOU DON'T NEED **ME?**
WAKE UP, WILLOW, ***WAKE UP!*** PLEASE WAKE UP, THIS ISN'T REAL...

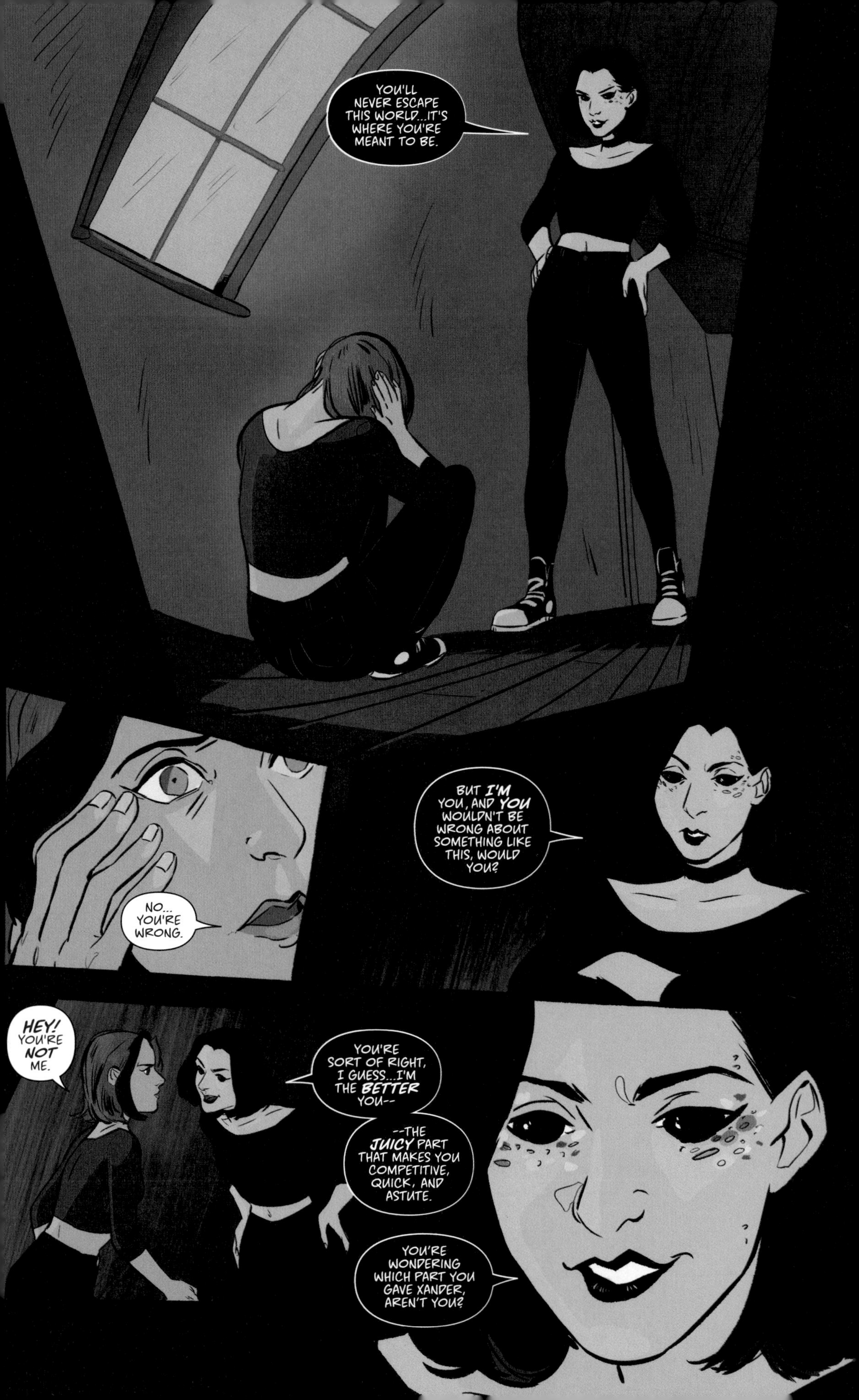
YOU'LL NEVER ESCAPE THIS WORLD...IT'S WHERE YOU'RE MEANT TO BE.
BUT I'M YOU, AND YOU WOULDN'T BE WRONG ABOUT SOMETHING LIKE THIS, WOULD YOU?
NO... YOU'RE WRONG.
HEY! YOU'RE NOT ME.
YOU'RE SORT OF RIGHT, I GUESS...I'M THE BETTER YOU--
--THE JUICY PART THAT MAKES YOU COMPETITIVE, QUICK, AND ASTUTE.
YOU'RE WONDERING WHICH PART YOU GAVE XANDER, AREN'T YOU?

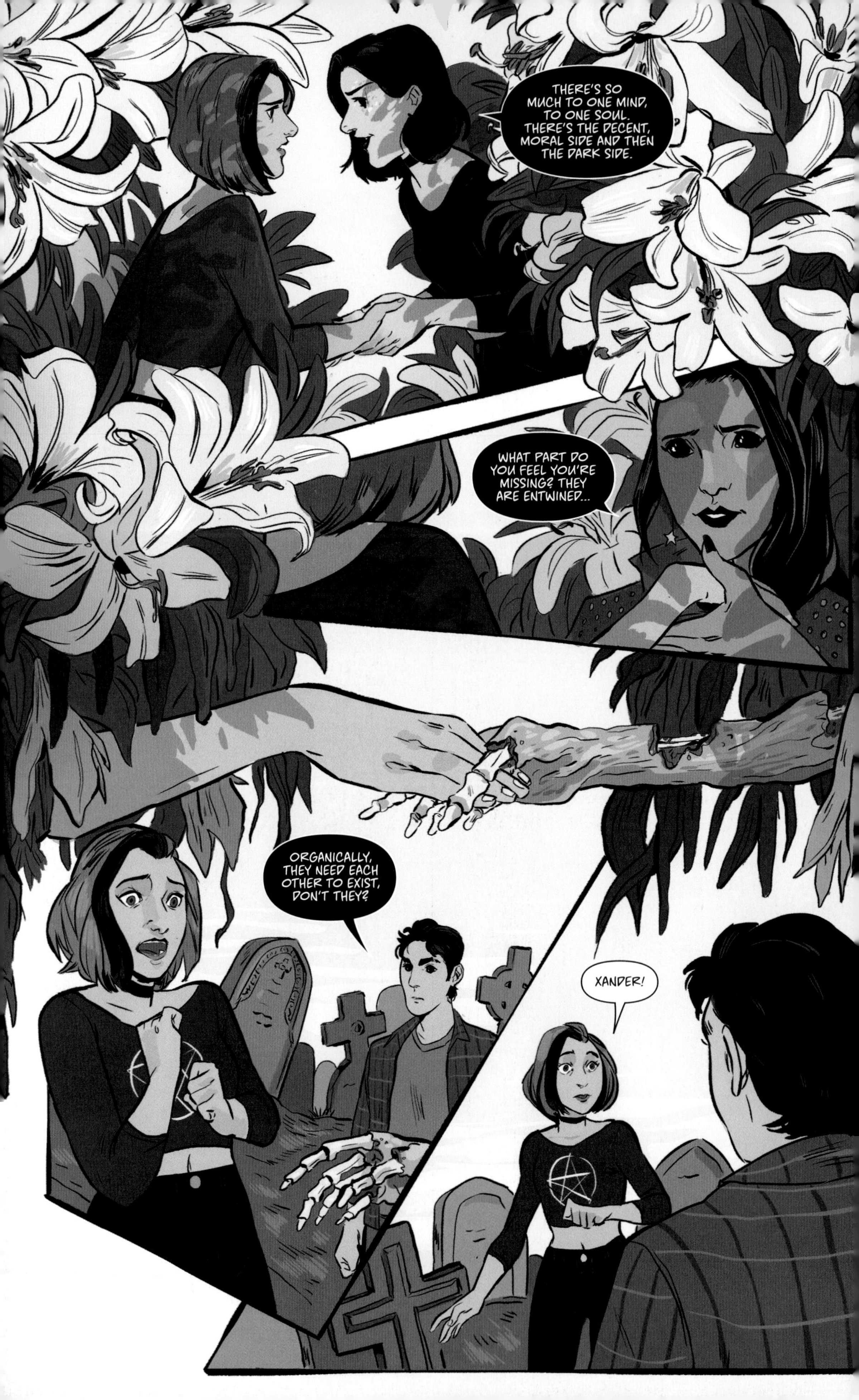
THERE'S SO MUCH TO ONE MIND, TO ONE SOUL. THERE'S THE DECENT, MORAL SIDE AND THEN THE DARK SIDE.
WHAT PART DO YOU FEEL YOU'RE MISSING? THEY ARE ENTWINED...
ORGANICALLY, THEY NEED EACH OTHER TO EXIST, DON'T THEY?
XANDER!

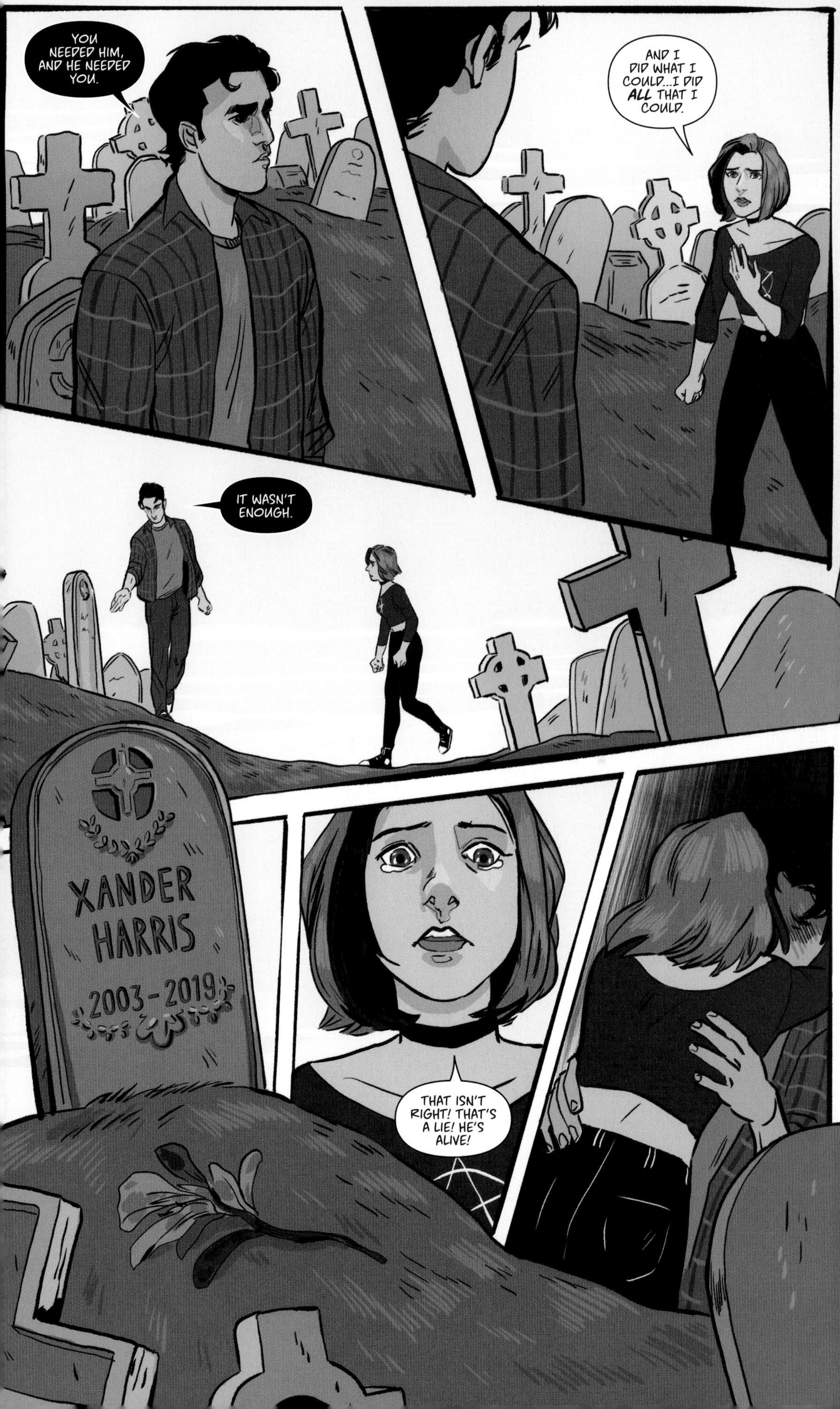
YOU NEEDED HIM, AND HE NEEDED YOU.
AND I DID WHAT I COULD...I DID **ALL** THAT I COULD.
IT WASN'T ENOUGH.
XANDER HARRIS
2003 - 2019
THAT ISN'T RIGHT! THAT'S A LIE! HE'S ALIVE!

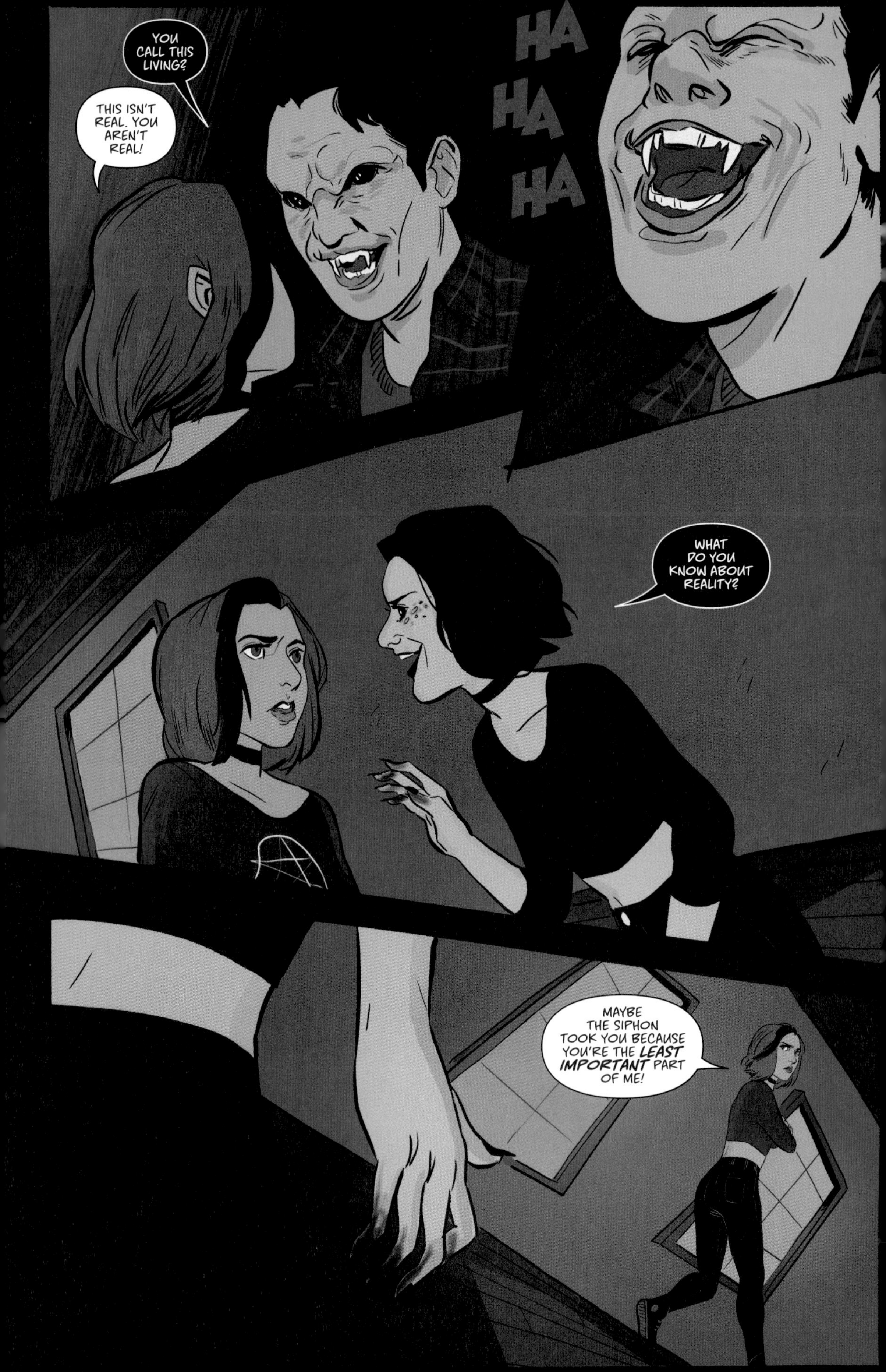
YOU CALL THIS LIVING?
THIS ISN'T REAL. YOU AREN'T REAL!
HA HA HA
WHAT DO YOU KNOW ABOUT REALITY?
MAYBE THE SIPHON TOOK YOU BECAUSE YOU'RE THE **LEAST IMPORTANT** PART OF ME!

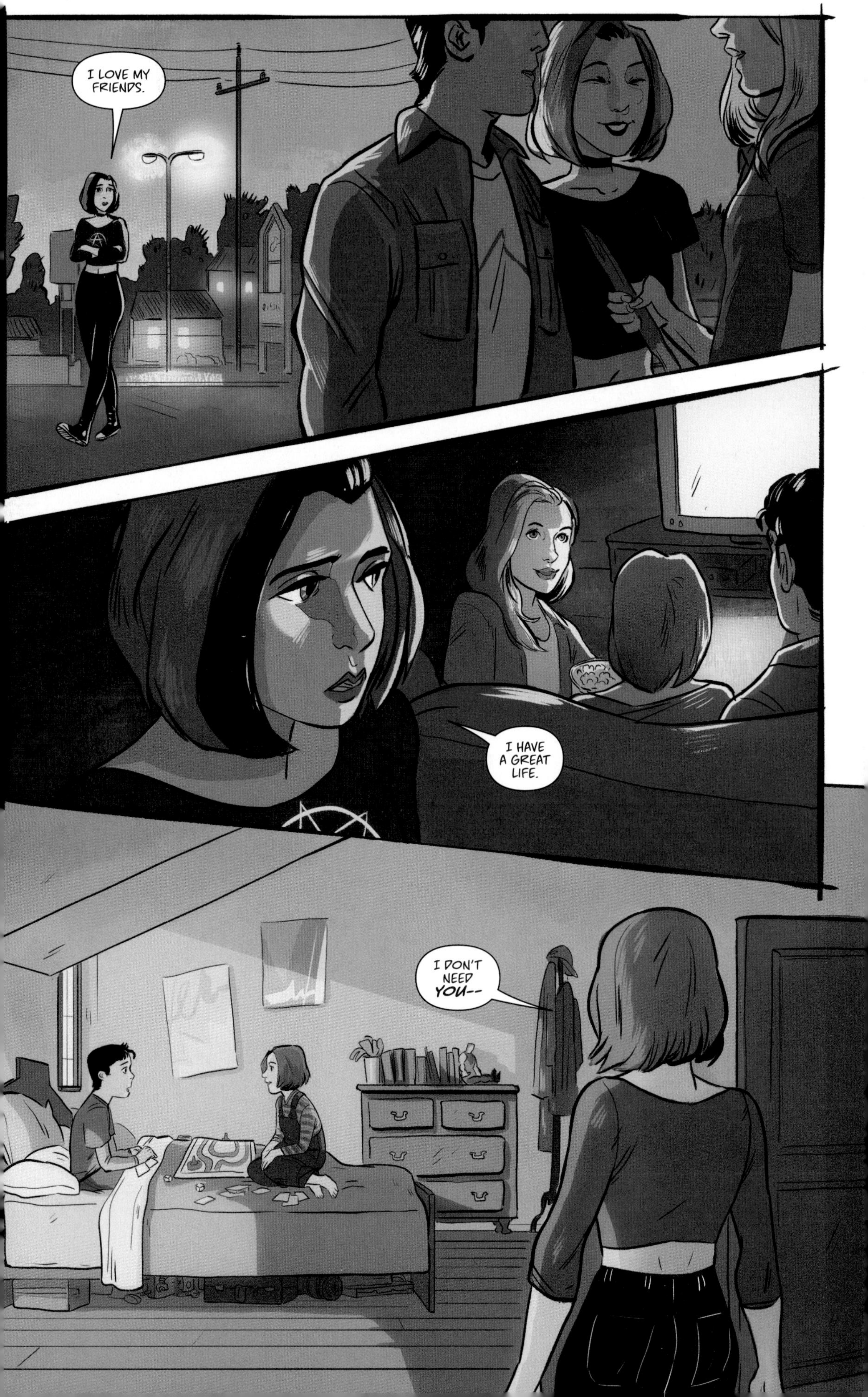
I LOVE MY FRIENDS.
I HAVE A GREAT LIFE.
I DON'T NEED YOU--

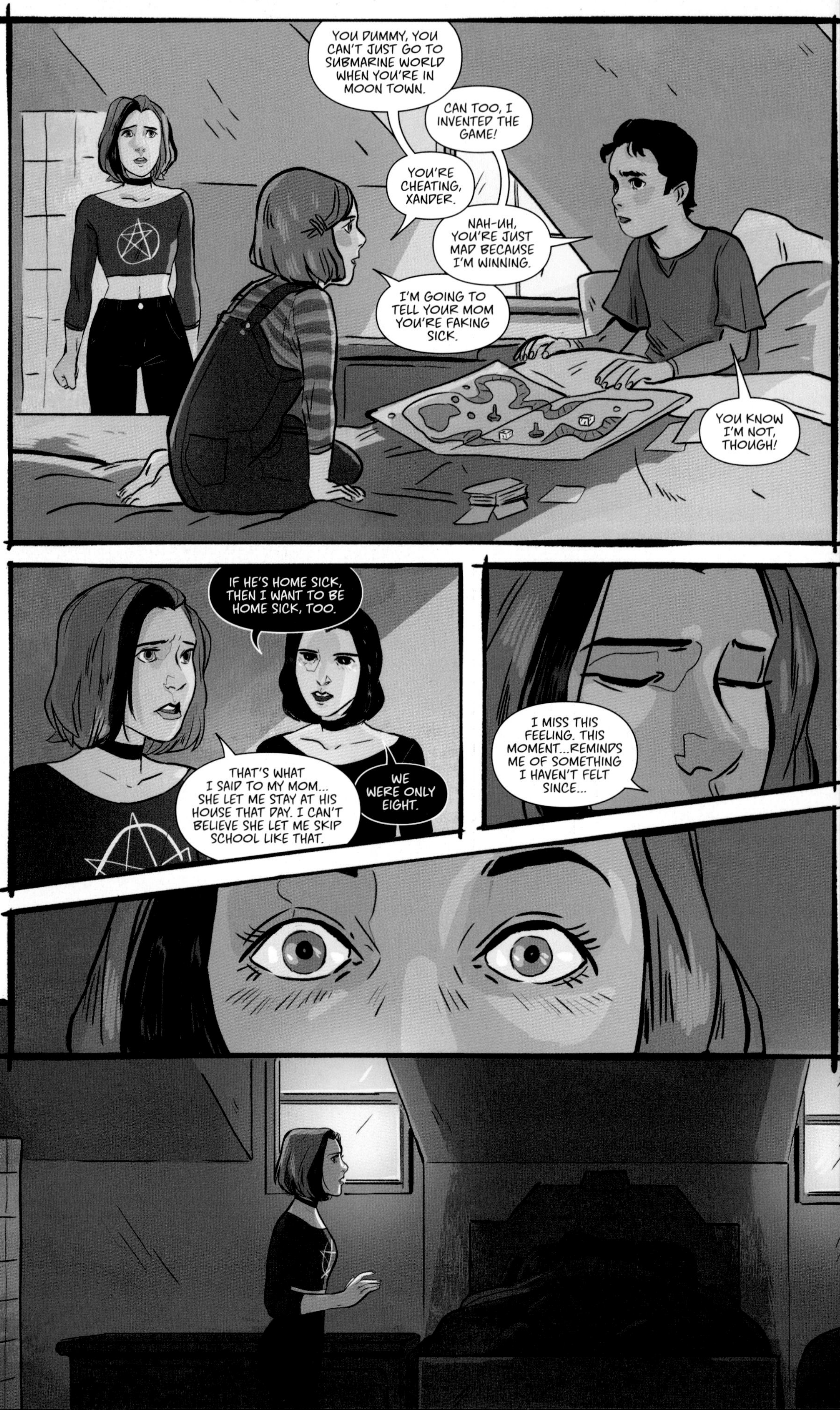
YOU DUMMY, YOU CAN'T JUST GO TO SUBMARINE WORLD WHEN YOU'RE IN MOON TOWN.
CAN TOO, I INVENTED THE GAME!
YOU'RE CHEATING, XANDER.
NAH-UH, YOU'RE JUST MAD BECAUSE I'M WINNING.
I'M GOING TO TELL YOUR MOM YOU'RE FAKING SICK.
YOU KNOW I'M NOT, THOUGH!
IF HE'S HOME SICK, THEN I WANT TO BE HOME SICK, TOO.
THAT'S WHAT I SAID TO MY MOM... SHE LET ME STAY AT HIS HOUSE THAT DAY. I CAN'T BELIEVE SHE LET ME SKIP SCHOOL LIKE THAT.
WE WERE ONLY EIGHT.
I MISS THIS FEELING. THIS MOMENT...REMINDS ME OF SOMETHING I HAVEN'T FELT SINCE...

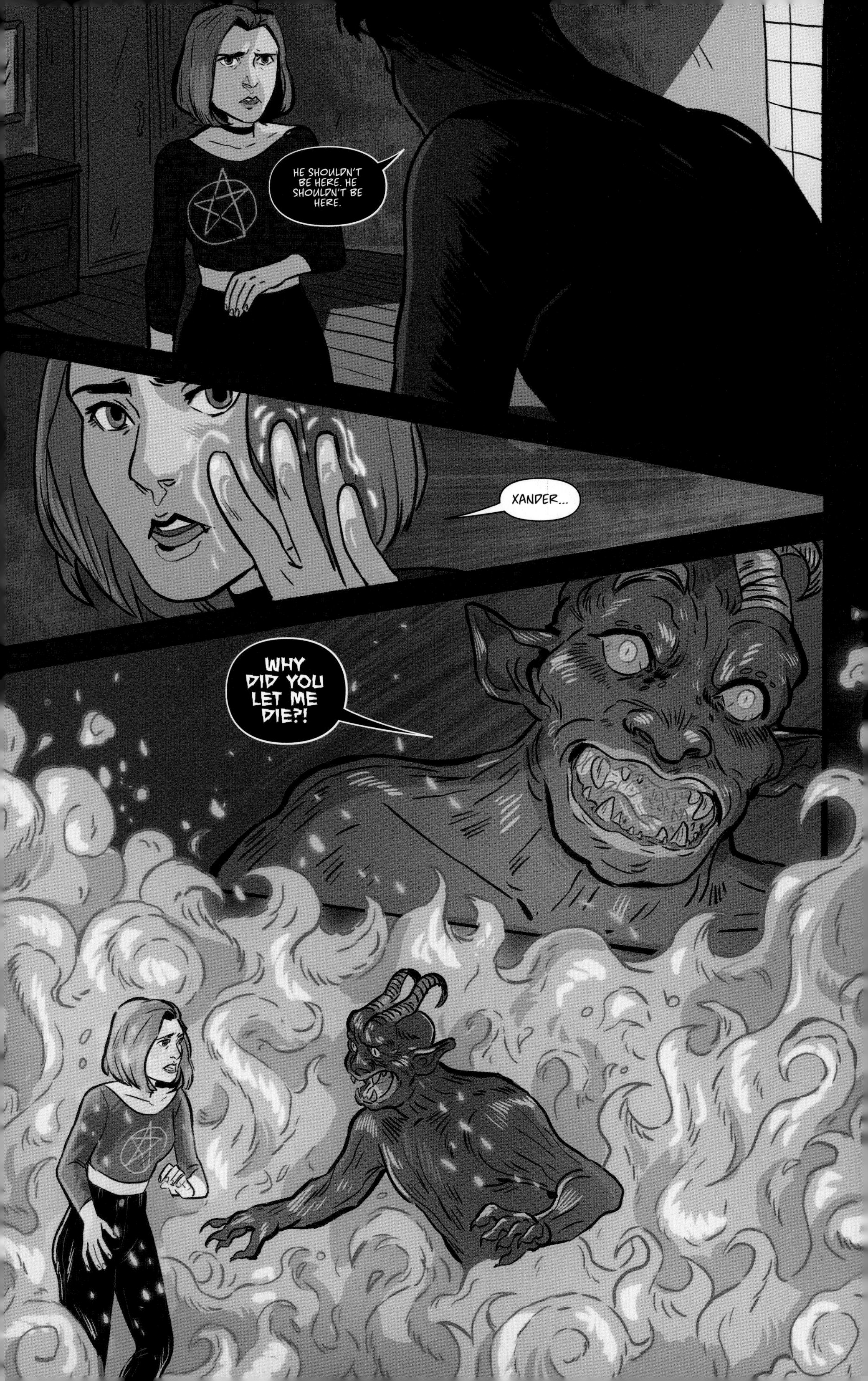
HE SHOULDN'T BE HERE. HE SHOULDN'T BE HERE.
XANDER...
WHY DID YOU LET ME DIE?!

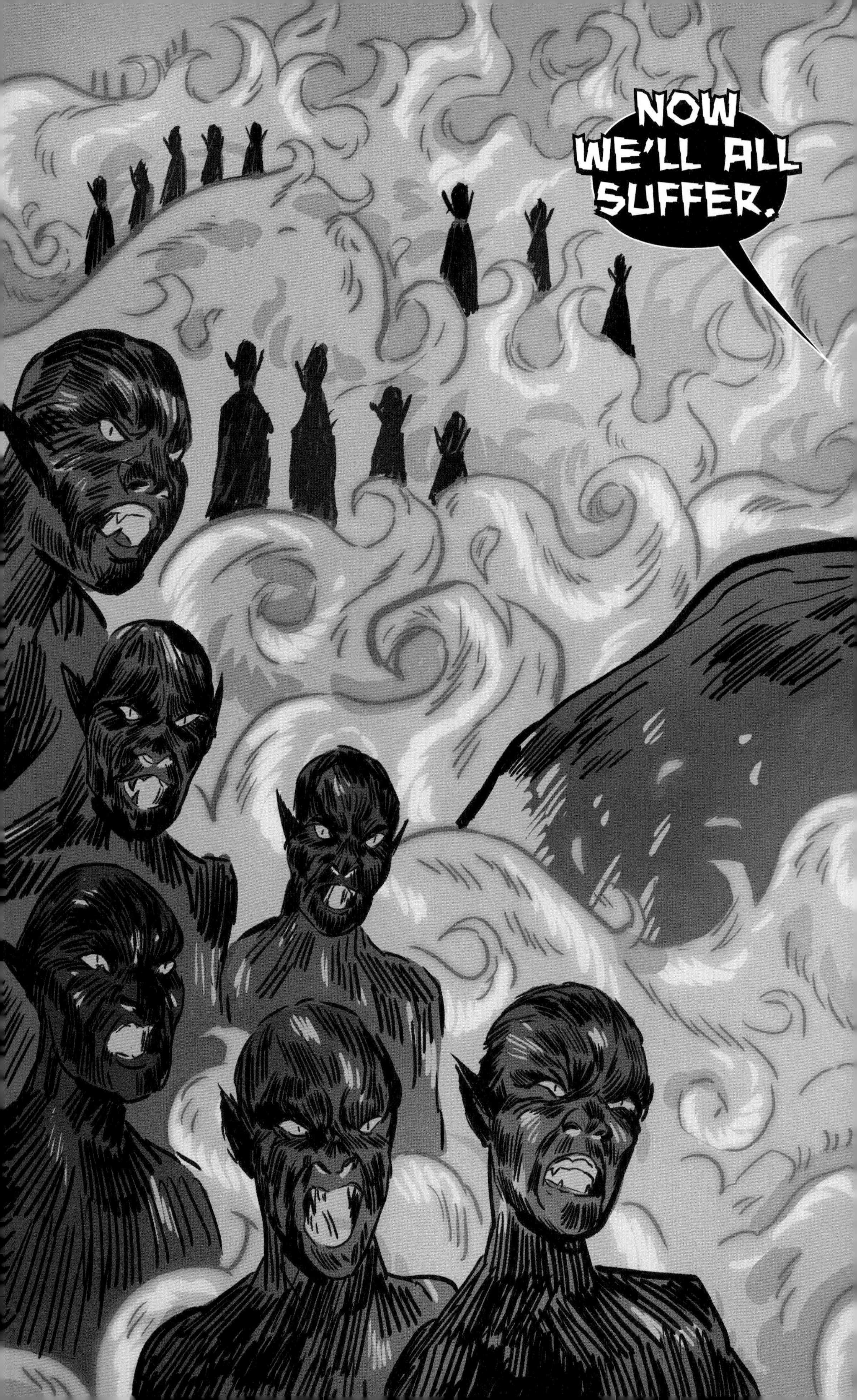
NOW WE'LL ALL SUFFER.

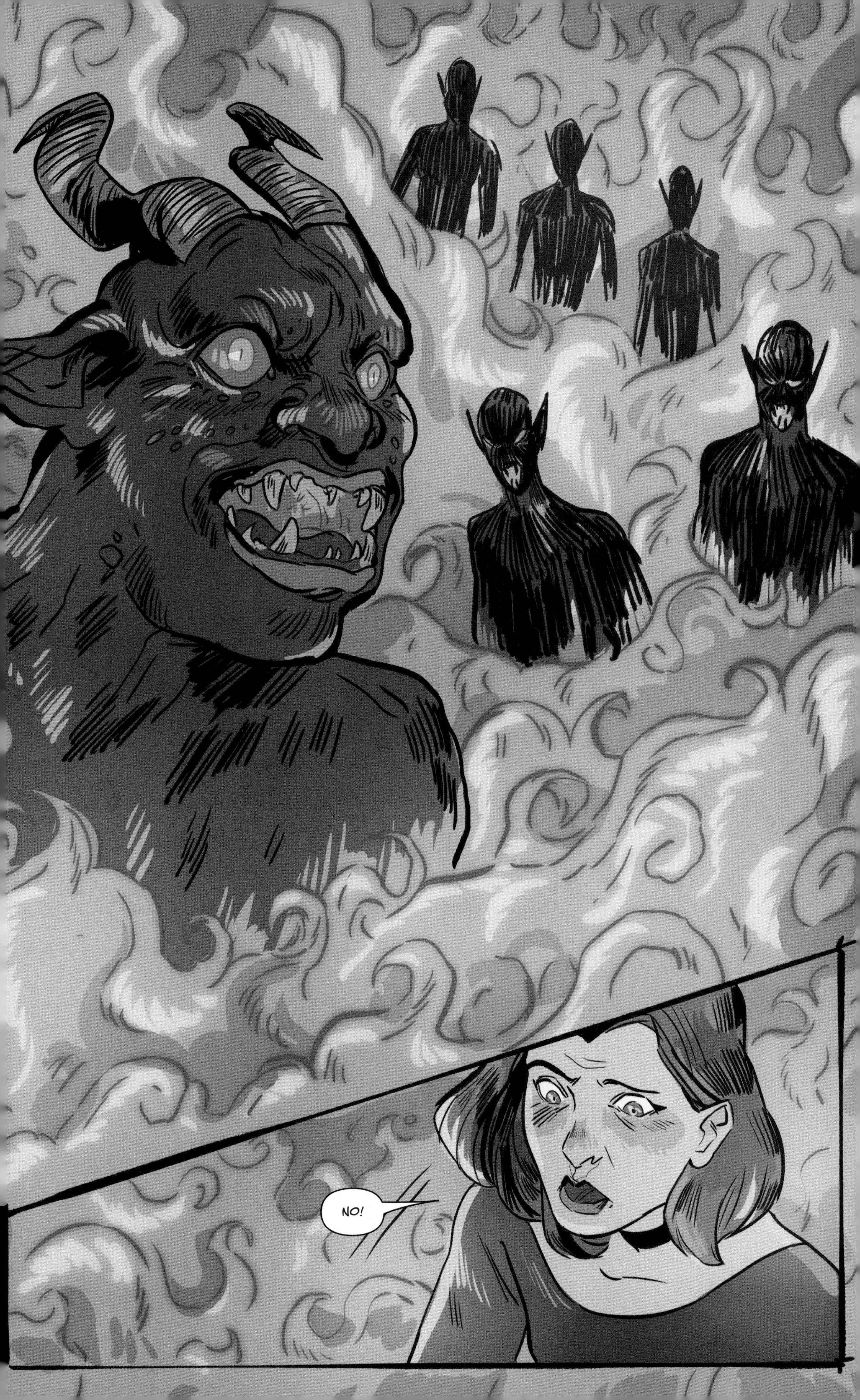
NO!

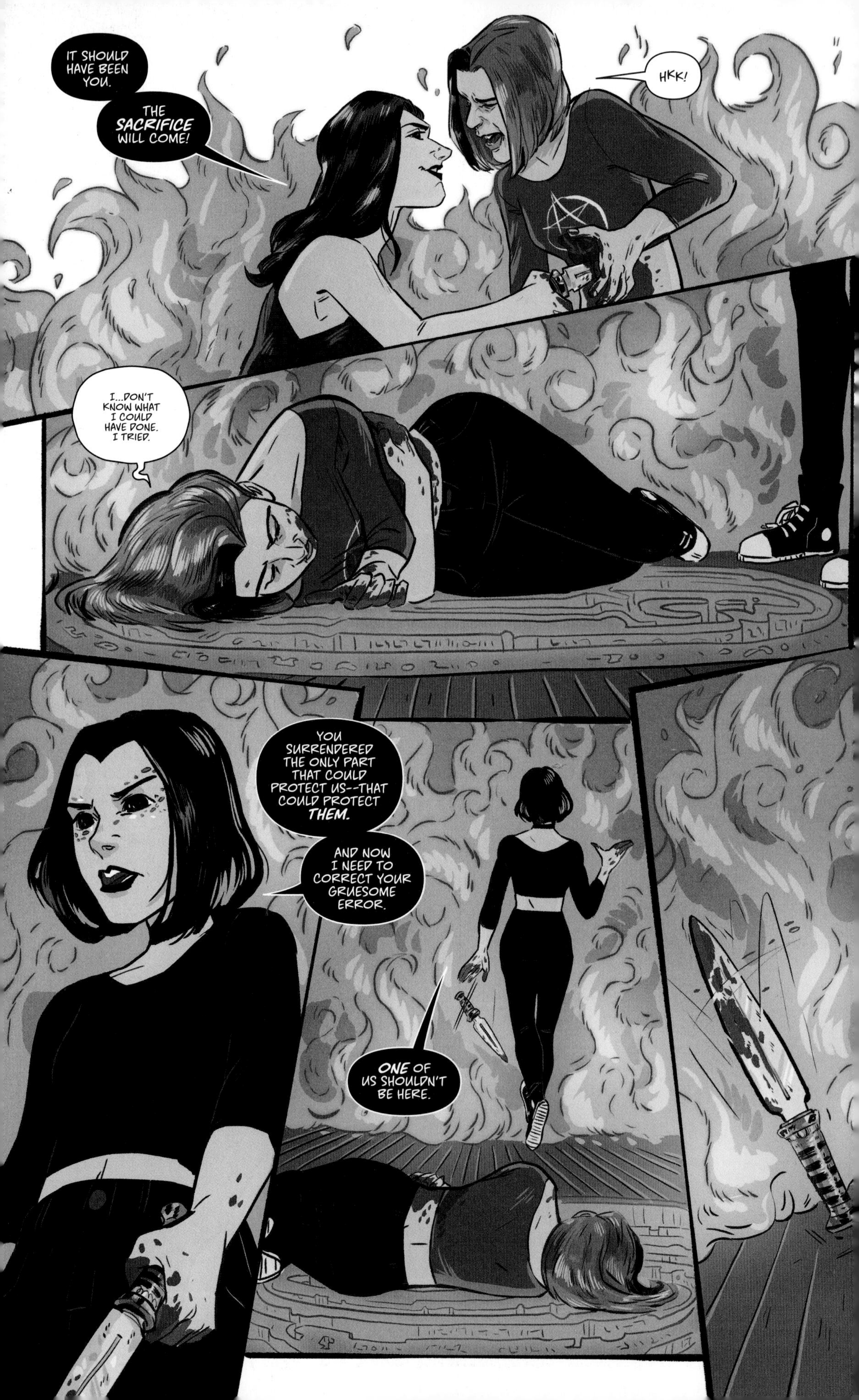
IT SHOULD HAVE BEEN YOU.
THE SACRIFICE WILL COME!
HKK!
I...DON'T KNOW WHAT I COULD HAVE DONE. I TRIED.
YOU SURRENDERED THE ONLY PART THAT COULD PROTECT US--THAT COULD PROTECT THEM.
AND NOW I NEED TO CORRECT YOUR GRUESOME ERROR.
ONE OF US SHOULDN'T BE HERE.

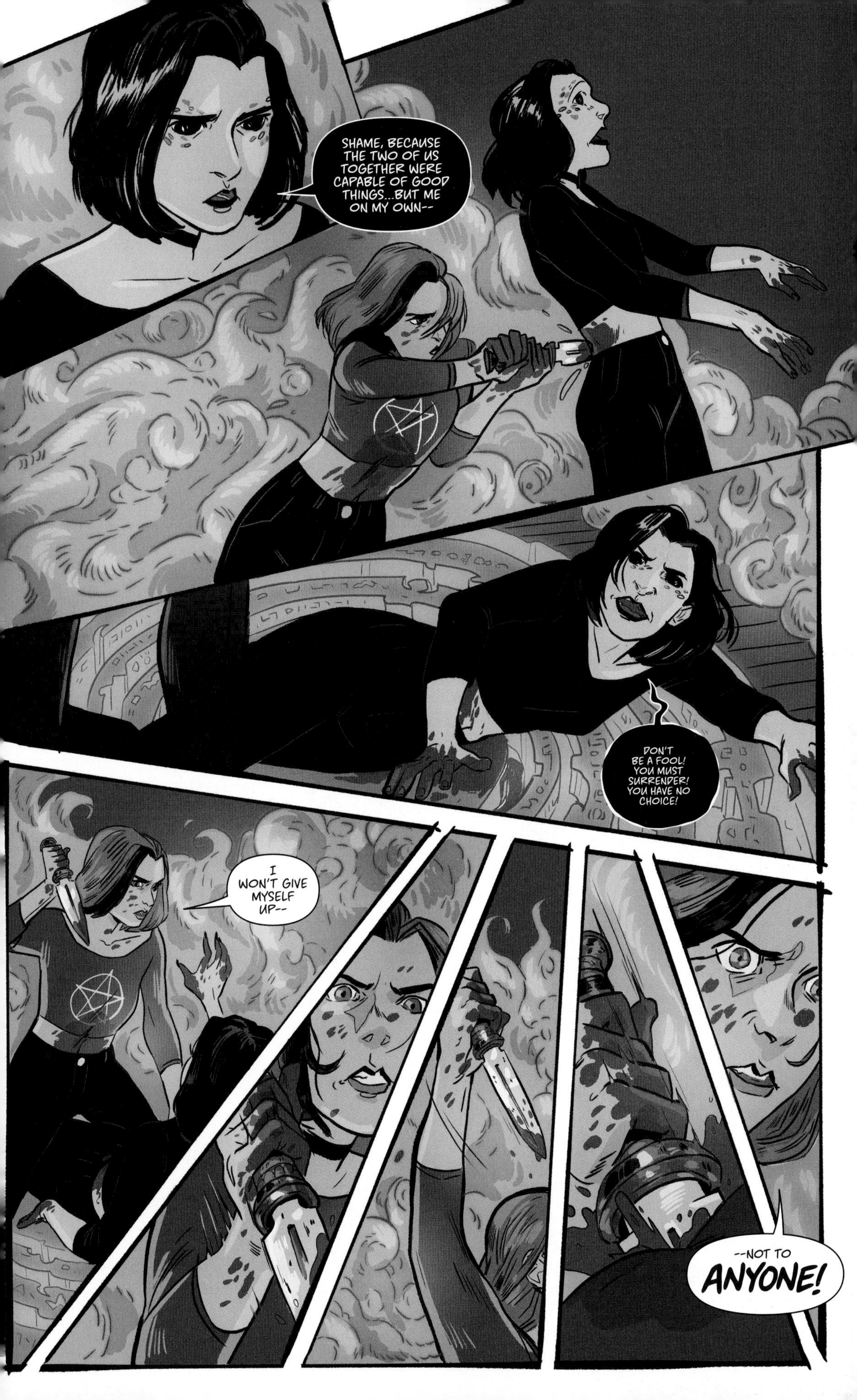
SHAME, BECAUSE THE TWO OF US TOGETHER WERE CAPABLE OF GOOD THINGS...BUT ME ON MY OWN--
DON'T BE A FOOL! YOU MUST SURRENDER! YOU HAVE NO CHOICE!
I WON'T GIVE MYSELF UP--
--NOT TO ANYONE!

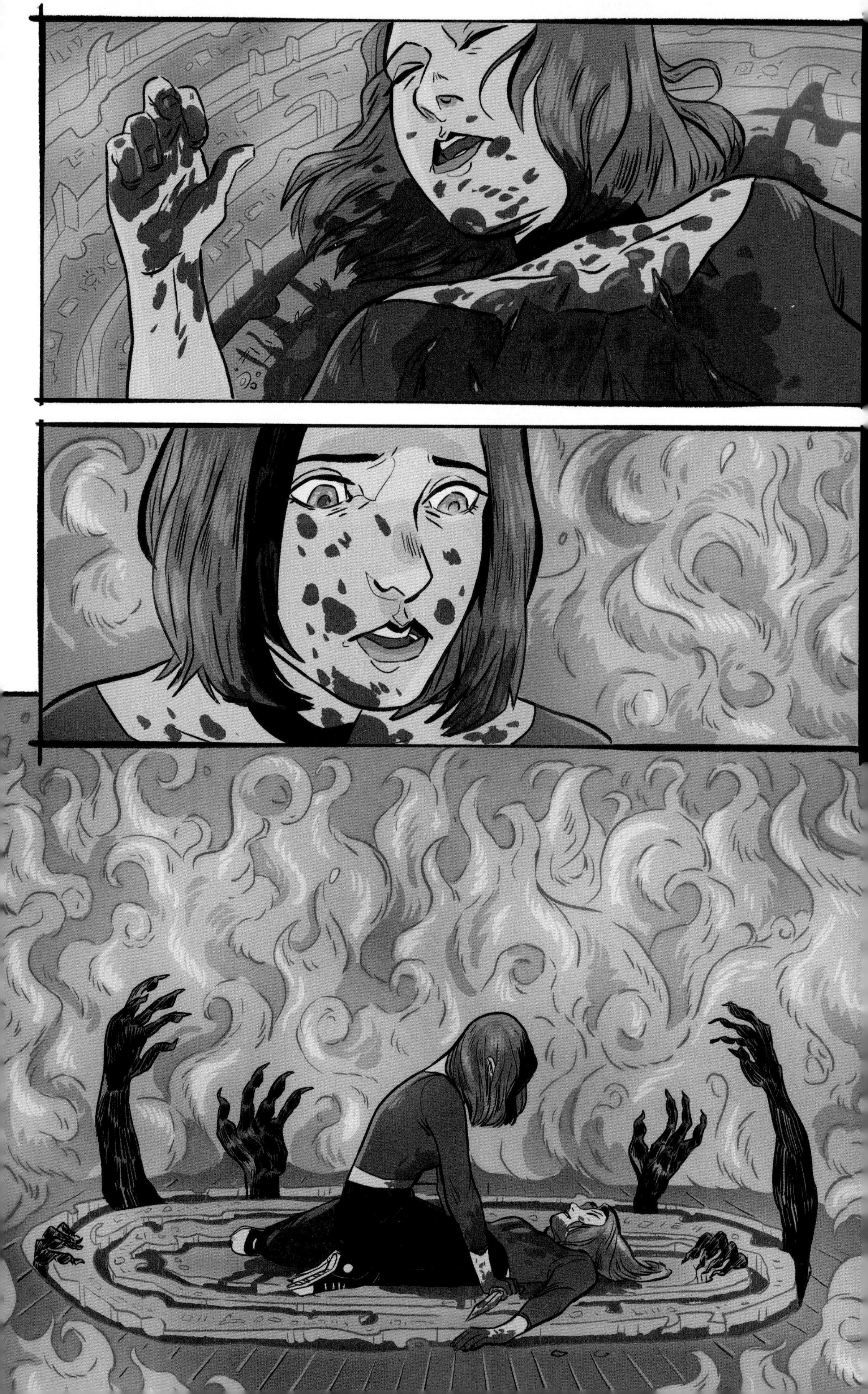

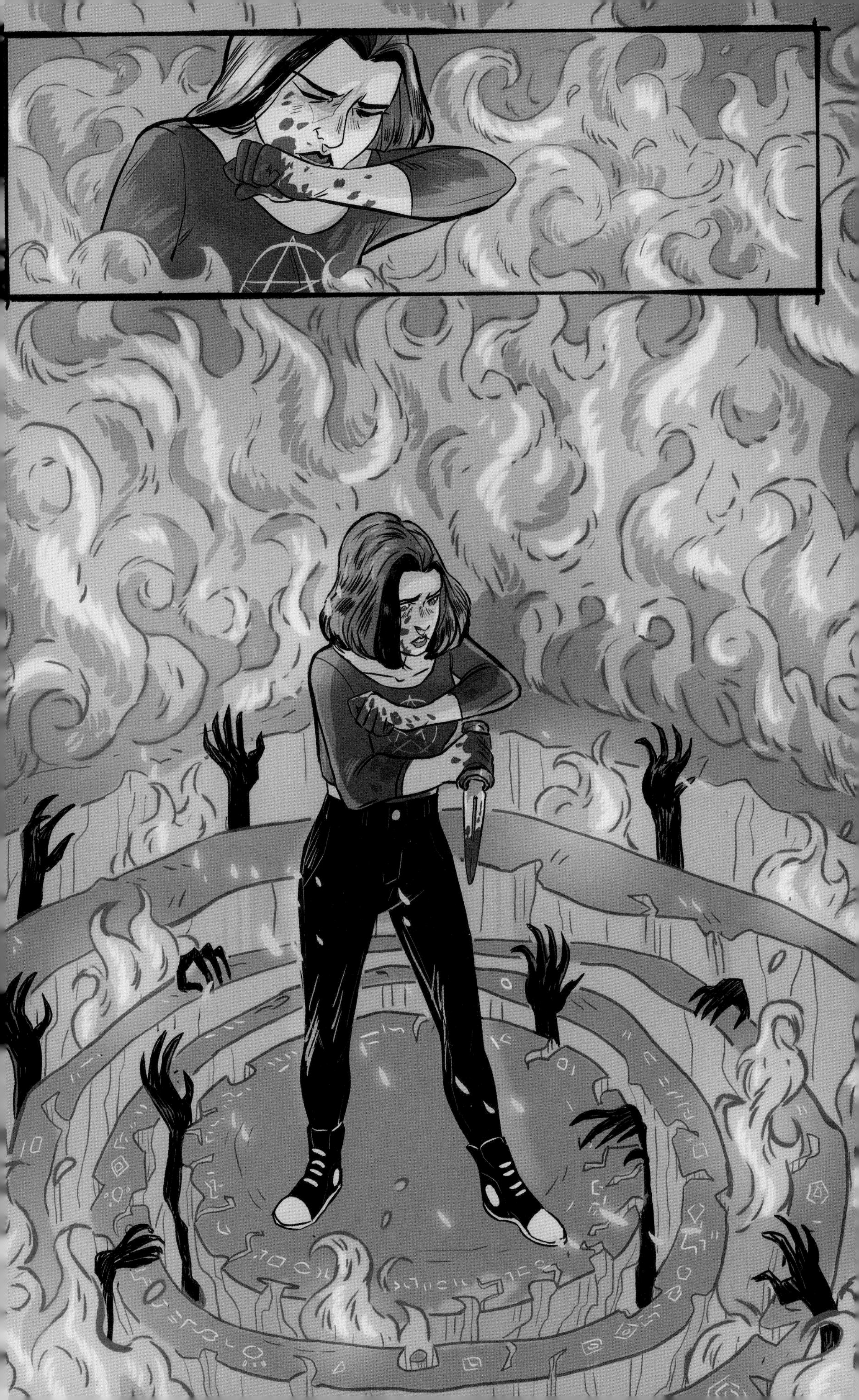

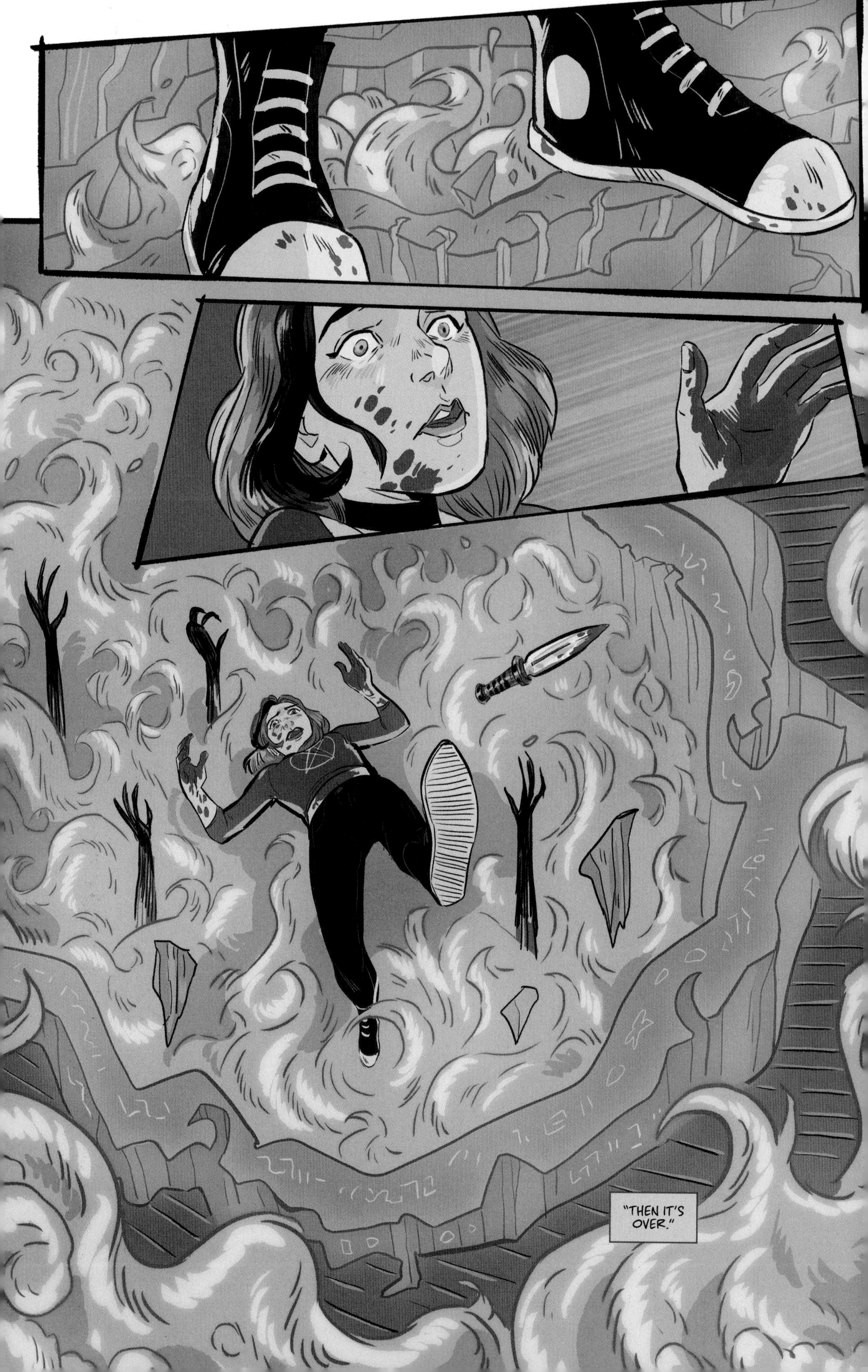
"THEN IT'S OVER."

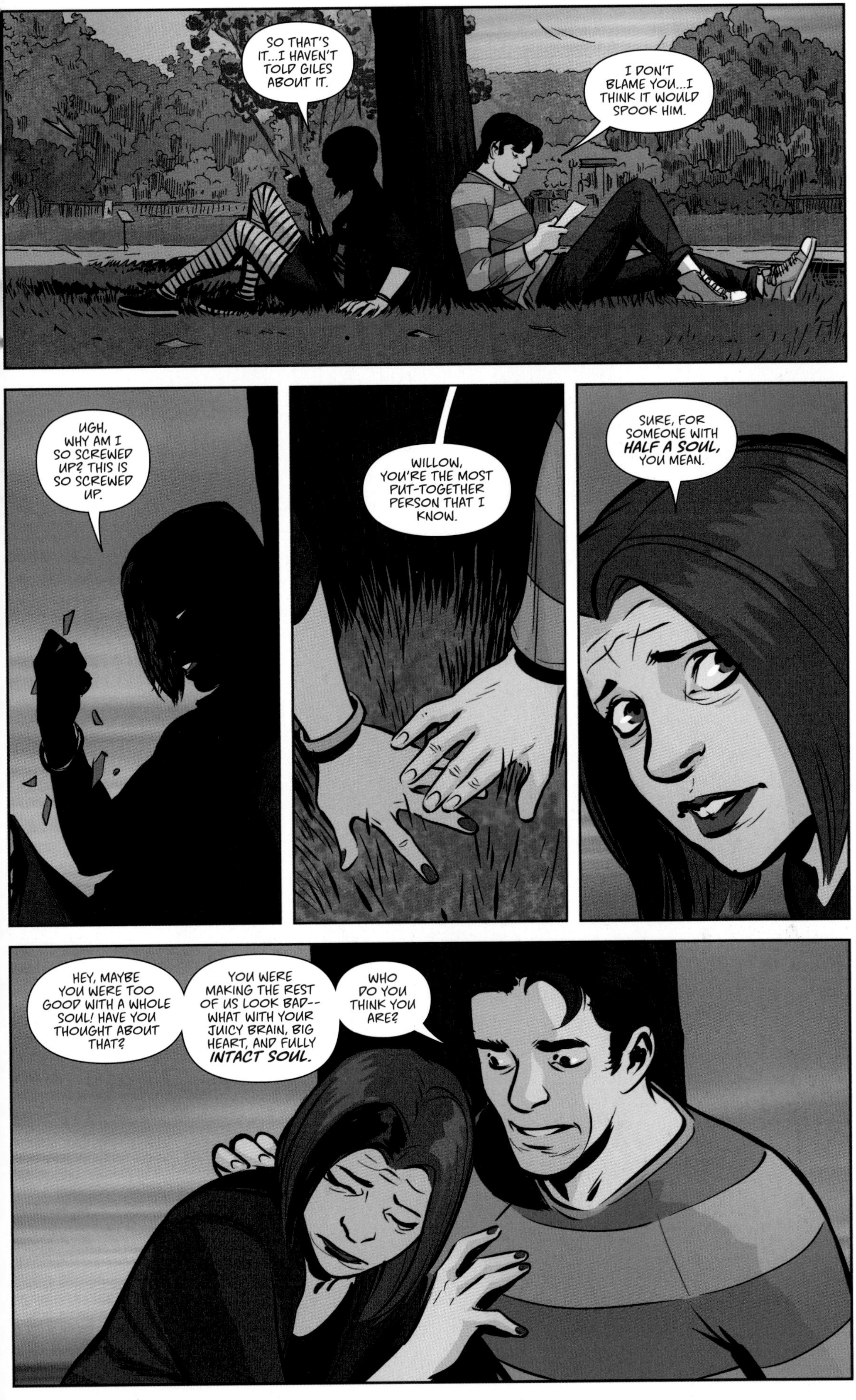
SO THAT'S IT...I HAVEN'T TOLD GILES ABOUT IT.
I DON'T BLAME YOU...I THINK IT WOULD SPOOK HIM.
UGH, WHY AM I SO SCREWED UP? THIS IS SO SCREWED UP.
WILLOW, YOU'RE THE MOST PUT-TOGETHER PERSON THAT I KNOW.
SURE, FOR SOMEONE WITH HALF A SOUL, YOU MEAN.
HEY, MAYBE YOU WERE TOO GOOD WITH A WHOLE SOUL! HAVE YOU THOUGHT ABOUT THAT?
YOU WERE MAKING THE REST OF US LOOK BAD--WHAT WITH YOUR JUICY BRAIN, BIG HEART, AND FULLY INTACT SOUL.
WHO DO YOU THINK YOU ARE?

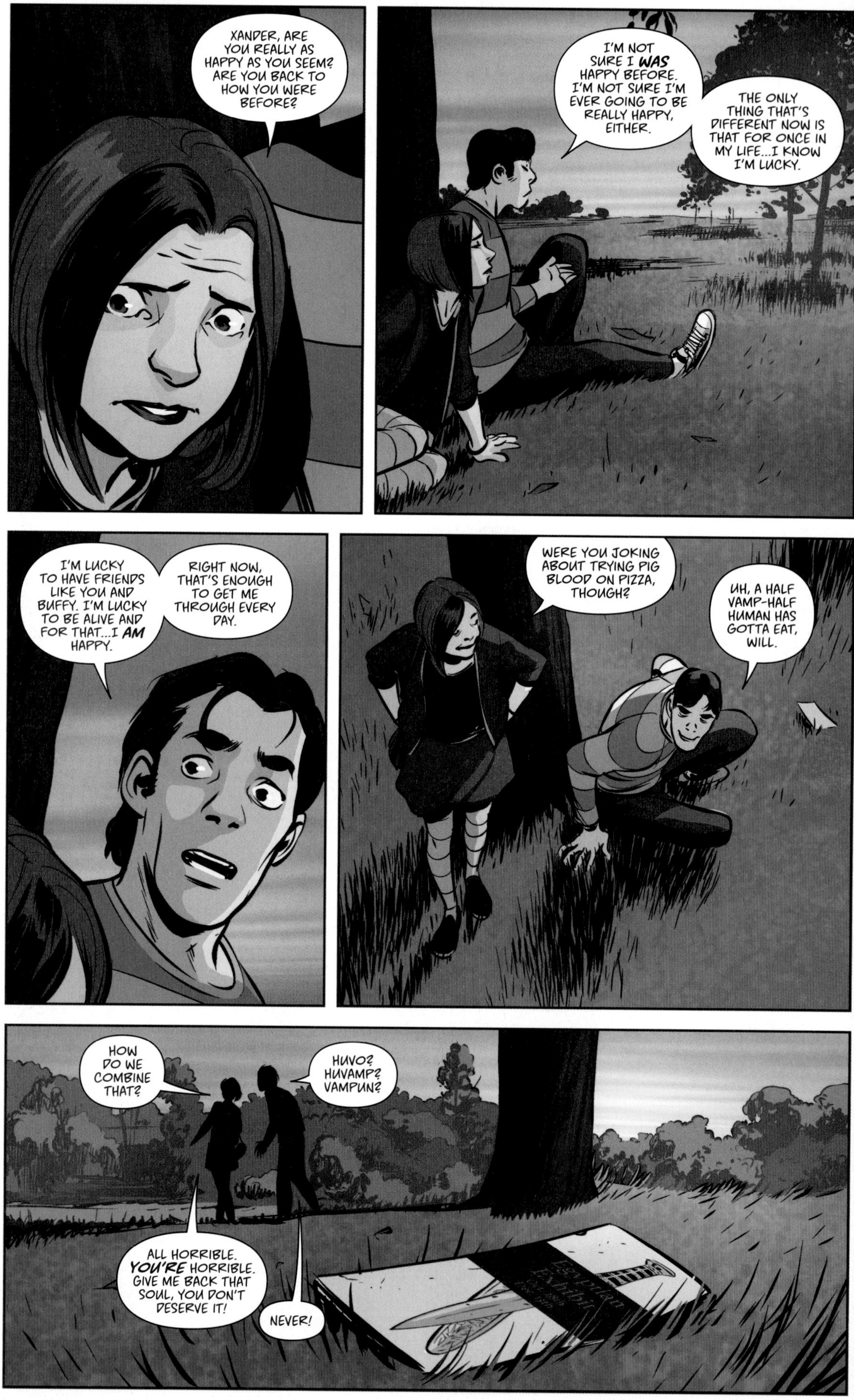
XANDER, ARE YOU REALLY AS HAPPY AS YOU SEEM? ARE YOU BACK TO HOW YOU WERE BEFORE?
I'M NOT SURE I WAS HAPPY BEFORE. I'M NOT SURE I'M EVER GOING TO BE REALLY HAPPY, EITHER.
THE ONLY THING THAT'S DIFFERENT NOW IS THAT FOR ONCE IN MY LIFE...I KNOW I'M LUCKY.
I'M LUCKY TO HAVE FRIENDS LIKE YOU AND BUFFY. I'M LUCKY TO BE ALIVE AND FOR THAT...I AM HAPPY.
RIGHT NOW, THAT'S ENOUGH TO GET ME THROUGH EVERY DAY.
WERE YOU JOKING ABOUT TRYING PIG BLOOD ON PIZZA, THOUGH?
UH, A HALF VAMP-HALF HUMAN HAS GOTTA EAT, WILL.
HOW DO WE COMBINE THAT?
HUVO? HUVAMP? VAMPUN?
ALL HORRIBLE. YOU'RE HORRIBLE. GIVE ME BACK THAT SOUL, YOU DON'T DESERVE IT!
NEVER!

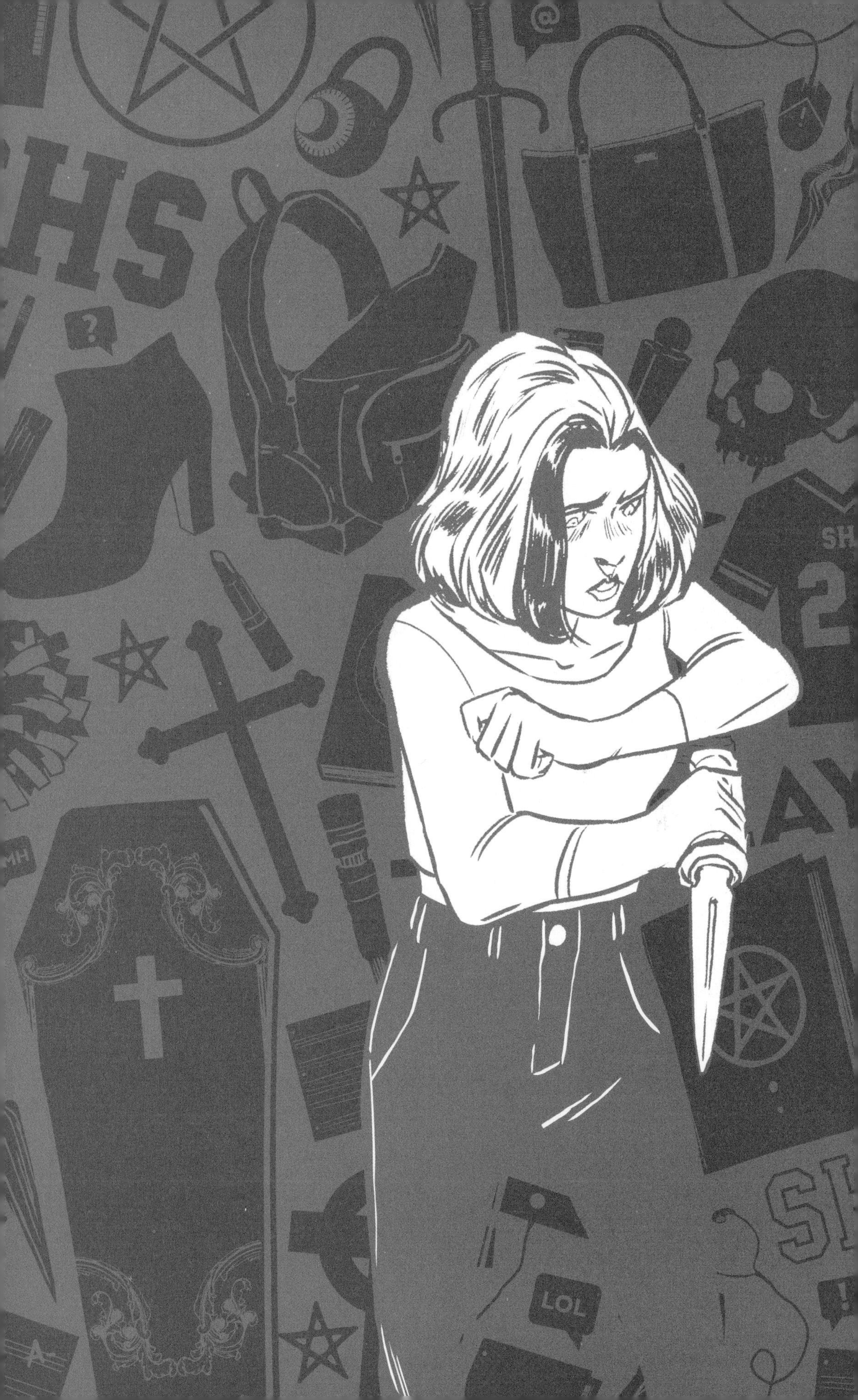
LOL

CHAPTER EIGHT

Issue Eight Cover by **Marc Aspinall**

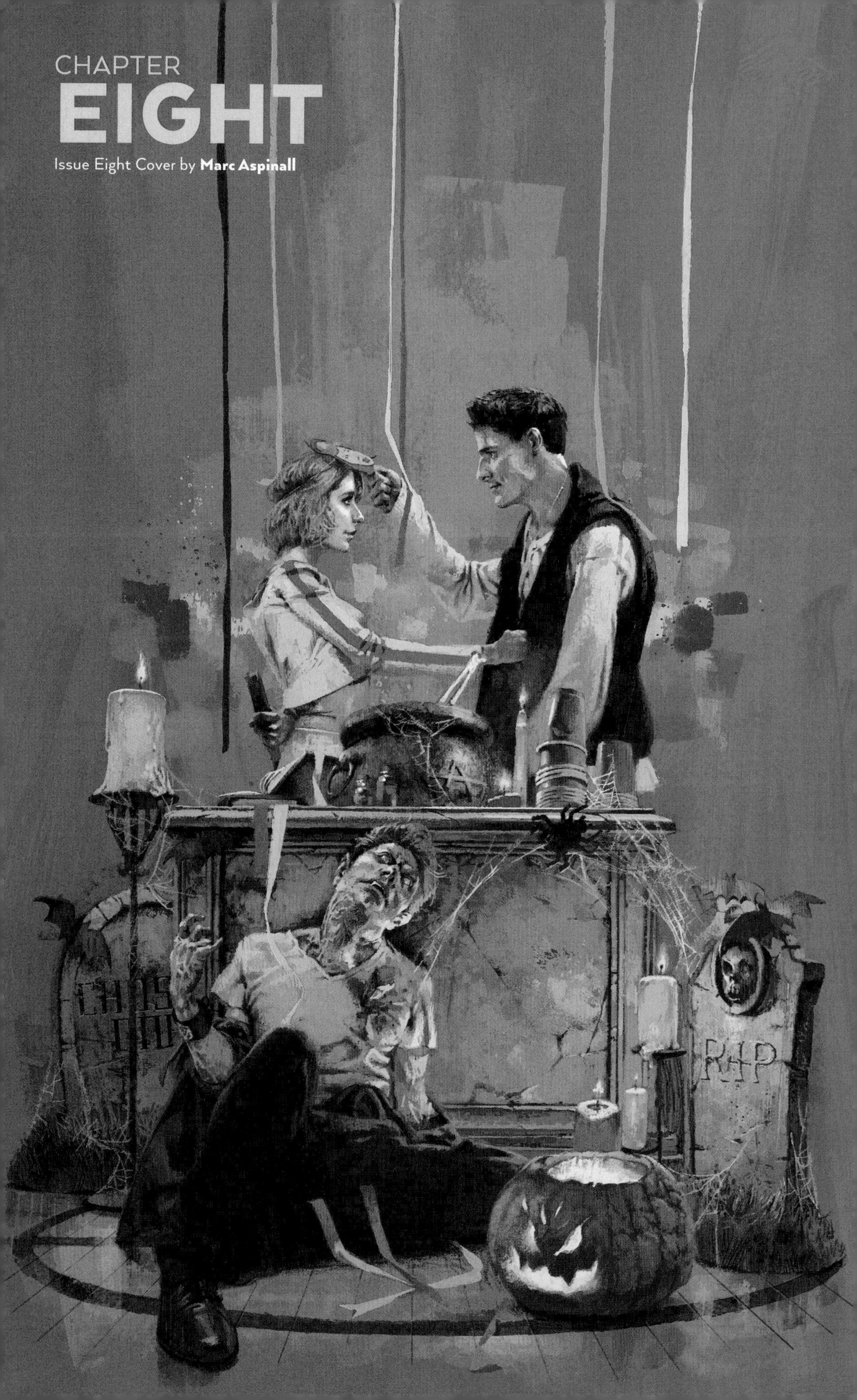

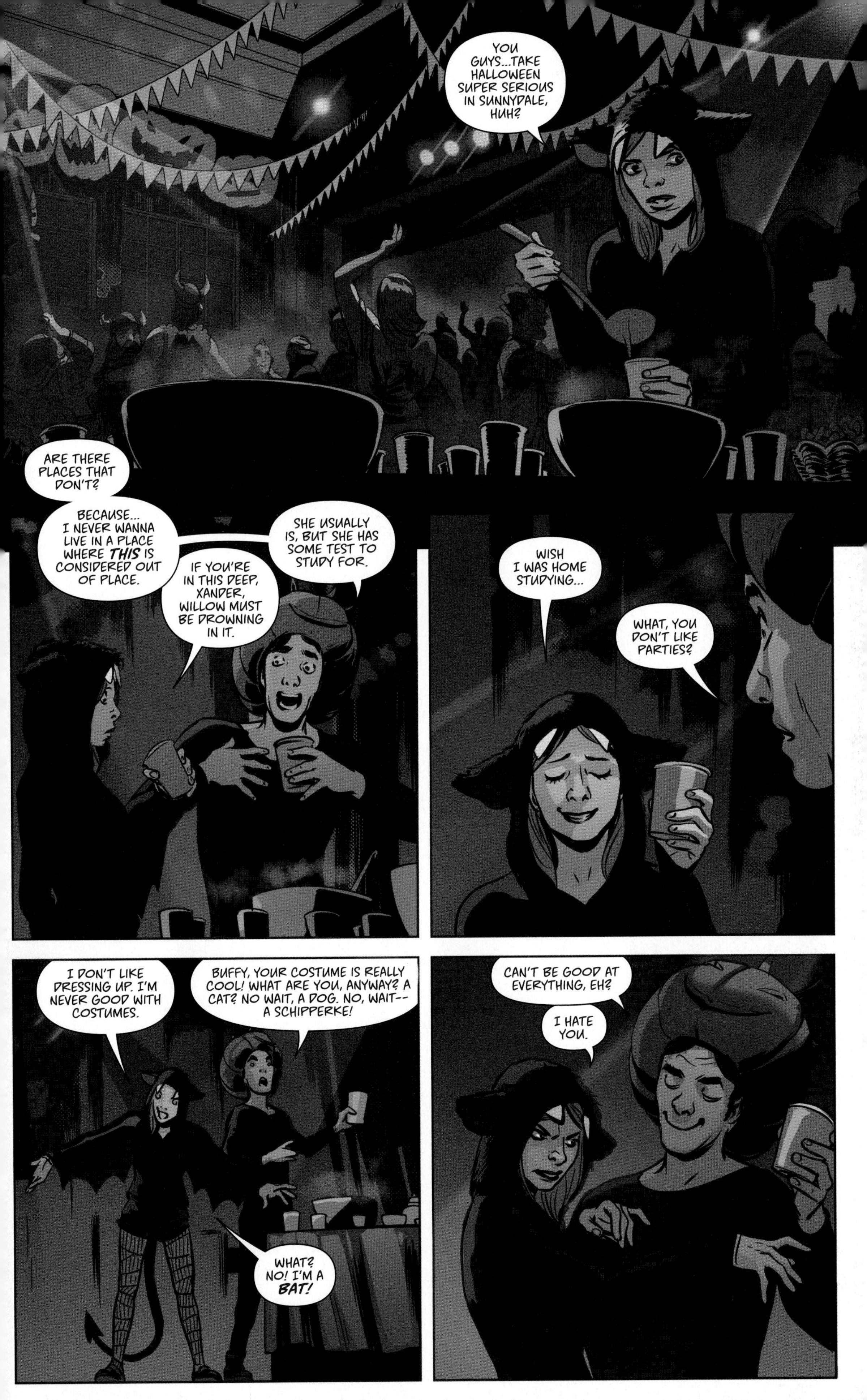
YOU GUYS...TAKE HALLOWEEN SUPER SERIOUS IN SUNNYDALE, HUH?
ARE THERE PLACES THAT DON'T?
BECAUSE... I NEVER WANNA LIVE IN A PLACE WHERE THIS IS CONSIDERED OUT OF PLACE.
IF YOU'RE IN THIS DEEP, XANDER, WILLOW MUST BE DROWNING IN IT.
SHE USUALLY IS, BUT SHE HAS SOME TEST TO STUDY FOR.
WISH I WAS HOME STUDYING...
WHAT, YOU DON'T LIKE PARTIES?
I DON'T LIKE DRESSING UP. I'M NEVER GOOD WITH COSTUMES.
BUFFY, YOUR COSTUME IS REALLY COOL! WHAT ARE YOU, ANYWAY? A CAT? NO WAIT, A DOG. NO, WAIT-- A SCHIPPERKE!
WHAT? NO! I'M A BAT!
CAN'T BE GOOD AT EVERYTHING, EH?
I HATE YOU.

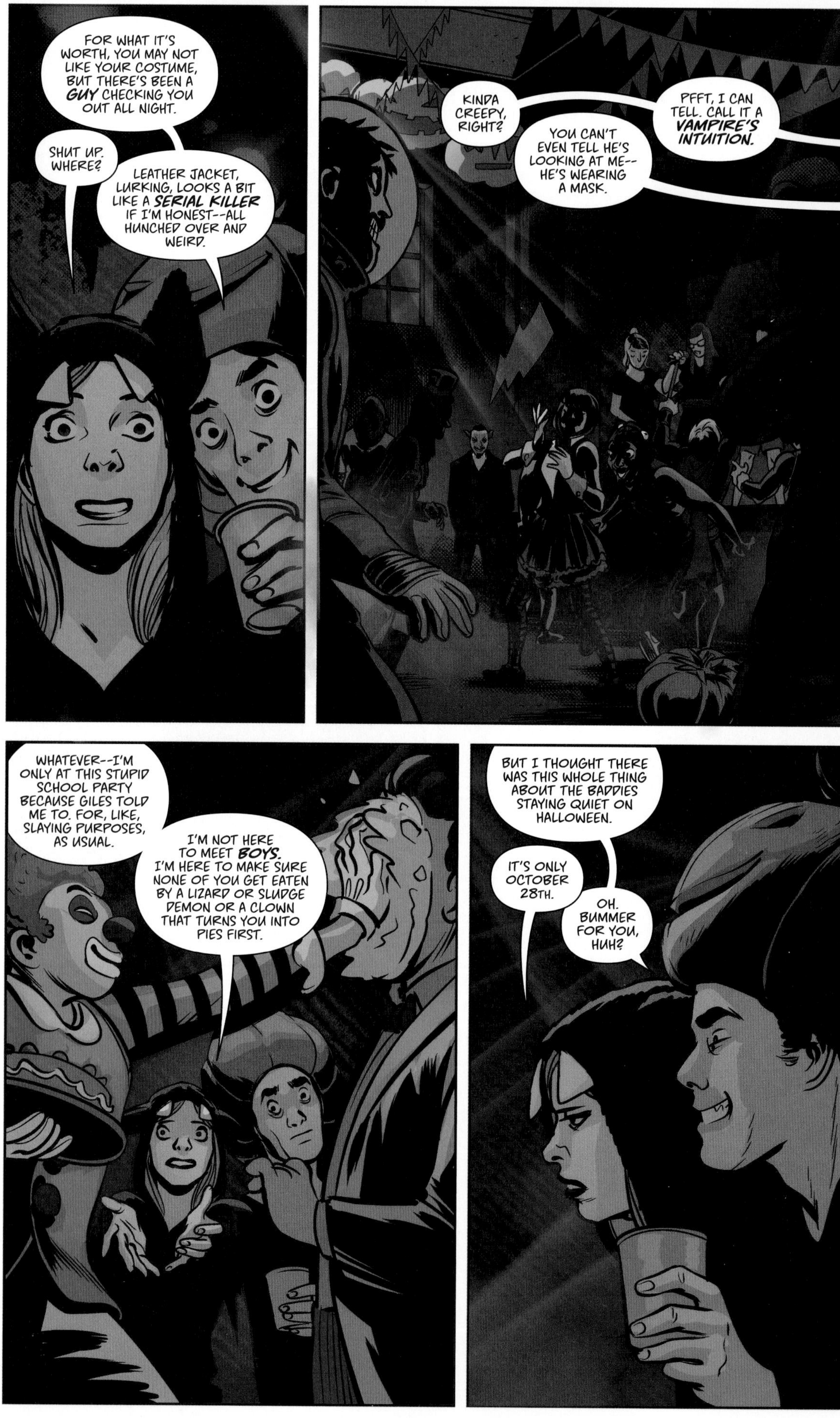
FOR WHAT IT'S WORTH, YOU MAY NOT LIKE YOUR COSTUME, BUT THERE'S BEEN A GUY CHECKING YOU OUT ALL NIGHT.
SHUT UP. WHERE?
LEATHER JACKET, LURKING, LOOKS A BIT LIKE A SERIAL KILLER IF I'M HONEST--ALL HUNCHED OVER AND WEIRD.
KINDA CREEPY, RIGHT?
YOU CAN'T EVEN TELL HE'S LOOKING AT ME-- HE'S WEARING A MASK.
PFFT, I CAN TELL. CALL IT A VAMPIRE'S INTUITION.
WHATEVER--I'M ONLY AT THIS STUPID SCHOOL PARTY BECAUSE GILES TOLD ME TO. FOR, LIKE, SLAYING PURPOSES, AS USUAL.
I'M NOT HERE TO MEET BOYS. I'M HERE TO MAKE SURE NONE OF YOU GET EATEN BY A LIZARD OR SLUDGE DEMON OR A CLOWN THAT TURNS YOU INTO PIES FIRST.
BUT I THOUGHT THERE WAS THIS WHOLE THING ABOUT THE BADDIES STAYING QUIET ON HALLOWEEN.
IT'S ONLY OCTOBER 28TH.
OH. BUMMER FOR YOU, HUH?

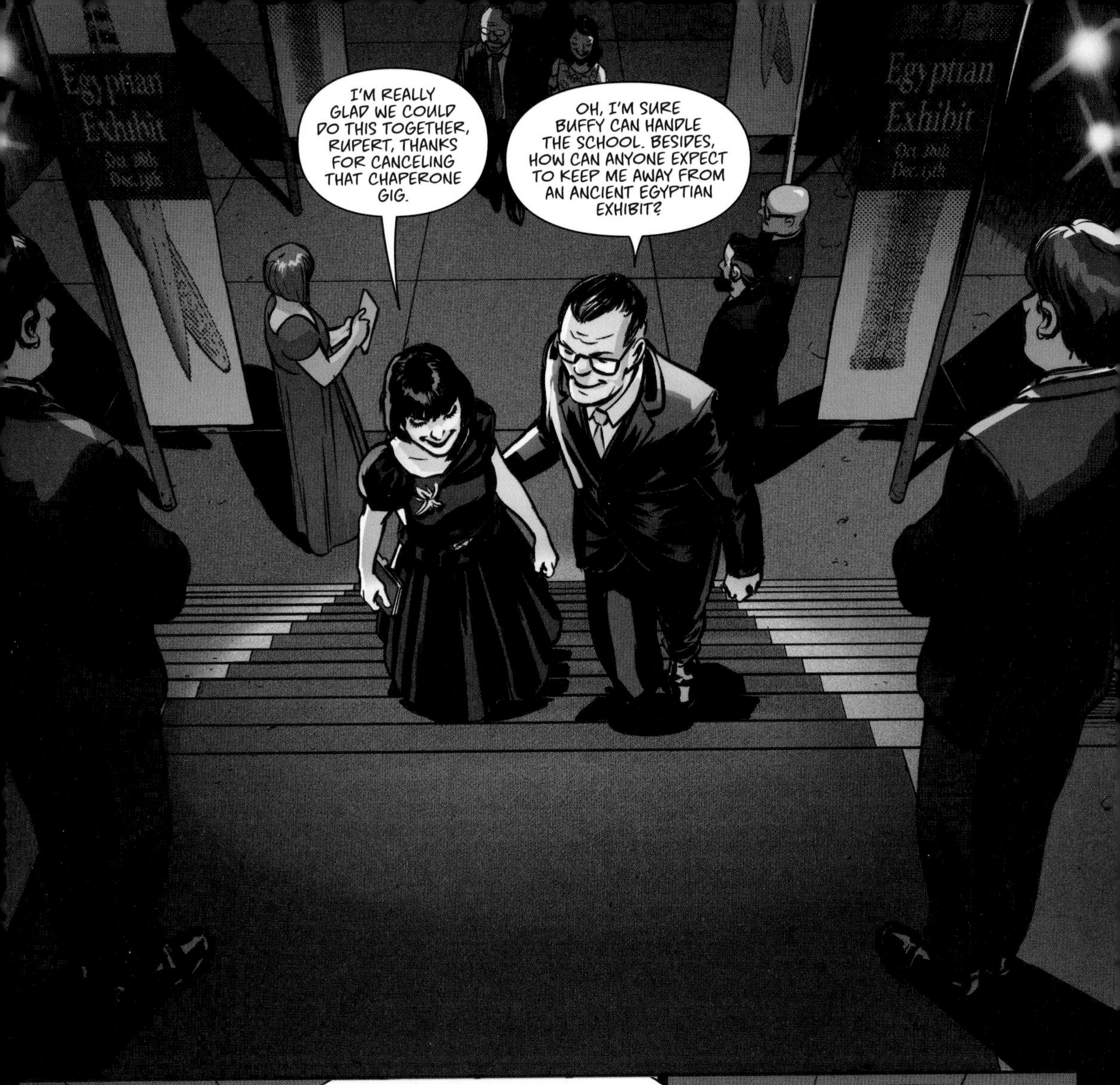
Egyptian Exhibit
I'M REALLY GLAD WE COULD DO THIS TOGETHER, RUPERT, THANKS FOR CANCELING THAT CHAPERONE GIG.
OH, I'M SURE BUFFY CAN HANDLE THE SCHOOL. BESIDES, HOW CAN ANYONE EXPECT TO KEEP ME AWAY FROM AN ANCIENT EGYPTIAN EXHIBIT?
Egyptian Exhibit

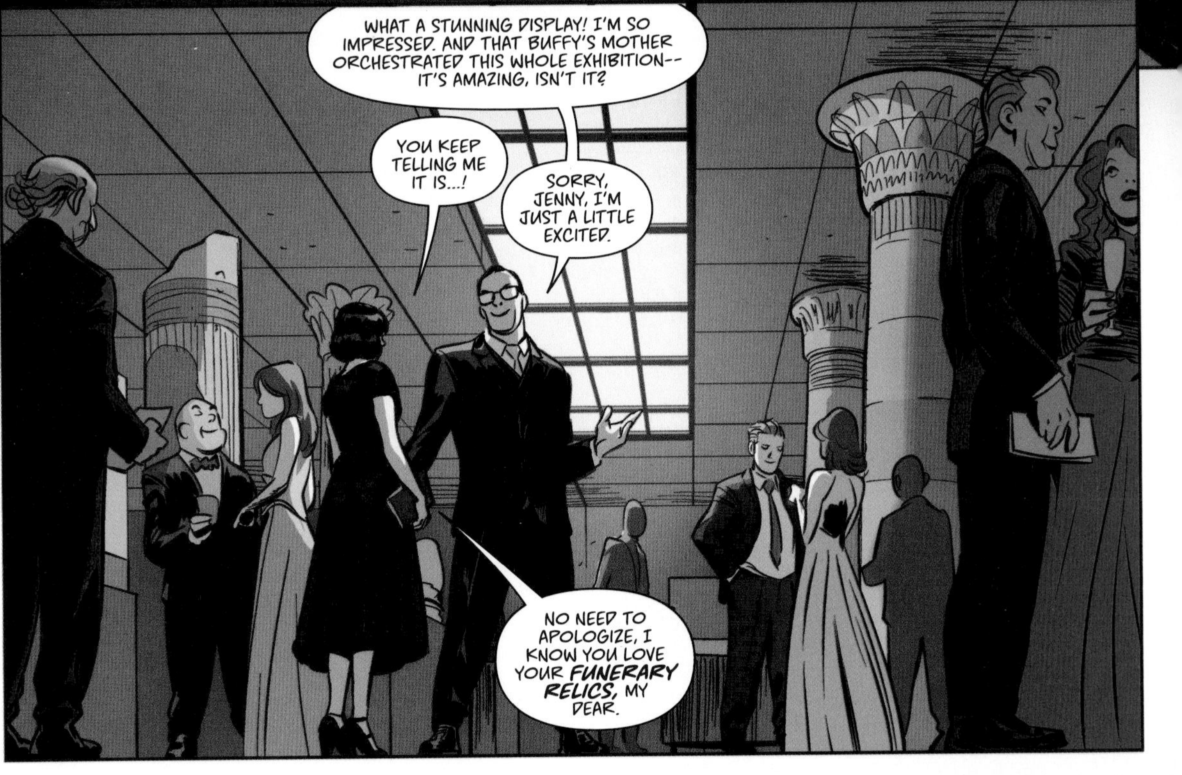
WHAT A STUNNING DISPLAY! I'M SO IMPRESSED. AND THAT BUFFY'S MOTHER ORCHESTRATED THIS WHOLE EXHIBITION-- IT'S AMAZING, ISN'T IT?
YOU KEEP TELLING ME IT IS...!
SORRY, JENNY, I'M JUST A LITTLE EXCITED.
NO NEED TO APOLOGIZE, I KNOW YOU LOVE YOUR **FUNERARY RELICS,** MY DEAR.

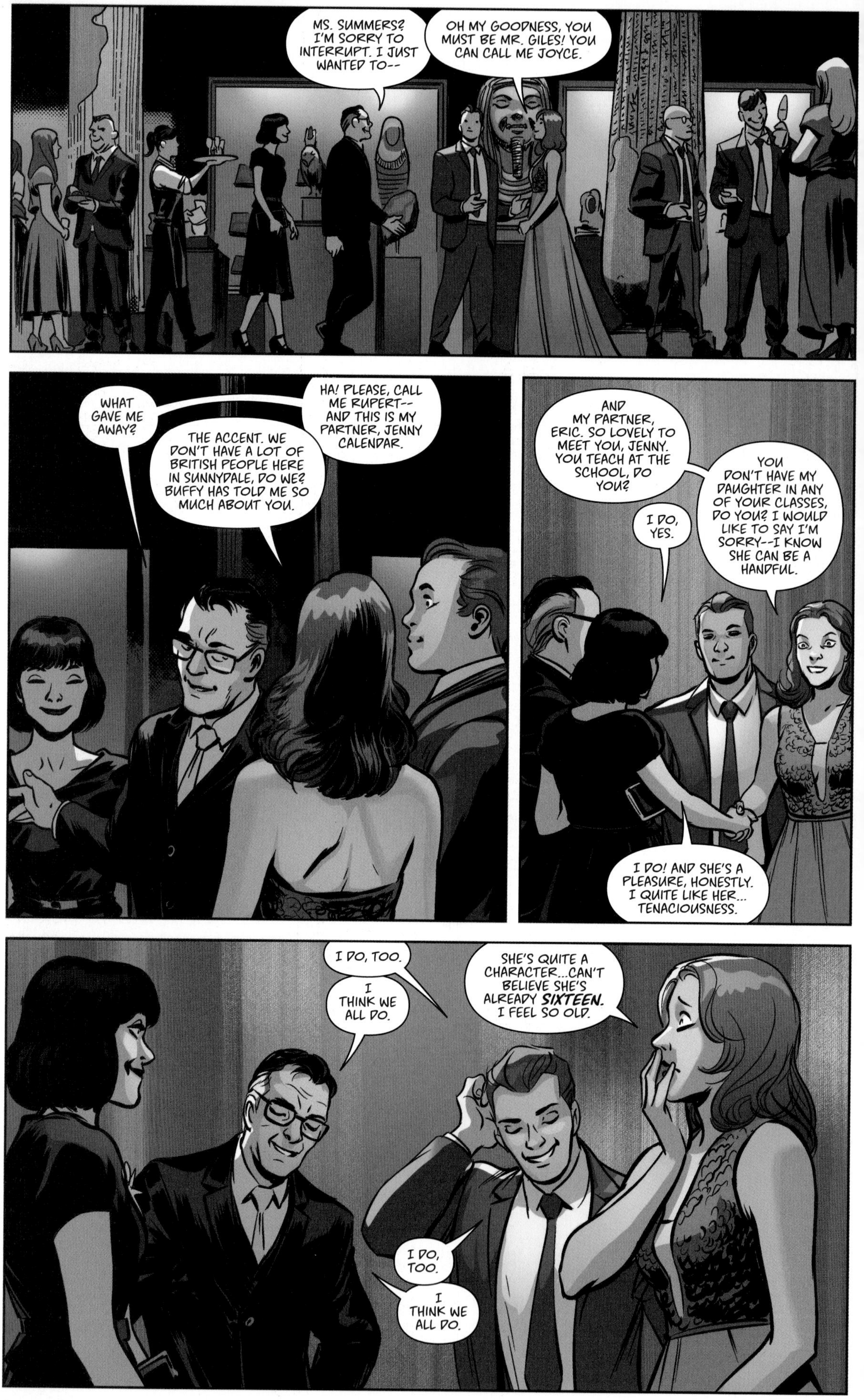
MS. SUMMERS? I'M SORRY TO INTERRUPT. I JUST WANTED TO--
OH MY GOODNESS, YOU MUST BE MR. GILES! YOU CAN CALL ME JOYCE.
WHAT GAVE ME AWAY?
THE ACCENT. WE DON'T HAVE A LOT OF BRITISH PEOPLE HERE IN SUNNYDALE, DO WE? BUFFY HAS TOLD ME SO MUCH ABOUT YOU.
HA! PLEASE, CALL ME RUPERT-- AND THIS IS MY PARTNER, JENNY CALENDAR.
AND MY PARTNER, ERIC. SO LOVELY TO MEET YOU, JENNY. YOU TEACH AT THE SCHOOL, DO YOU?
I DO, YES.
YOU DON'T HAVE MY DAUGHTER IN ANY OF YOUR CLASSES, DO YOU? I WOULD LIKE TO SAY I'M SORRY--I KNOW SHE CAN BE A HANDFUL.
I DO! AND SHE'S A PLEASURE, HONESTLY. I QUITE LIKE HER... TENACIOUSNESS.
I DO, TOO.
I THINK WE ALL DO.
SHE'S QUITE A CHARACTER...CAN'T BELIEVE SHE'S ALREADY SIXTEEN. I FEEL SO OLD.
I DO, TOO.
I THINK WE ALL DO.

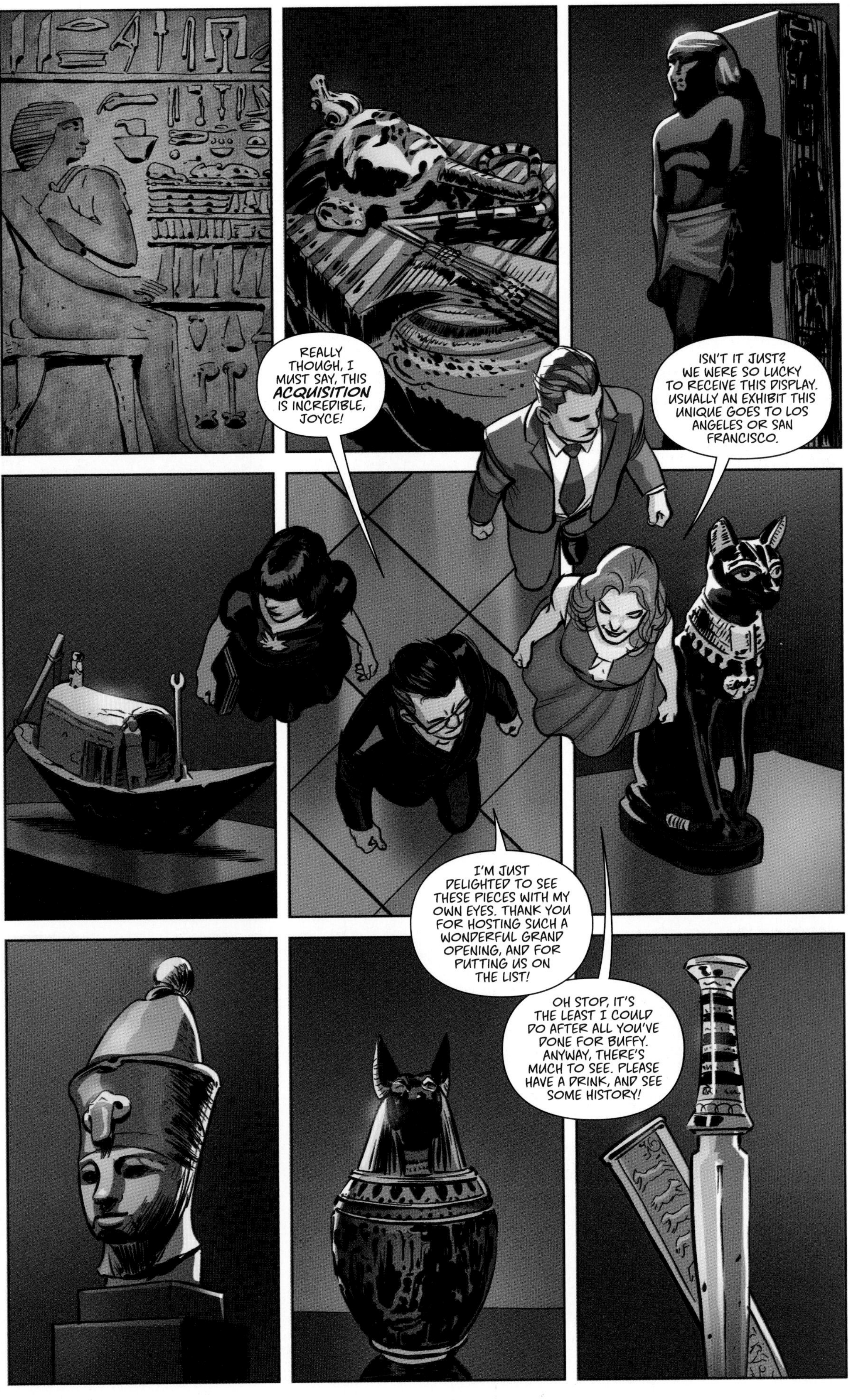
REALLY THOUGH, I MUST SAY, THIS ACQUISITION IS INCREDIBLE, JOYCE!
ISN'T IT JUST? WE WERE SO LUCKY TO RECEIVE THIS DISPLAY. USUALLY AN EXHIBIT THIS UNIQUE GOES TO LOS ANGELES OR SAN FRANCISCO.
I'M JUST DELIGHTED TO SEE THESE PIECES WITH MY OWN EYES. THANK YOU FOR HOSTING SUCH A WONDERFUL GRAND OPENING, AND FOR PUTTING US ON THE LIST!
OH STOP, IT'S THE LEAST I COULD DO AFTER ALL YOU'VE DONE FOR BUFFY. ANYWAY, THERE'S MUCH TO SEE. PLEASE HAVE A DRINK, AND SEE SOME HISTORY!

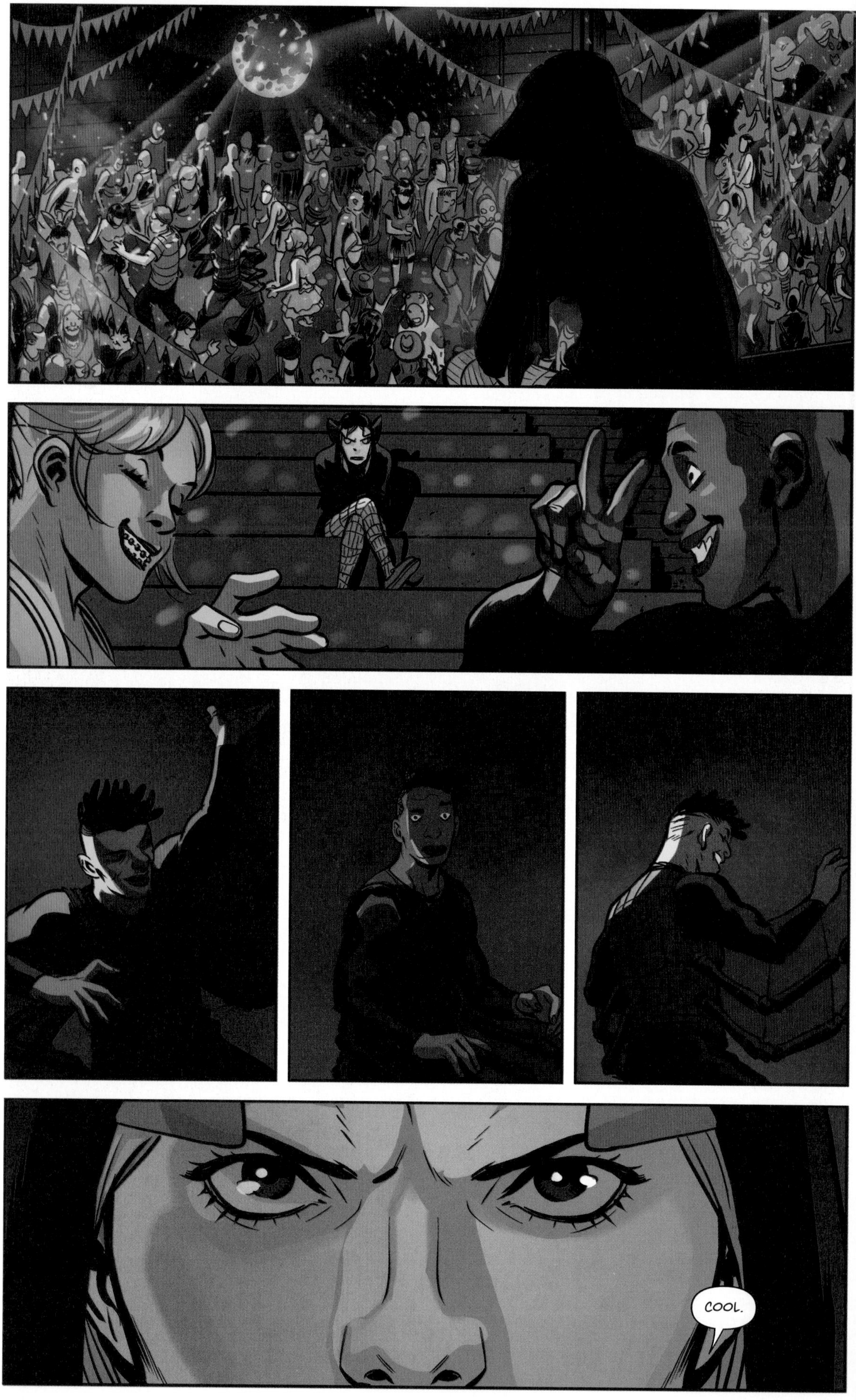
COOL.

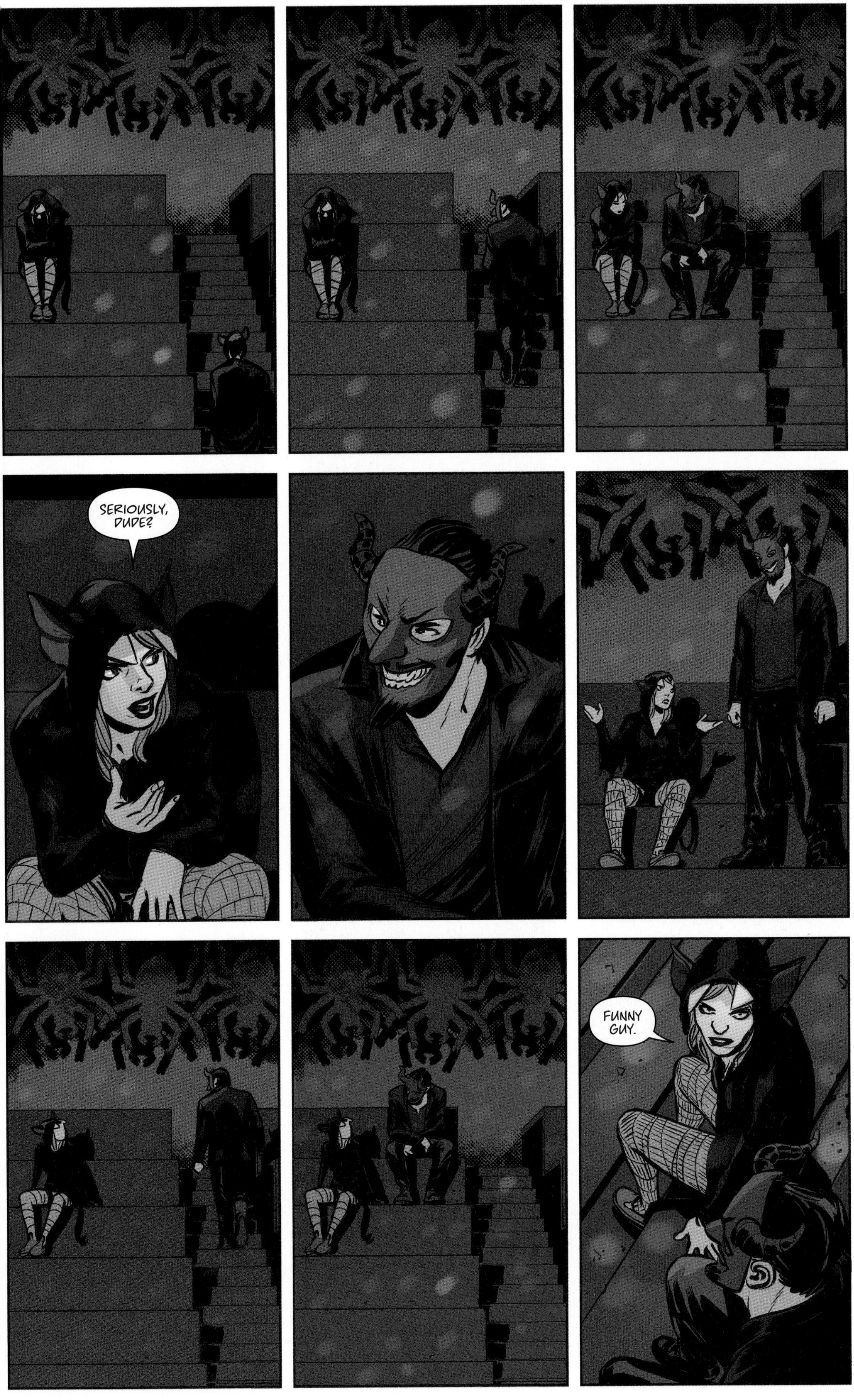
SERIOUSLY, DUDE?
FUNNY GUY.

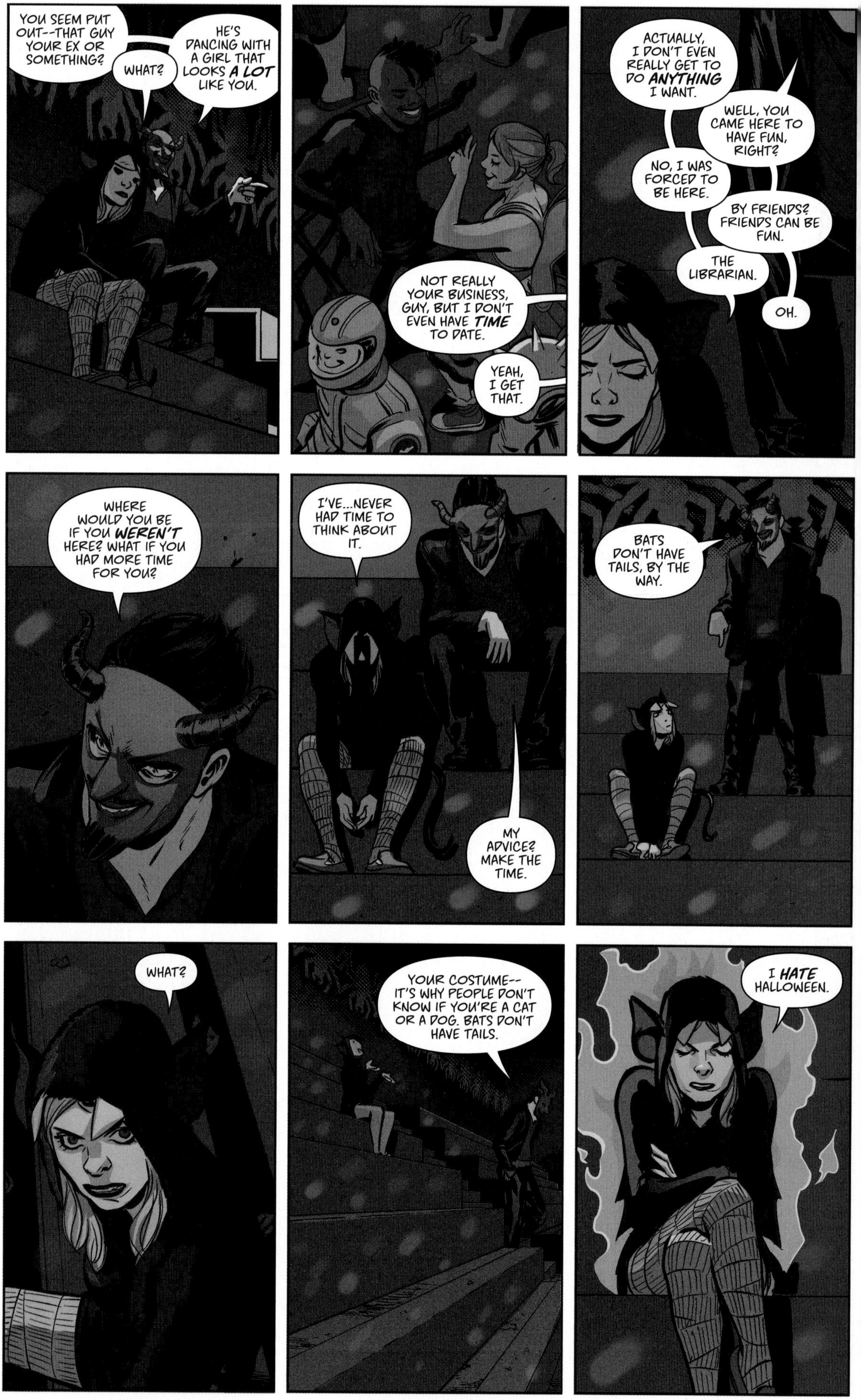
YOU SEEM PUT OUT--THAT GUY YOUR EX OR SOMETHING?
WHAT?
HE'S DANCING WITH A GIRL THAT LOOKS A LOT LIKE YOU.
NOT REALLY YOUR BUSINESS, GUY, BUT I DON'T EVEN HAVE TIME TO DATE.
YEAH, I GET THAT.
ACTUALLY, I DON'T EVEN REALLY GET TO DO ANYTHING I WANT.
WELL, YOU CAME HERE TO HAVE FUN, RIGHT?
NO, I WAS FORCED TO BE HERE.
BY FRIENDS? FRIENDS CAN BE FUN.
THE LIBRARIAN.
OH.
WHERE WOULD YOU BE IF YOU WEREN'T HERE? WHAT IF YOU HAD MORE TIME FOR YOU?
I'VE...NEVER HAD TIME TO THINK ABOUT IT.
MY ADVICE? MAKE THE TIME.
BATS DON'T HAVE TAILS, BY THE WAY.
WHAT?
YOUR COSTUME--IT'S WHY PEOPLE DON'T KNOW IF YOU'RE A CAT OR A DOG. BATS DON'T HAVE TAILS.
I HATE HALLOWEEN.

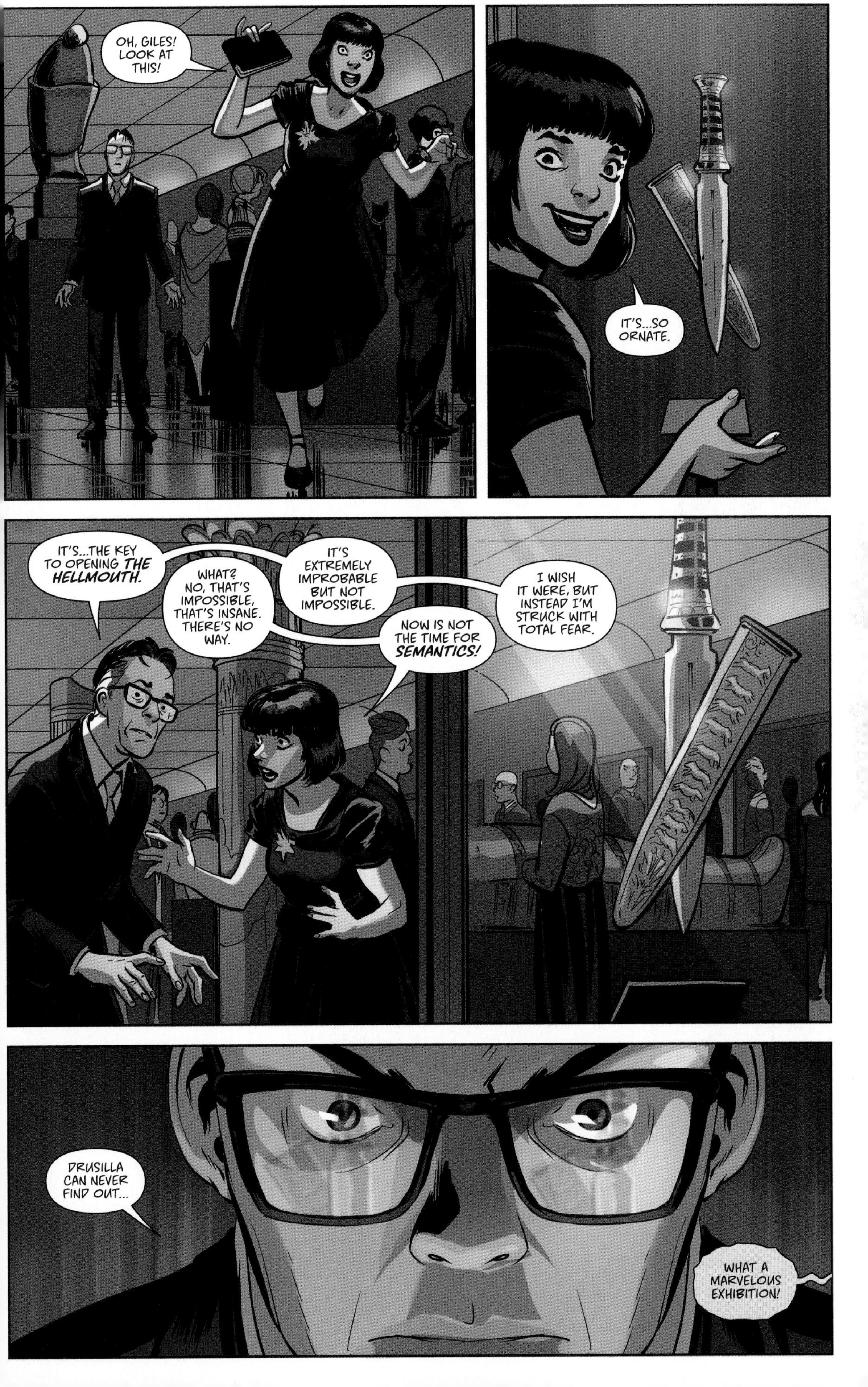
OH, GILES! LOOK AT THIS!
IT'S...SO ORNATE.
IT'S...THE KEY TO OPENING THE HELLMOUTH.
WHAT? NO, THAT'S IMPOSSIBLE, THAT'S INSANE. THERE'S NO WAY.
IT'S EXTREMELY IMPROBABLE BUT NOT IMPOSSIBLE.
NOW IS NOT THE TIME FOR SEMANTICS!
I WISH IT WERE, BUT INSTEAD I'M STRUCK WITH TOTAL FEAR.
DRUSILLA CAN NEVER FIND OUT...
WHAT A MARVELOUS EXHIBITION!

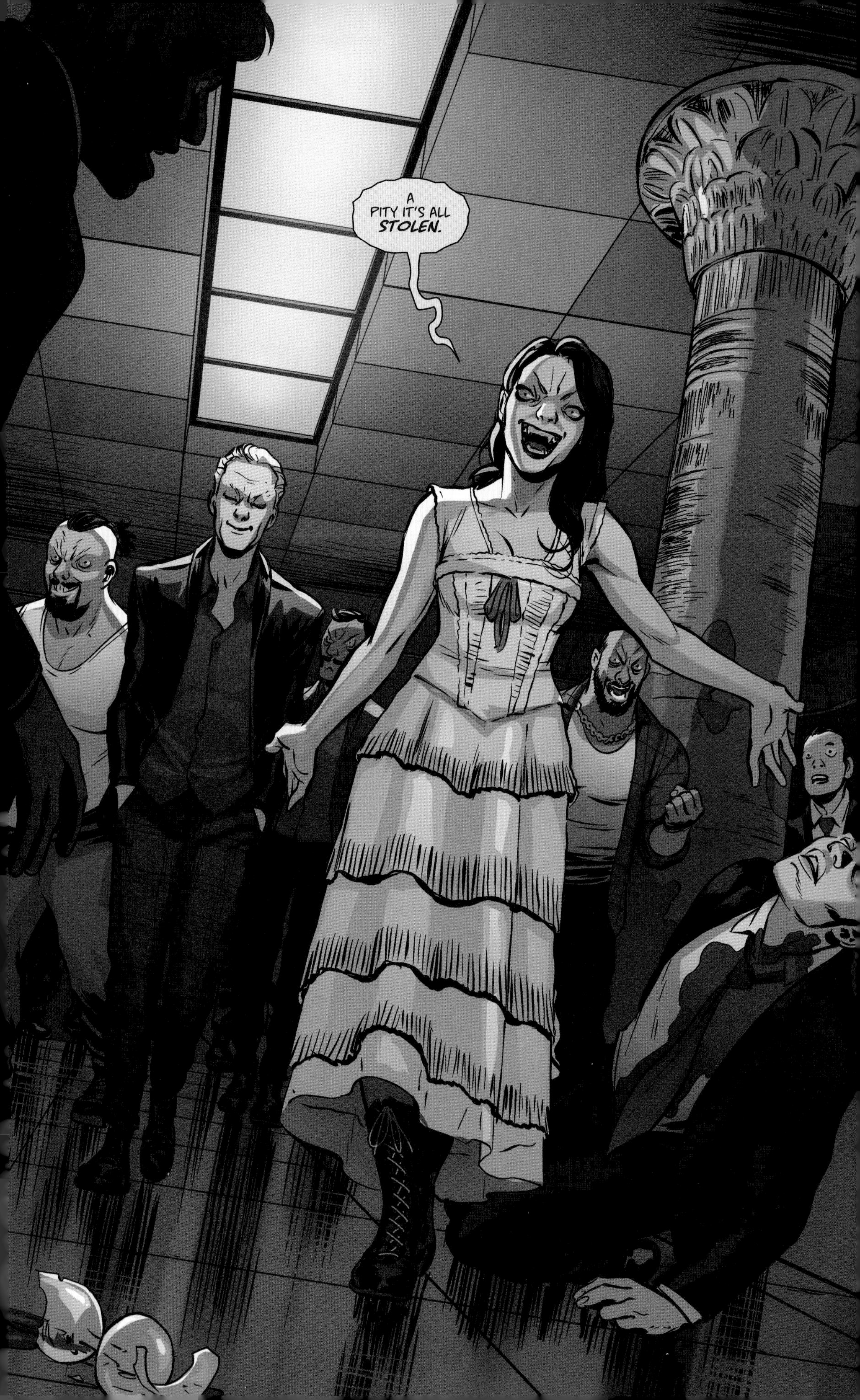
A PITY IT'S ALL STOLEN.

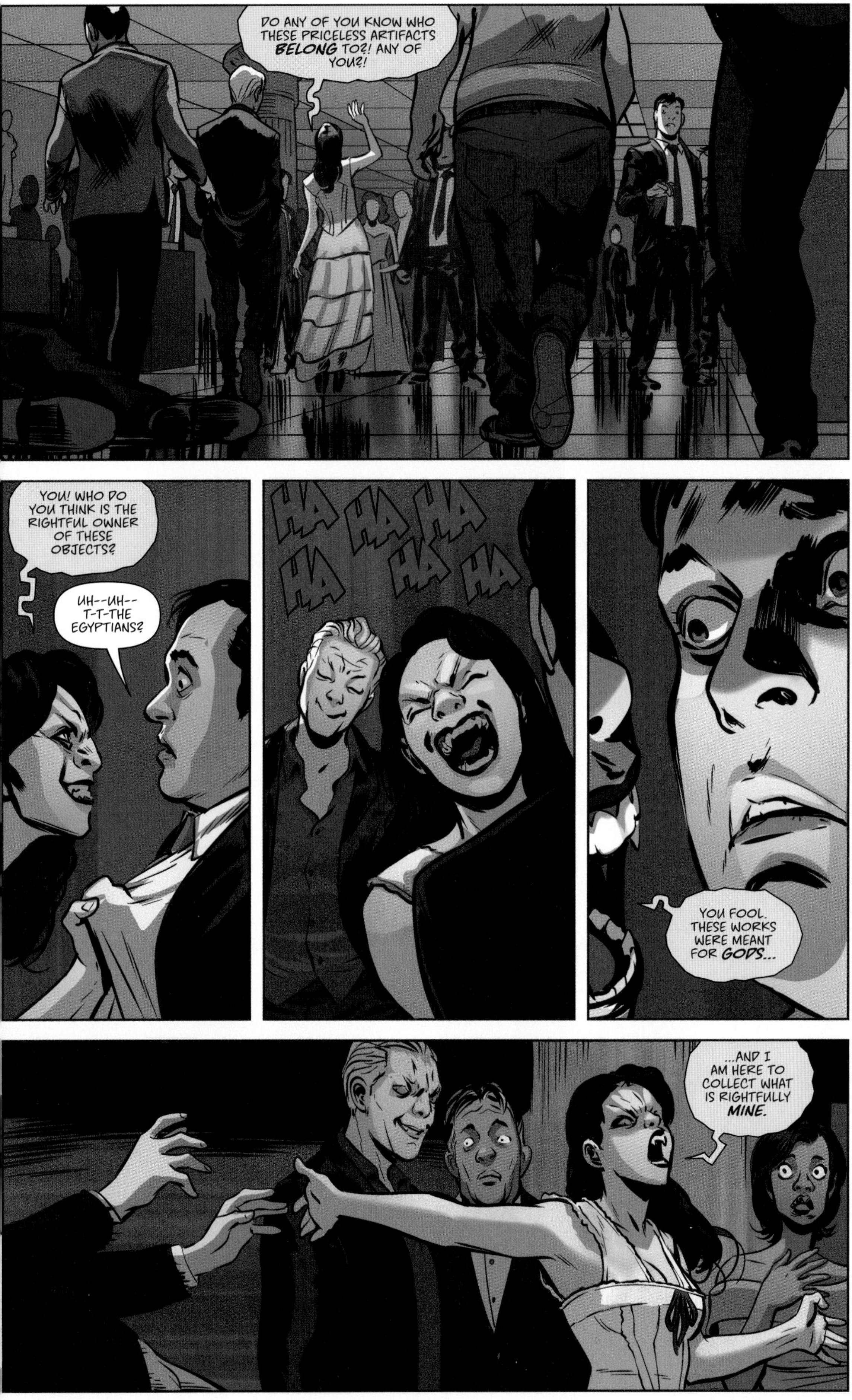
DO ANY OF YOU KNOW WHO THESE PRICELESS ARTIFACTS **BELONG** TO?! ANY OF YOU?!
YOU! WHO DO YOU THINK IS THE RIGHTFUL OWNER OF THESE OBJECTS?
UH--UH--T-T-THE EGYPTIANS?
HA HA HA HA HA HA HA
YOU FOOL. THESE WORKS WERE MEANT FOR **GODS**...
...AND I AM HERE TO COLLECT WHAT IS RIGHTFULLY **MINE**.

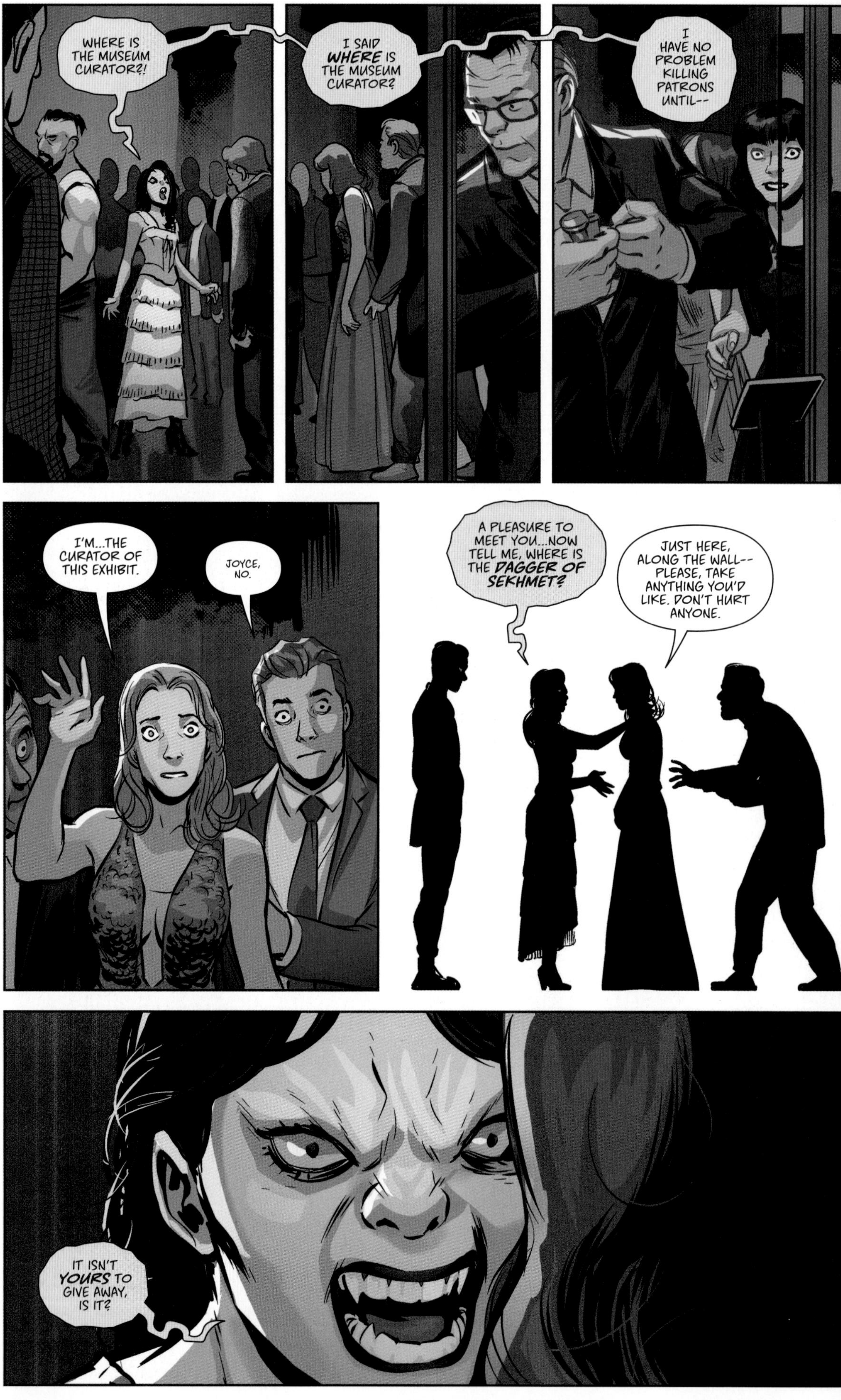
WHERE IS THE MUSEUM CURATOR?!
I SAID WHERE IS THE MUSEUM CURATOR?
I HAVE NO PROBLEM KILLING PATRONS UNTIL--
I'M...THE CURATOR OF THIS EXHIBIT.
JOYCE, NO.
A PLEASURE TO MEET YOU...NOW TELL ME, WHERE IS THE DAGGER OF SEKHMET?
JUST HERE, ALONG THE WALL--PLEASE, TAKE ANYTHING YOU'D LIKE. DON'T HURT ANYONE.
IT ISN'T YOURS TO GIVE AWAY, IS IT?

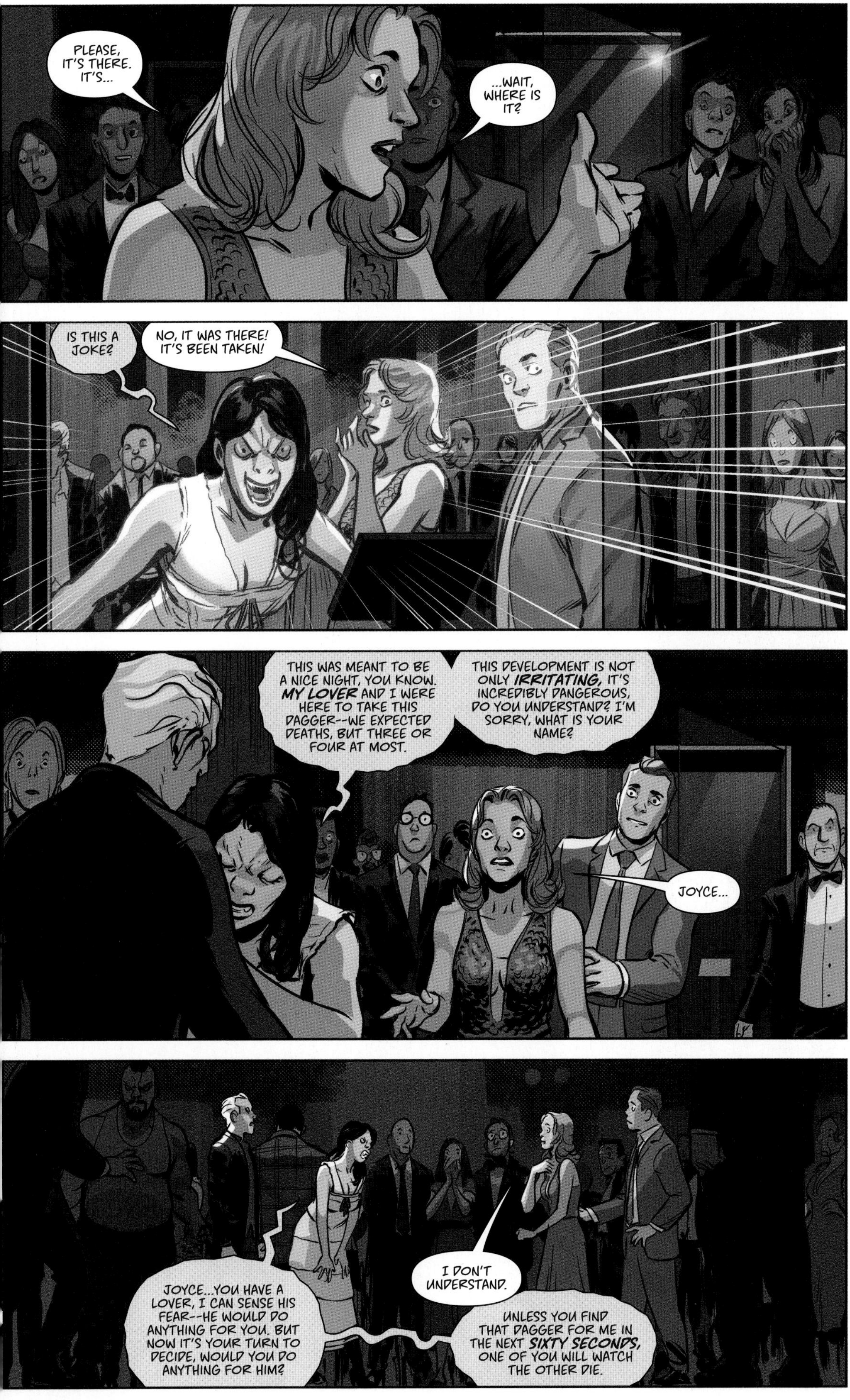
PLEASE, IT'S THERE. IT'S...
...WAIT, WHERE IS IT?
IS THIS A JOKE?
NO, IT WAS THERE! IT'S BEEN TAKEN!
THIS WAS MEANT TO BE A NICE NIGHT, YOU KNOW. MY LOVER AND I WERE HERE TO TAKE THIS DAGGER--WE EXPECTED DEATHS, BUT THREE OR FOUR AT MOST.
THIS DEVELOPMENT IS NOT ONLY IRRITATING, IT'S INCREDIBLY DANGEROUS, DO YOU UNDERSTAND? I'M SORRY, WHAT IS YOUR NAME?
JOYCE...
I DON'T UNDERSTAND.
JOYCE...YOU HAVE A LOVER, I CAN SENSE HIS FEAR--HE WOULD DO ANYTHING FOR YOU. BUT NOW IT'S YOUR TURN TO DECIDE, WOULD YOU DO ANYTHING FOR HIM?
UNLESS YOU FIND THAT DAGGER FOR ME IN THE NEXT SIXTY SECONDS, ONE OF YOU WILL WATCH THE OTHER DIE.

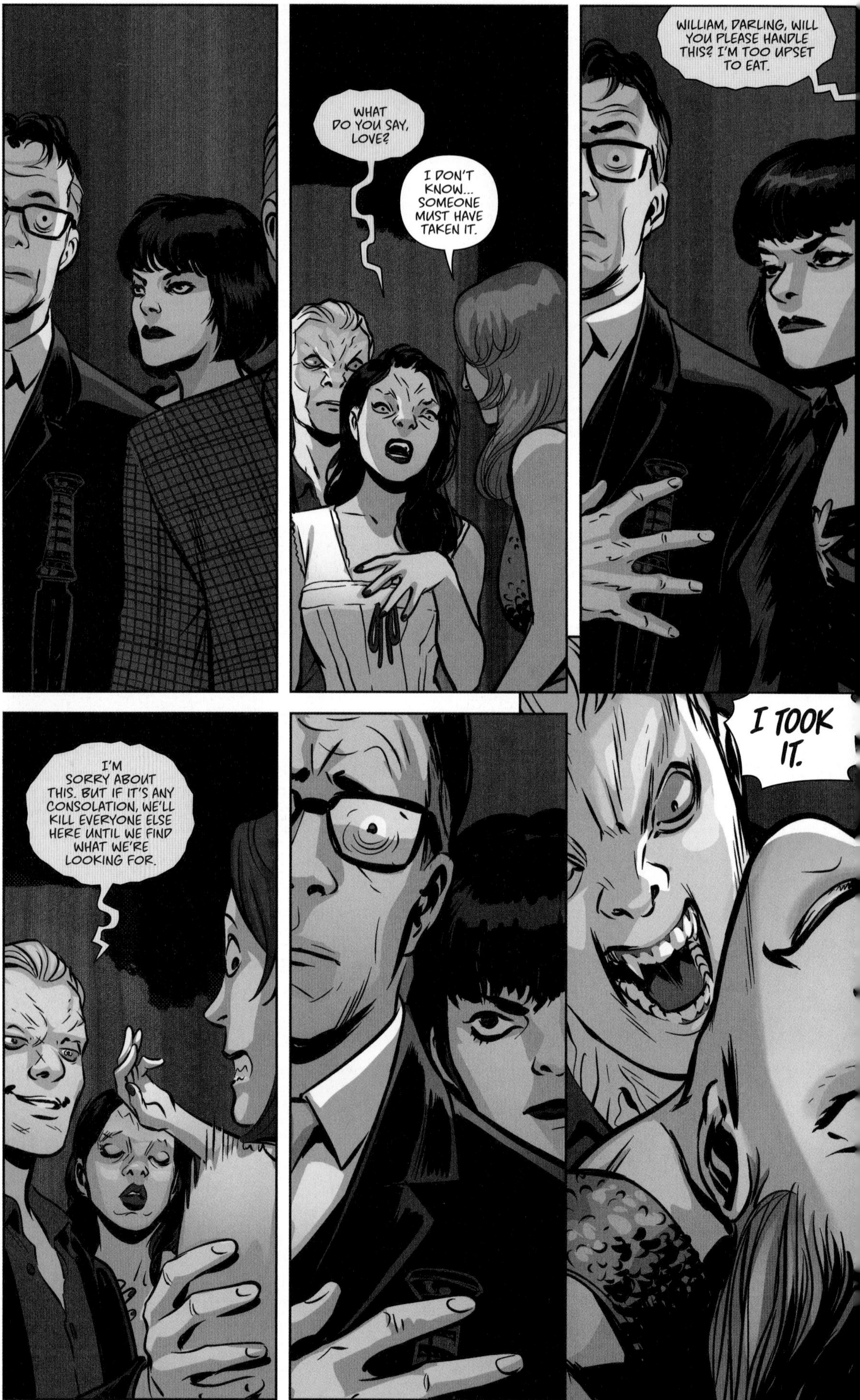
WHAT DO YOU SAY, LOVE?
I DON'T KNOW... SOMEONE MUST HAVE TAKEN IT.
WILLIAM, DARLING, WILL YOU PLEASE HANDLE THIS? I'M TOO UPSET TO EAT.
I'M SORRY ABOUT THIS. BUT IF IT'S ANY CONSOLATION, WE'LL KILL EVERYONE ELSE HERE UNTIL WE FIND WHAT WE'RE LOOKING FOR.
I TOOK IT.

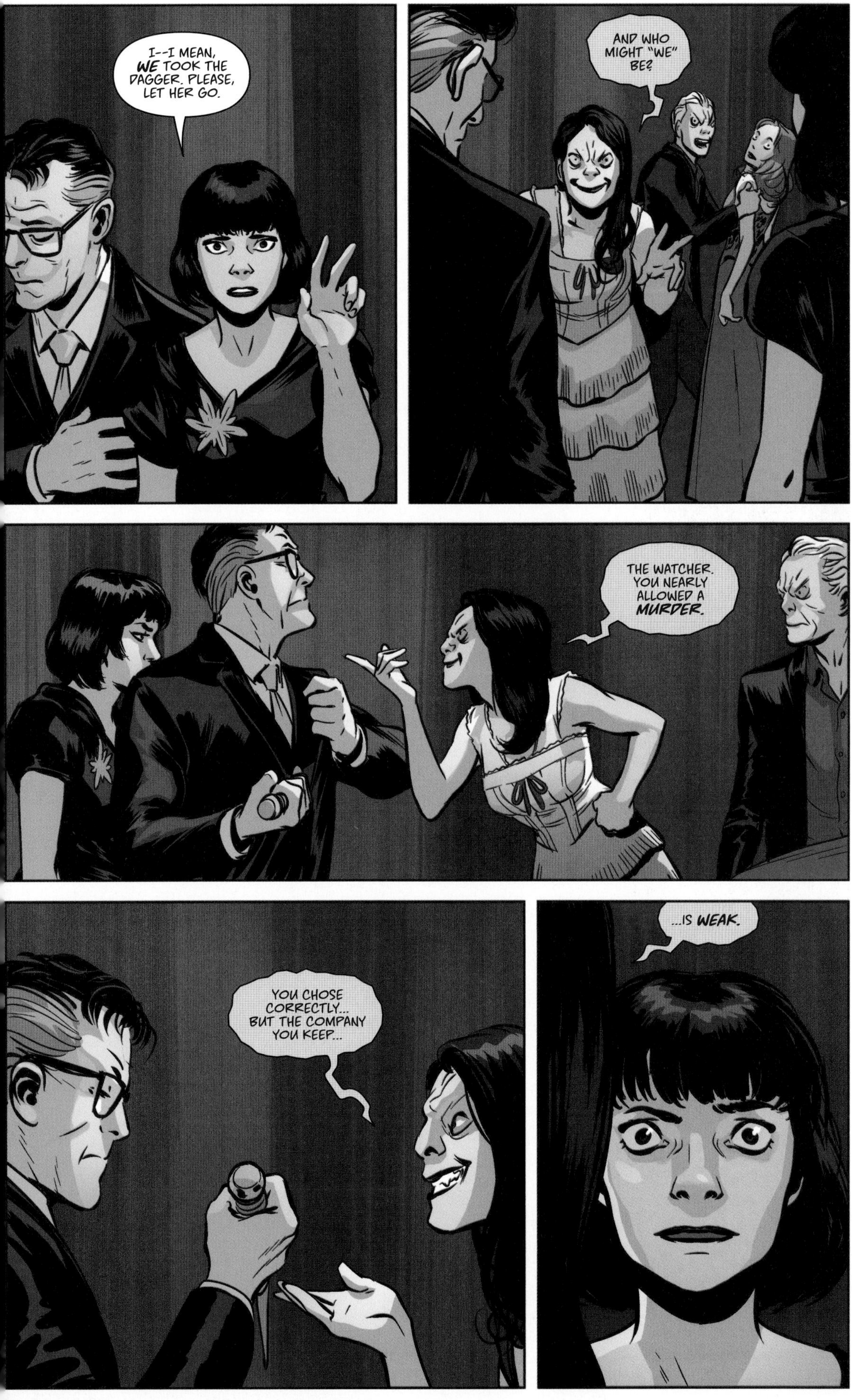
I--I MEAN, WE TOOK THE DAGGER. PLEASE, LET HER GO.
AND WHO MIGHT "WE" BE?
THE WATCHER. YOU NEARLY ALLOWED A MURDER.
YOU CHOSE CORRECTLY... BUT THE COMPANY YOU KEEP...
...IS WEAK.

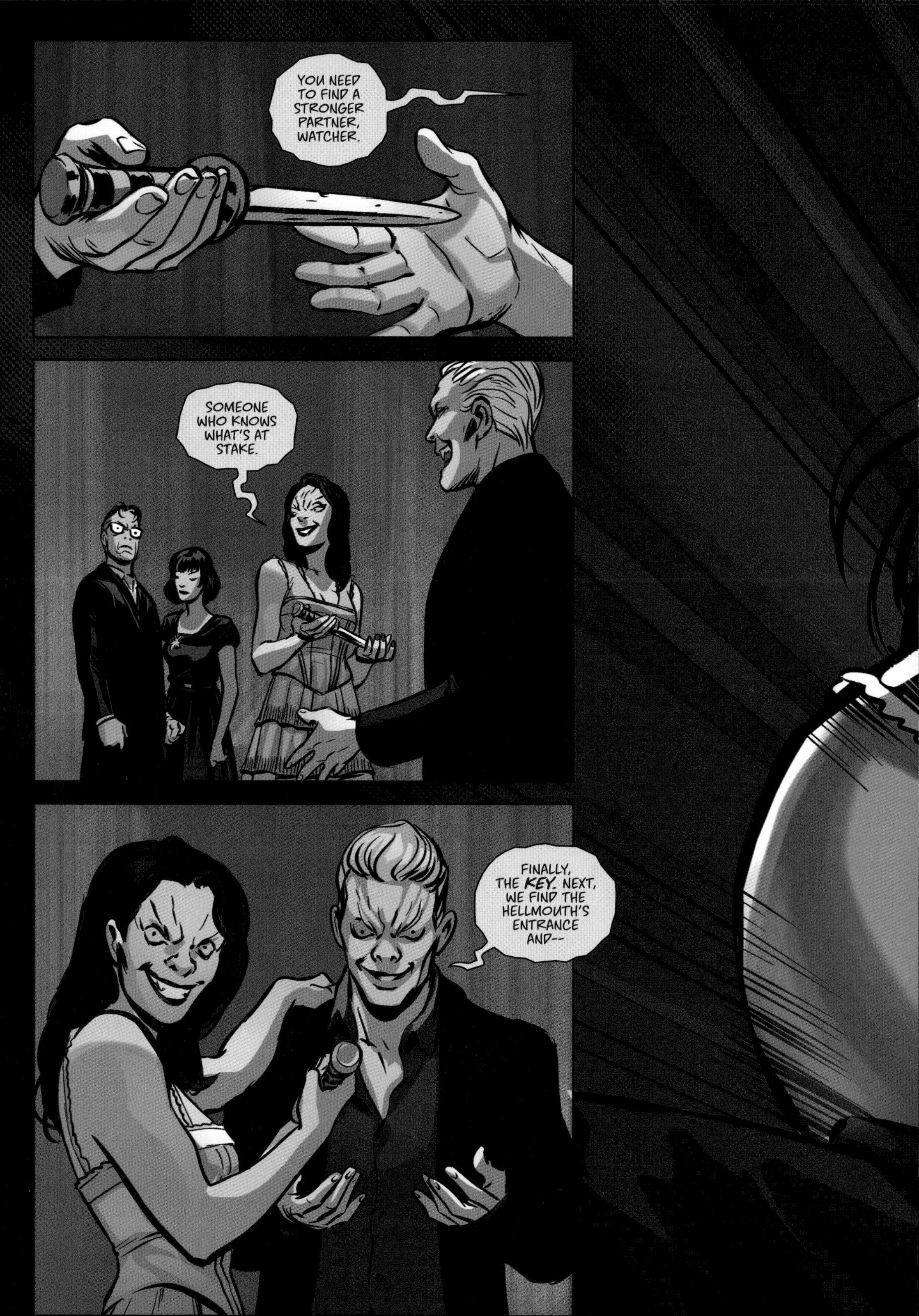
YOU NEED TO FIND A STRONGER PARTNER, WATCHER.
SOMEONE WHO KNOWS WHAT'S AT STAKE.
FINALLY, THE **KEY.** NEXT, WE FIND THE HELLMOUTH'S ENTRANCE AND--

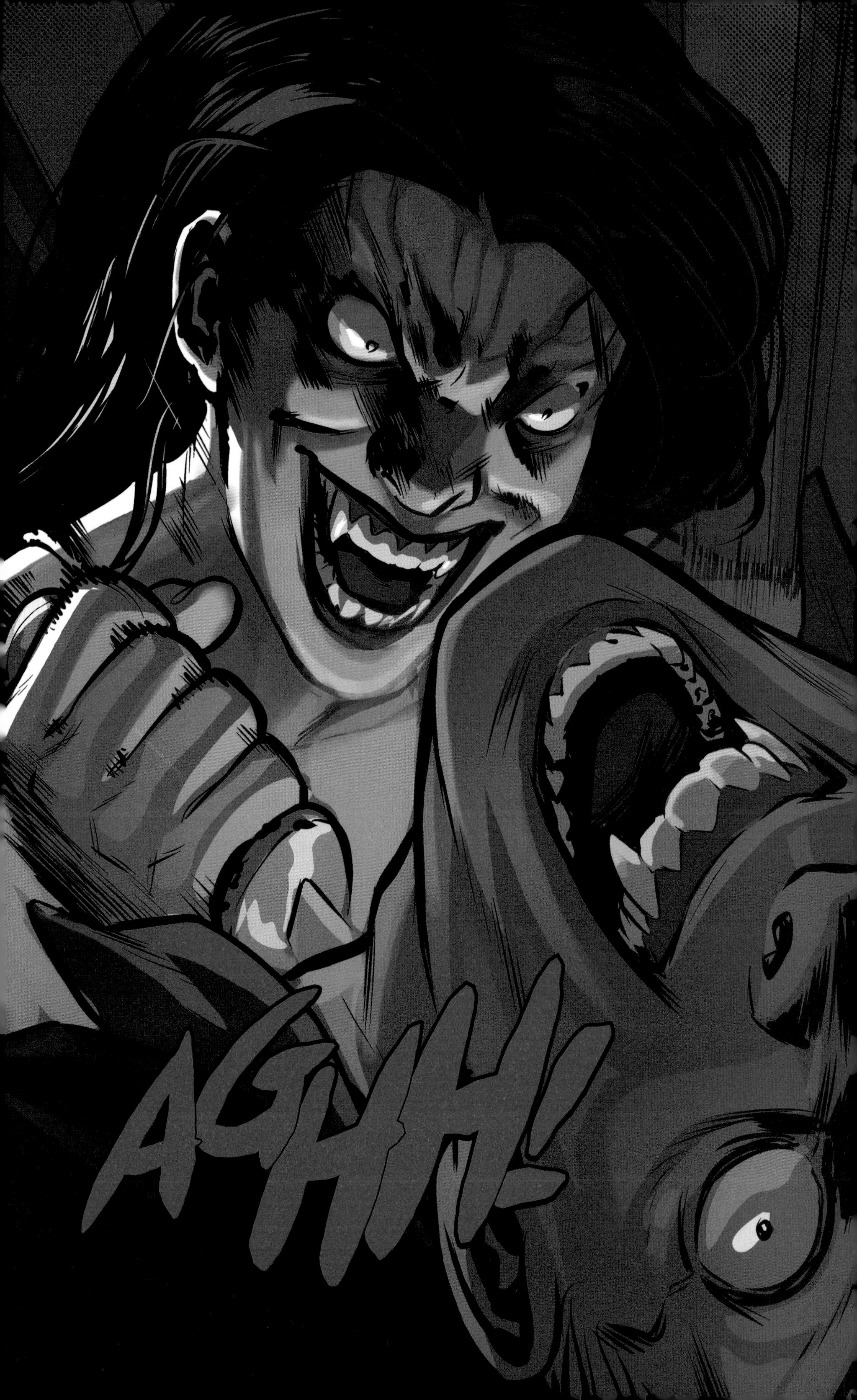
AGHH!

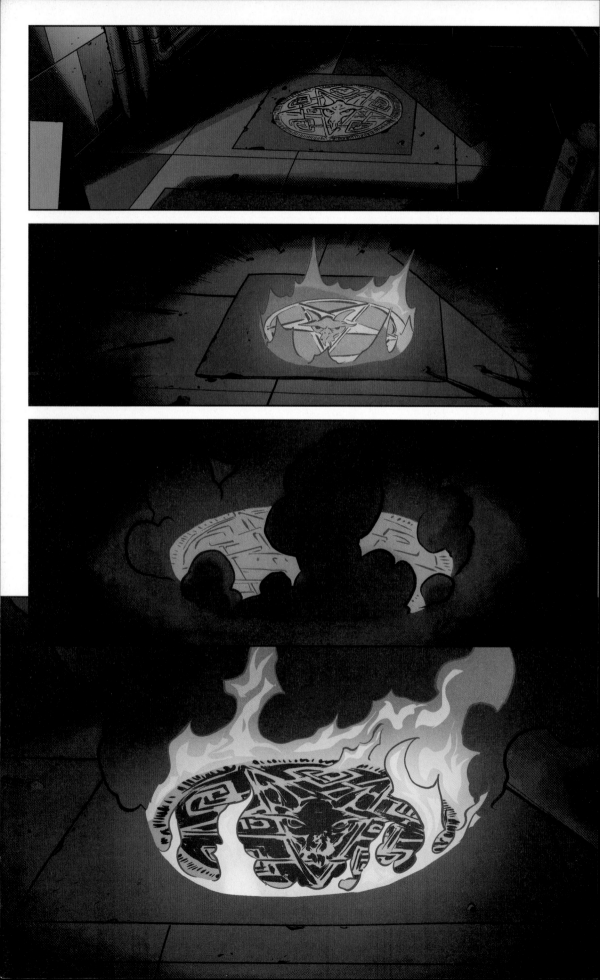

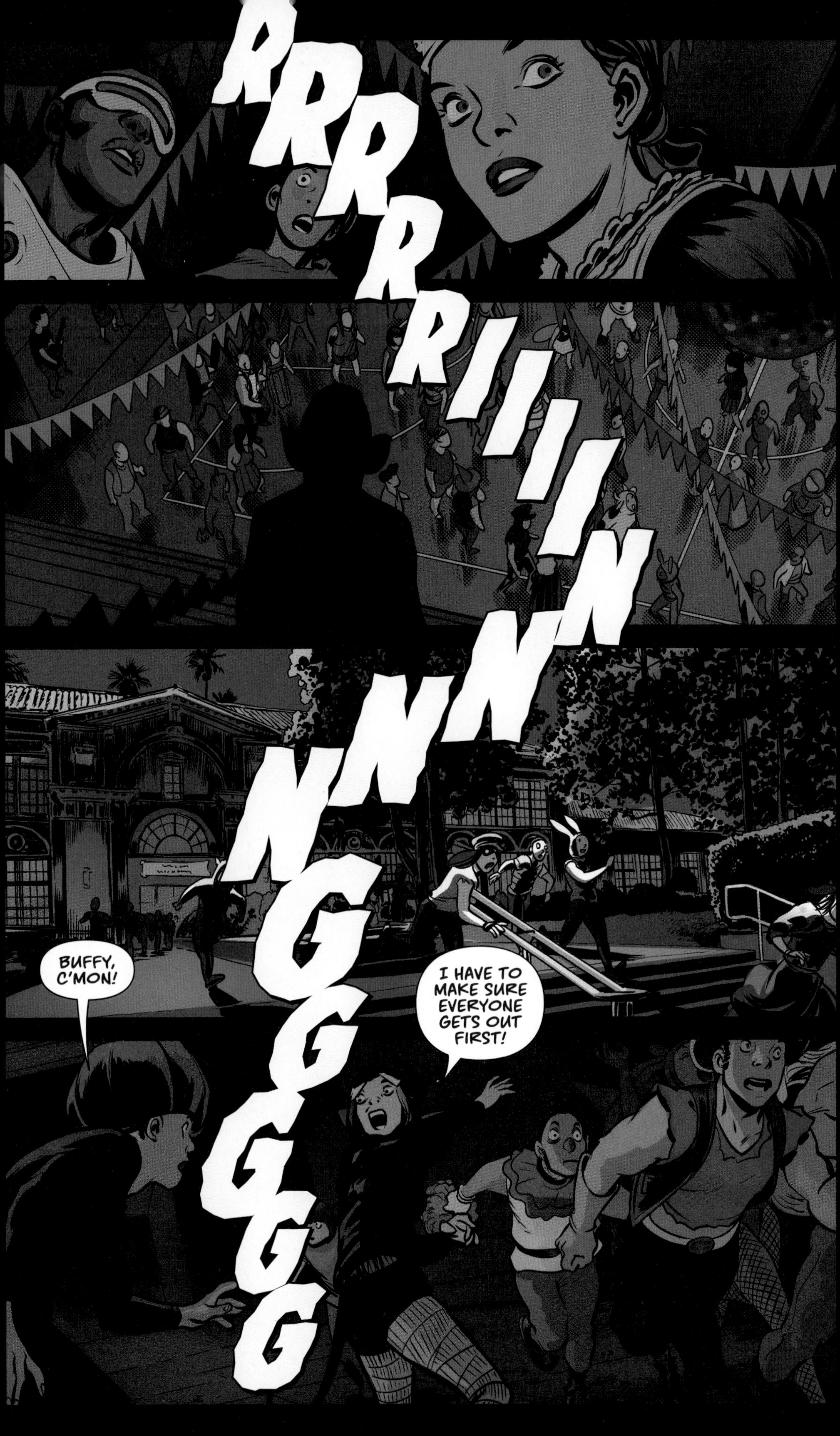
RRRRRRIIIIINNNNNGGGGGG
BUFFY, C'MON!
I HAVE TO MAKE SURE EVERYONE GETS OUT FIRST!

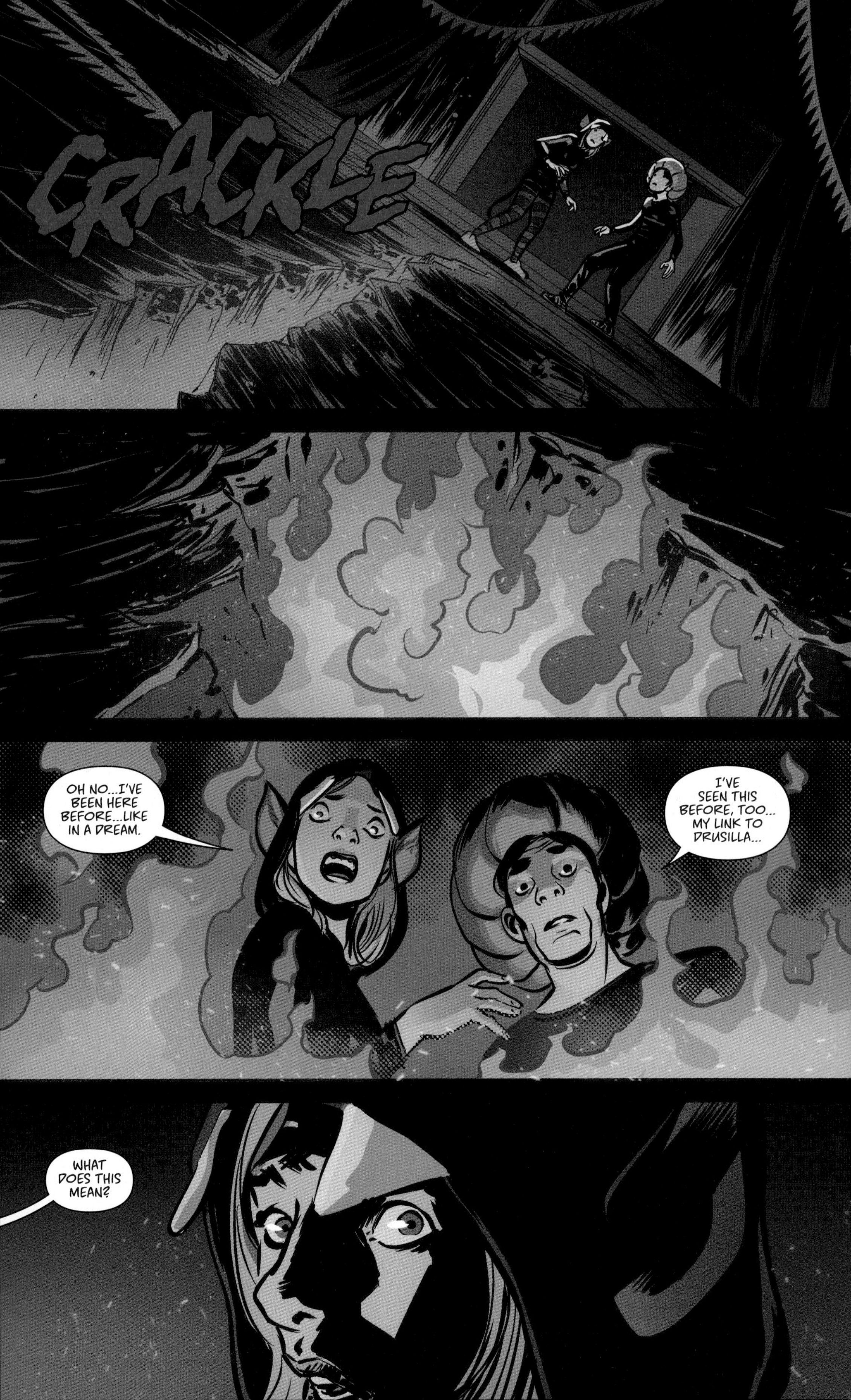
CRACKLE
OH NO...I'VE BEEN HERE BEFORE...LIKE IN A DREAM.
I'VE SEEN THIS BEFORE, TOO... MY LINK TO DRUSILLA...
WHAT DOES THIS MEAN?

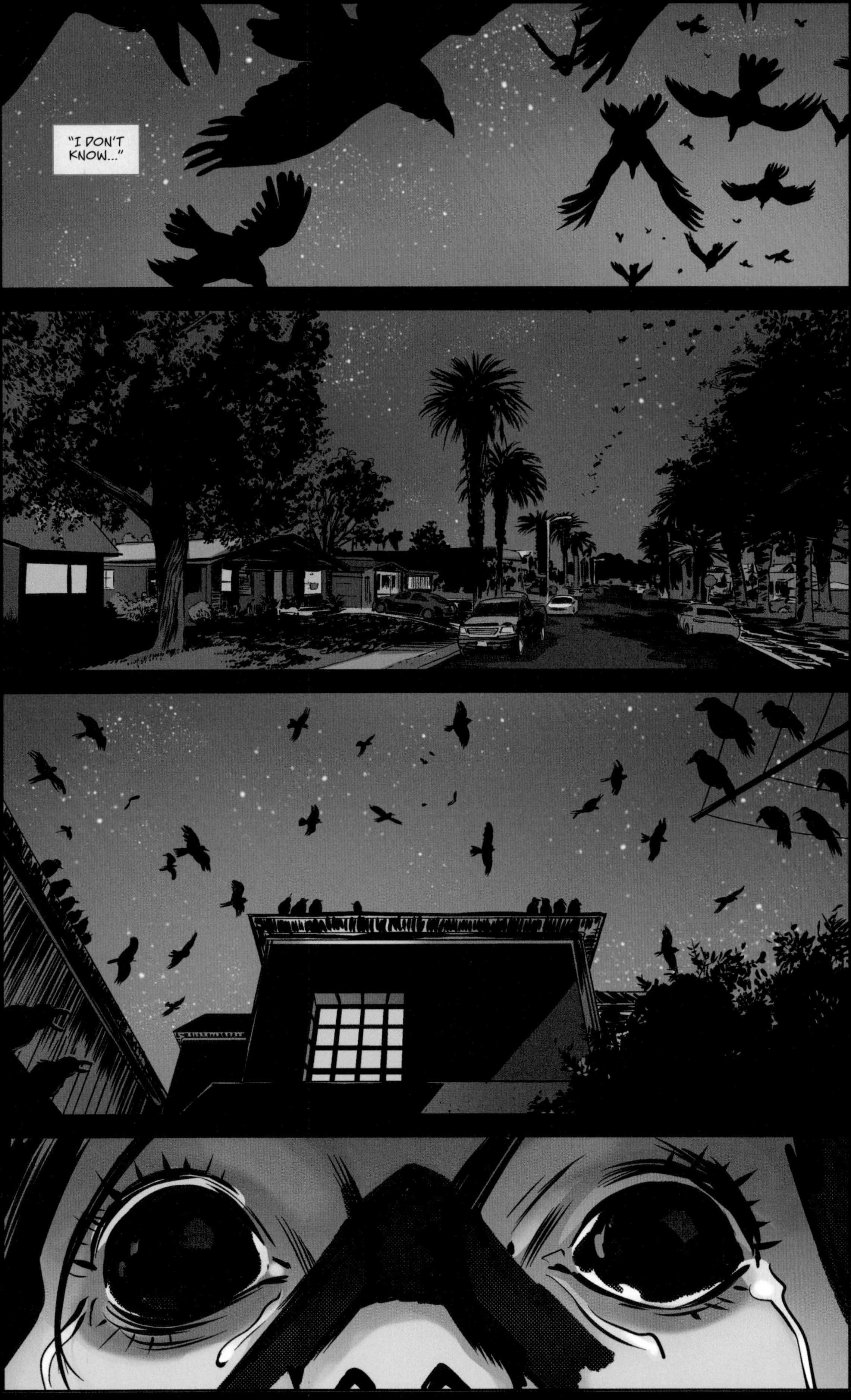
"I DON'T KNOW..."

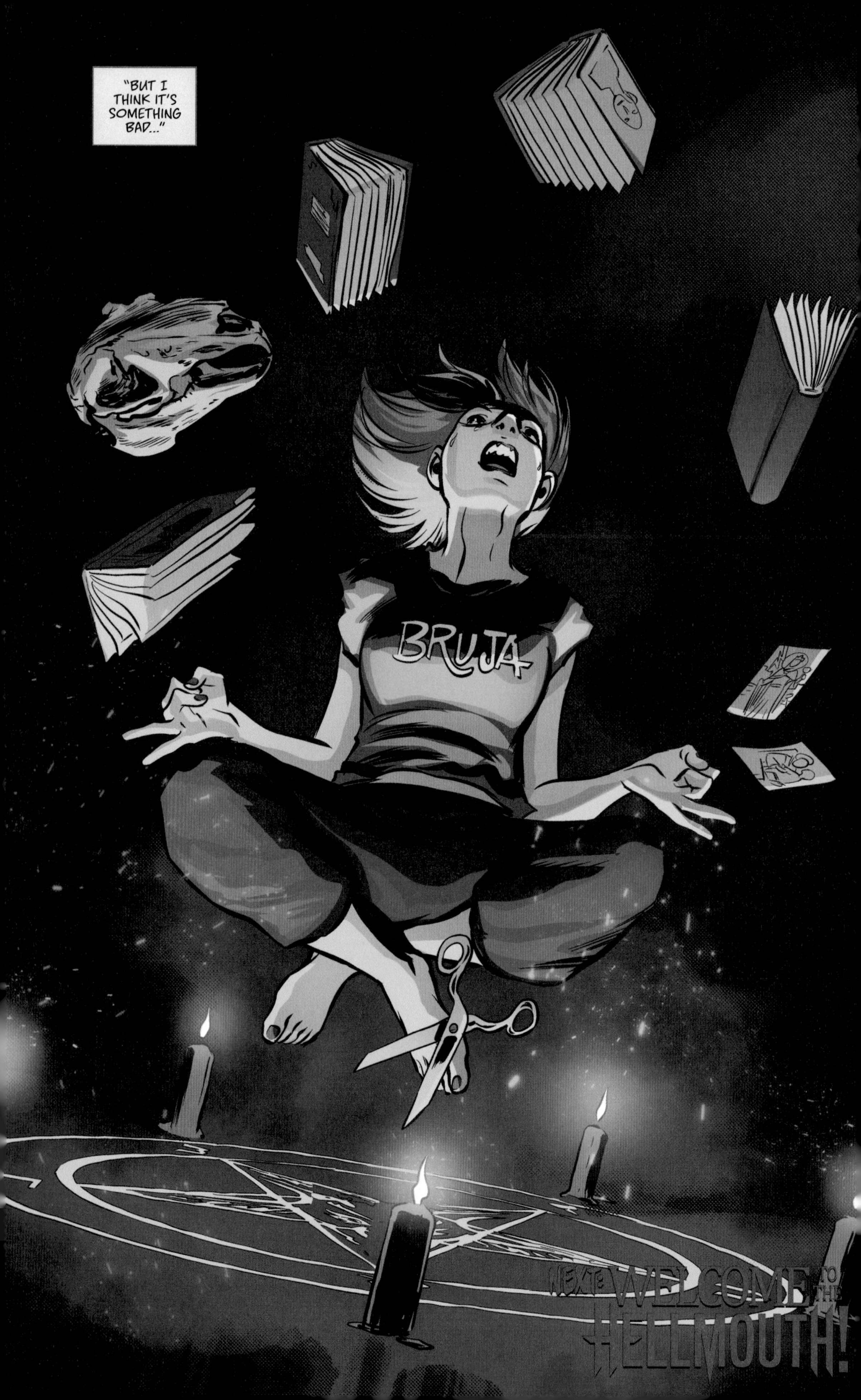
"BUT I THINK IT'S SOMETHING BAD..."
BRUJA
NEXT: WELCOME TO THE HELLMOUTH!

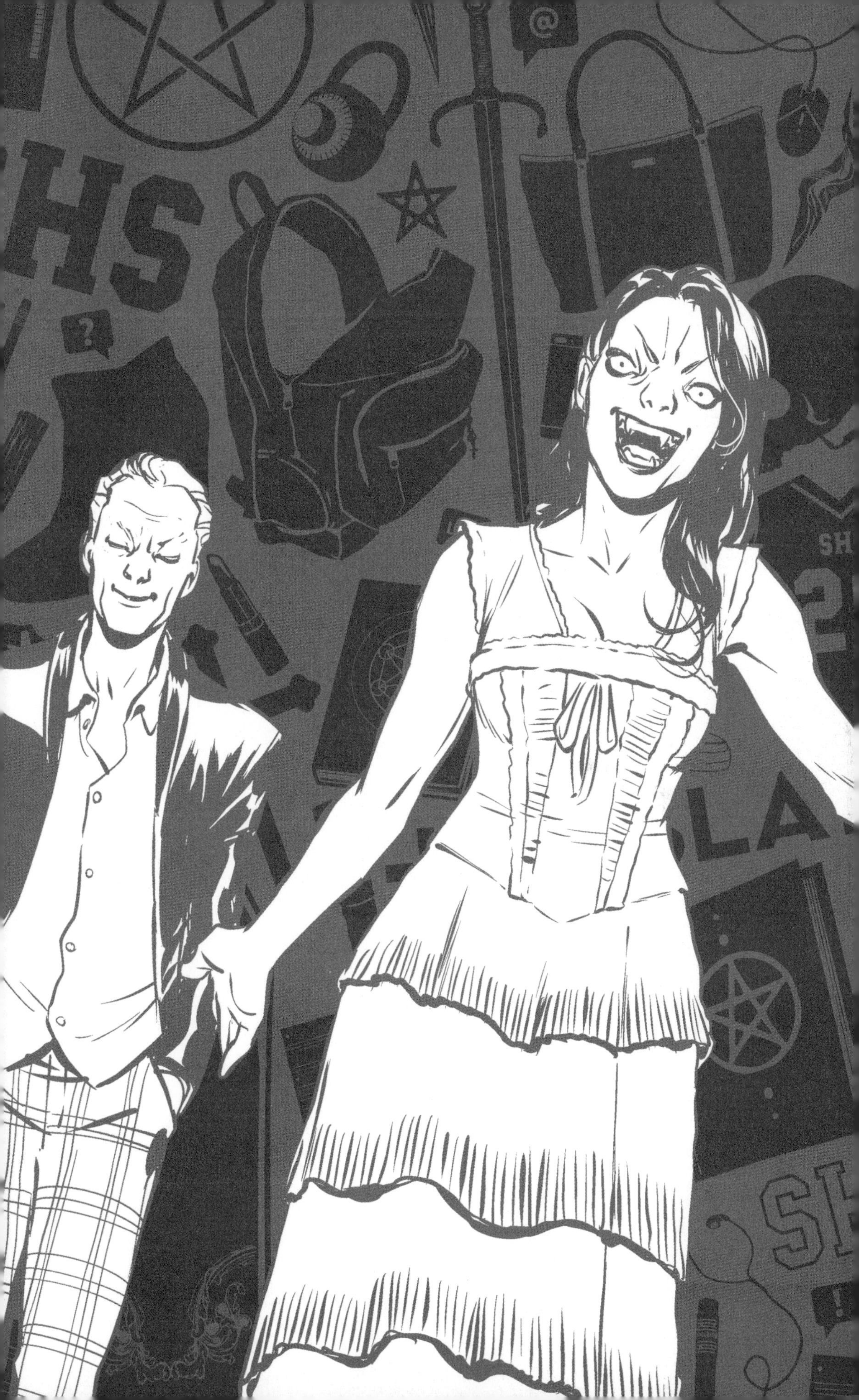

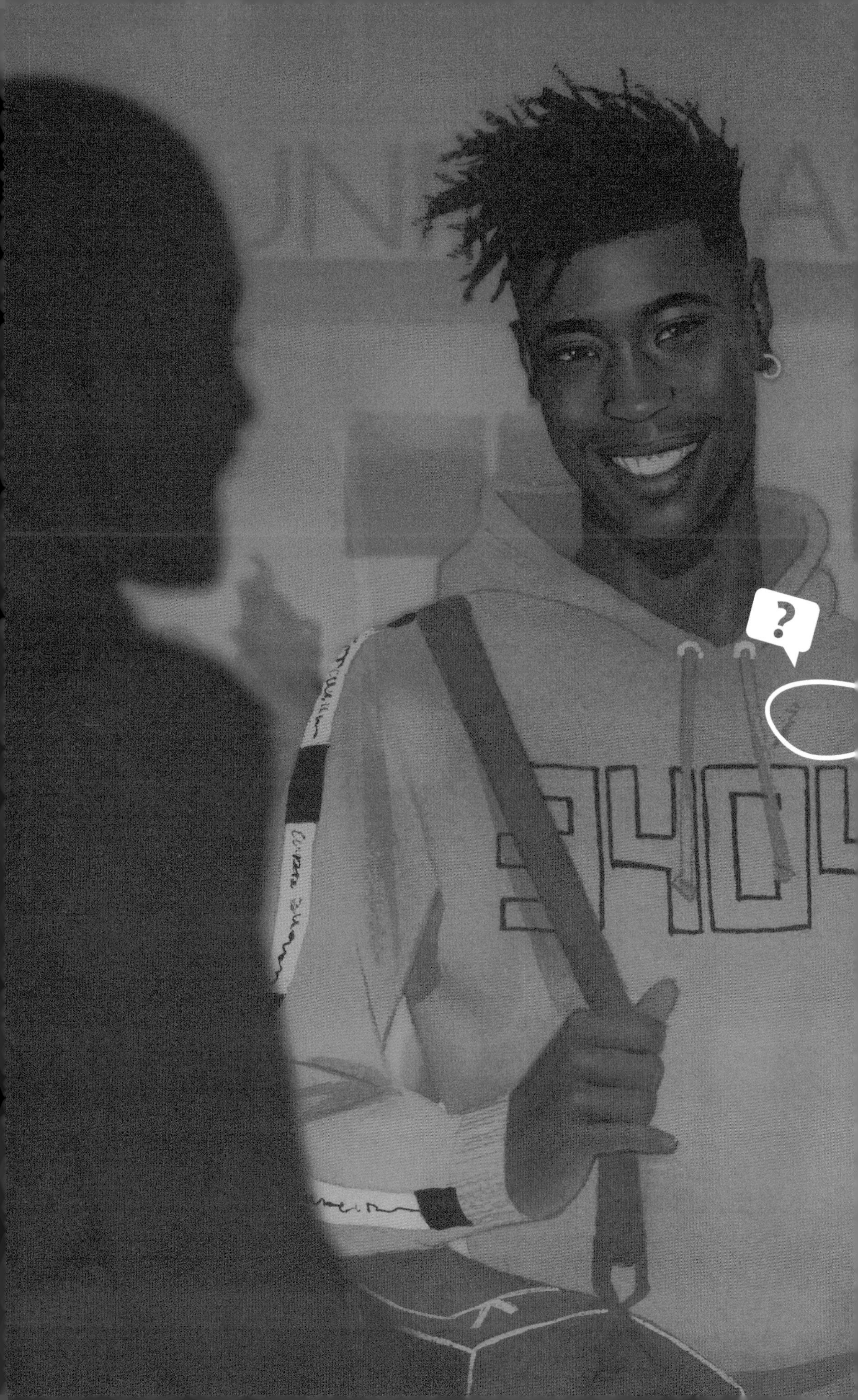
?

COVER GALLERY

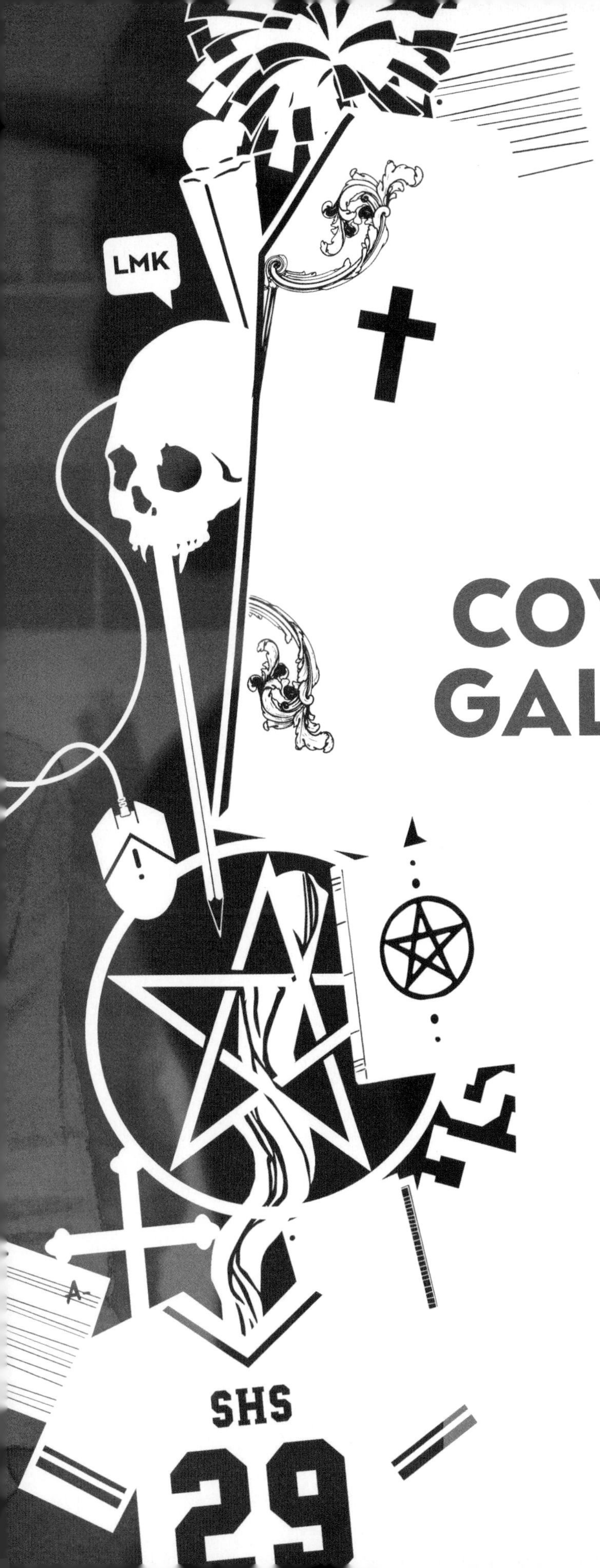
LMK
A-
SHS
29

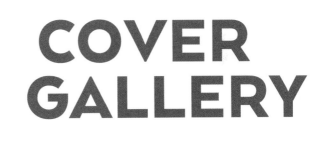

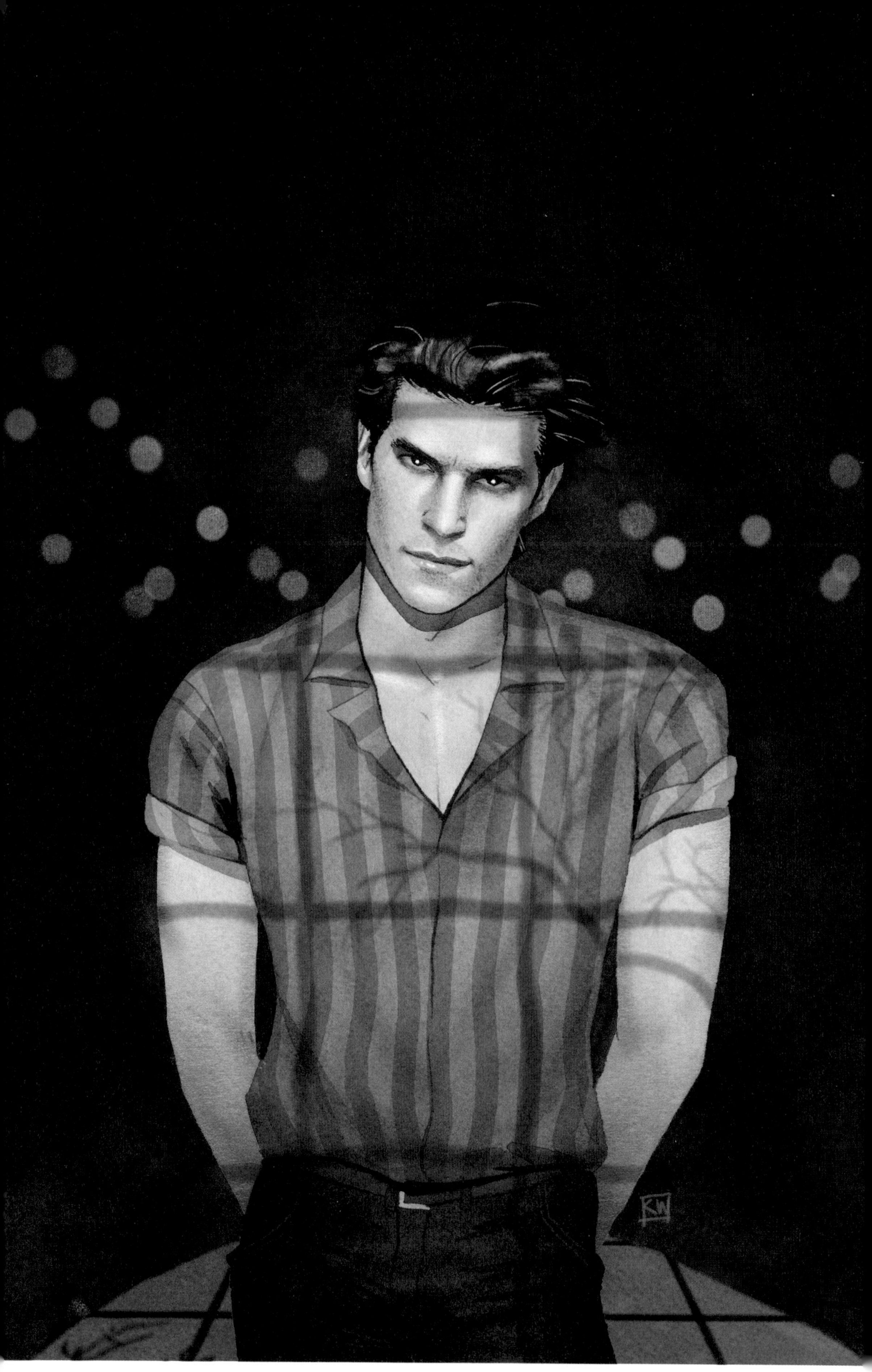

Issue Five Spotlight Variant by **Kevin Wada**

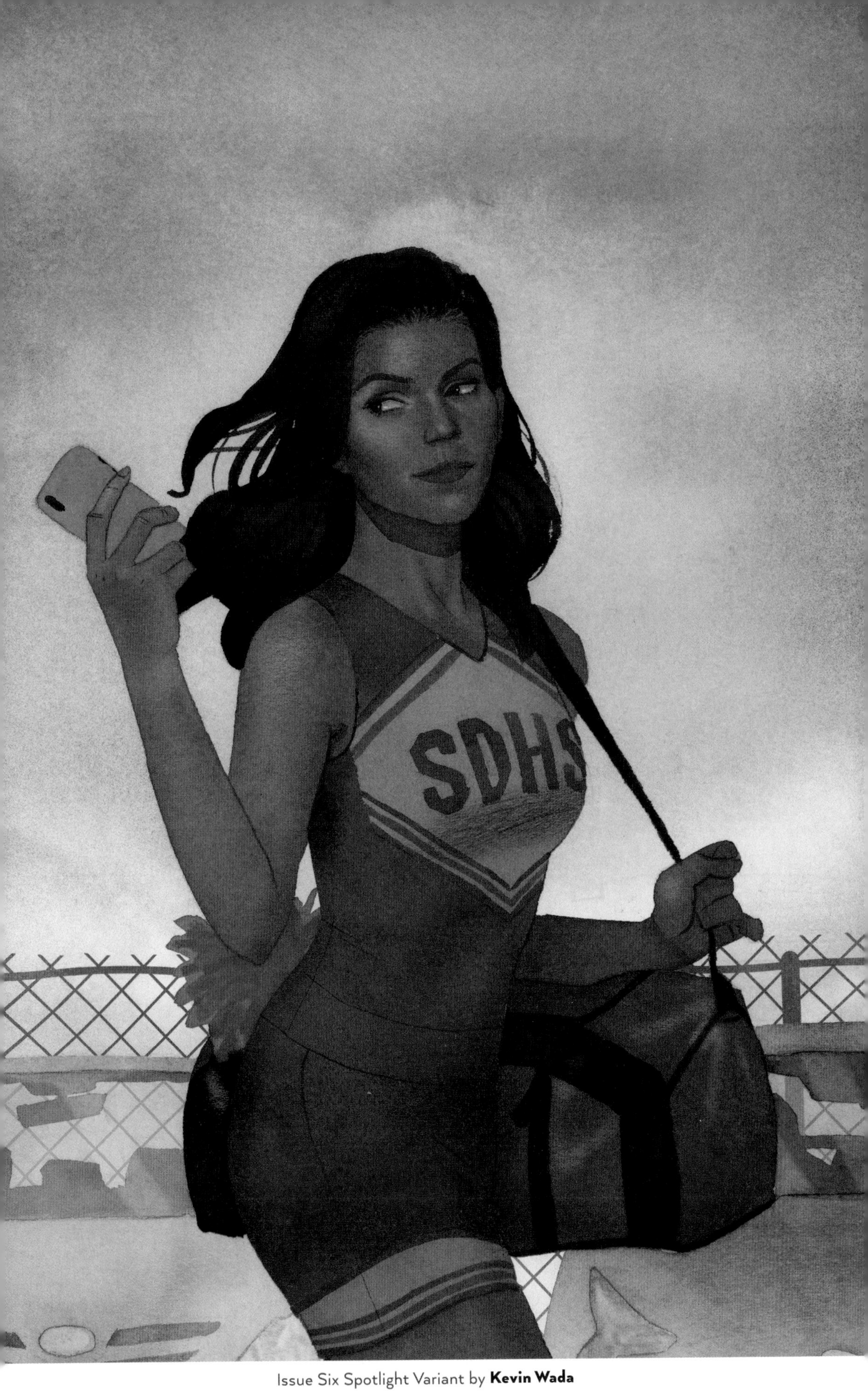
SDHS

Issue Six Spotlight Variant by **Kevin Wada**

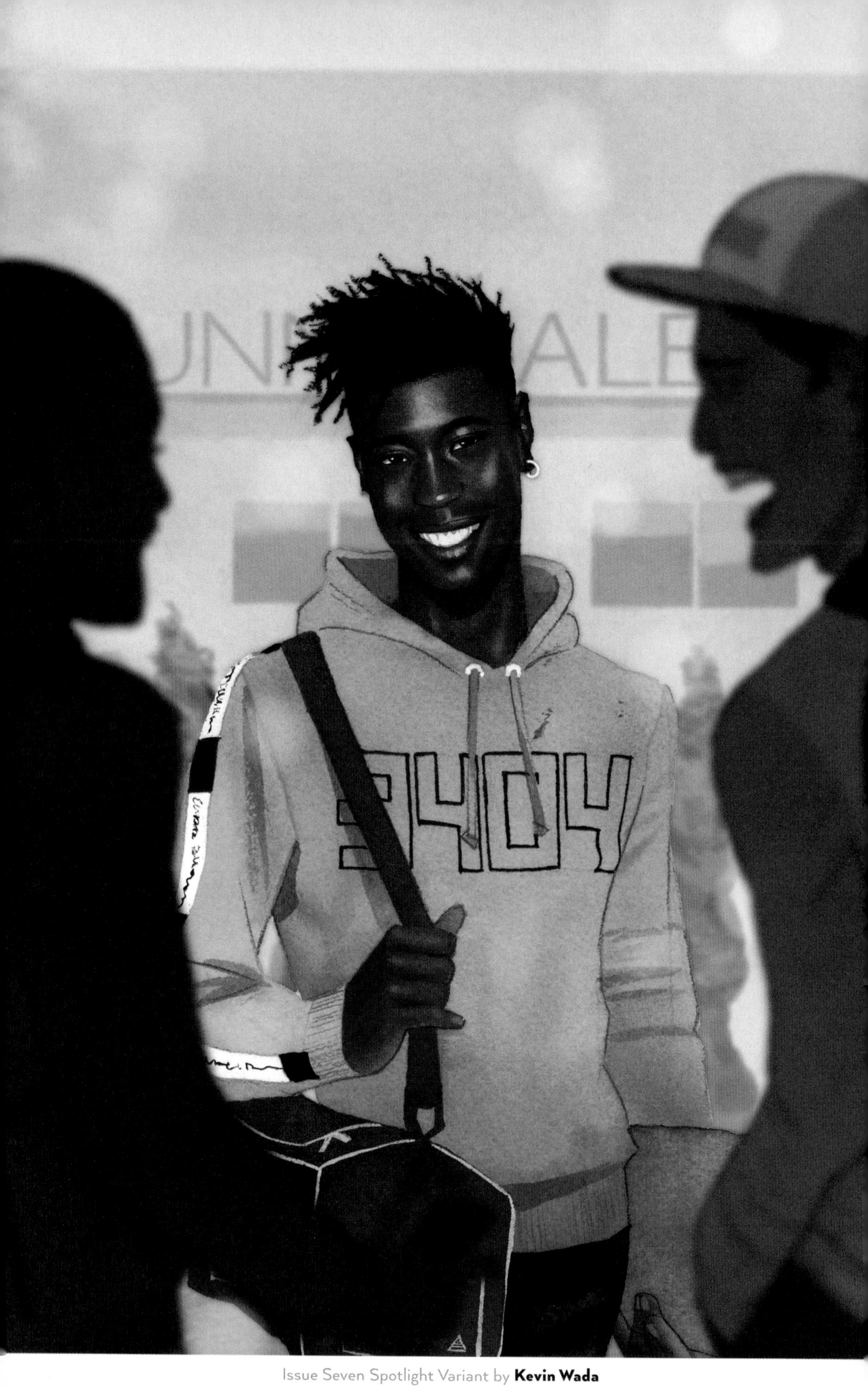

Issue Seven Spotlight Variant by **Kevin Wada**

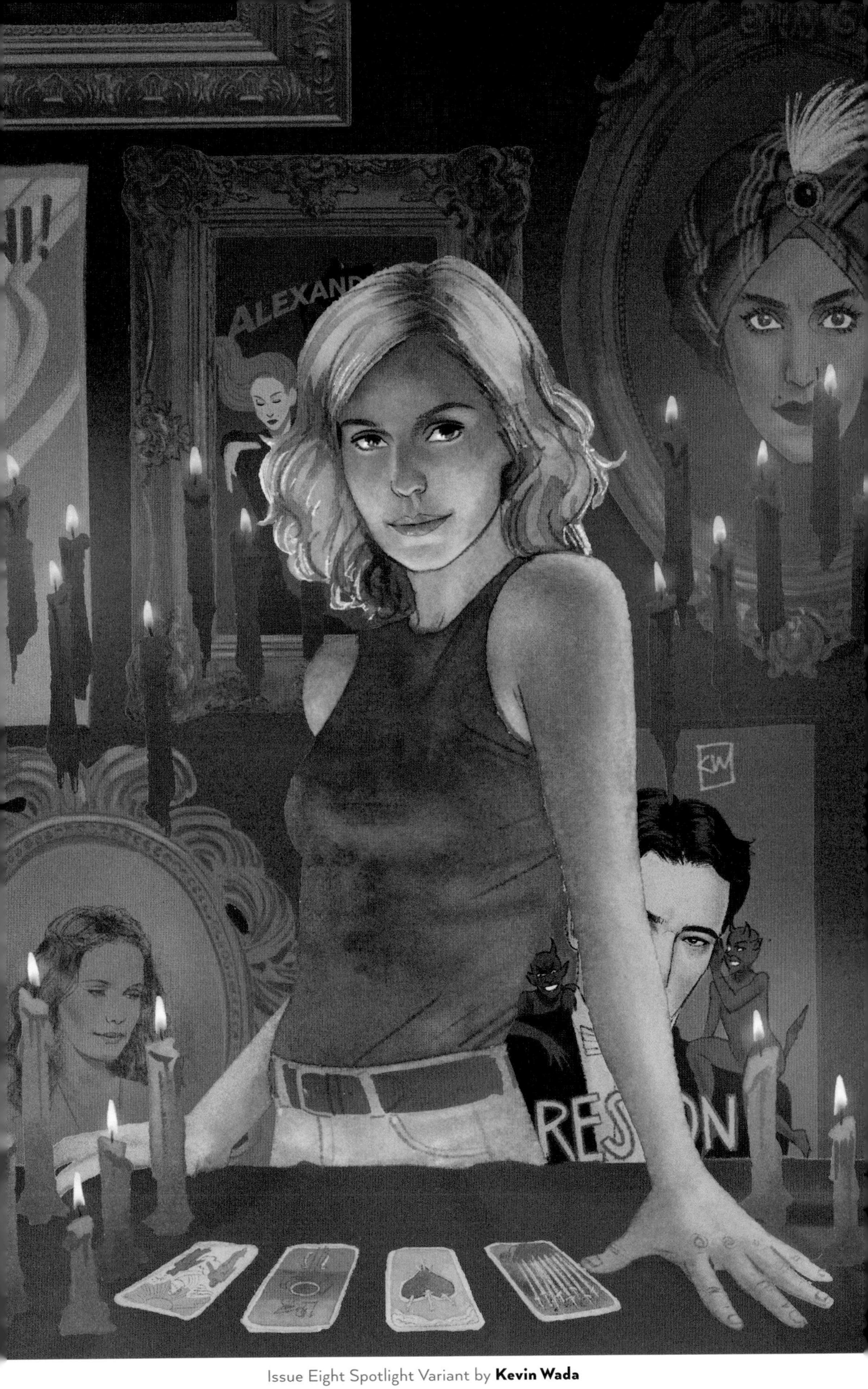
ALEXAND

Issue Eight Spotlight Variant by **Kevin Wada**

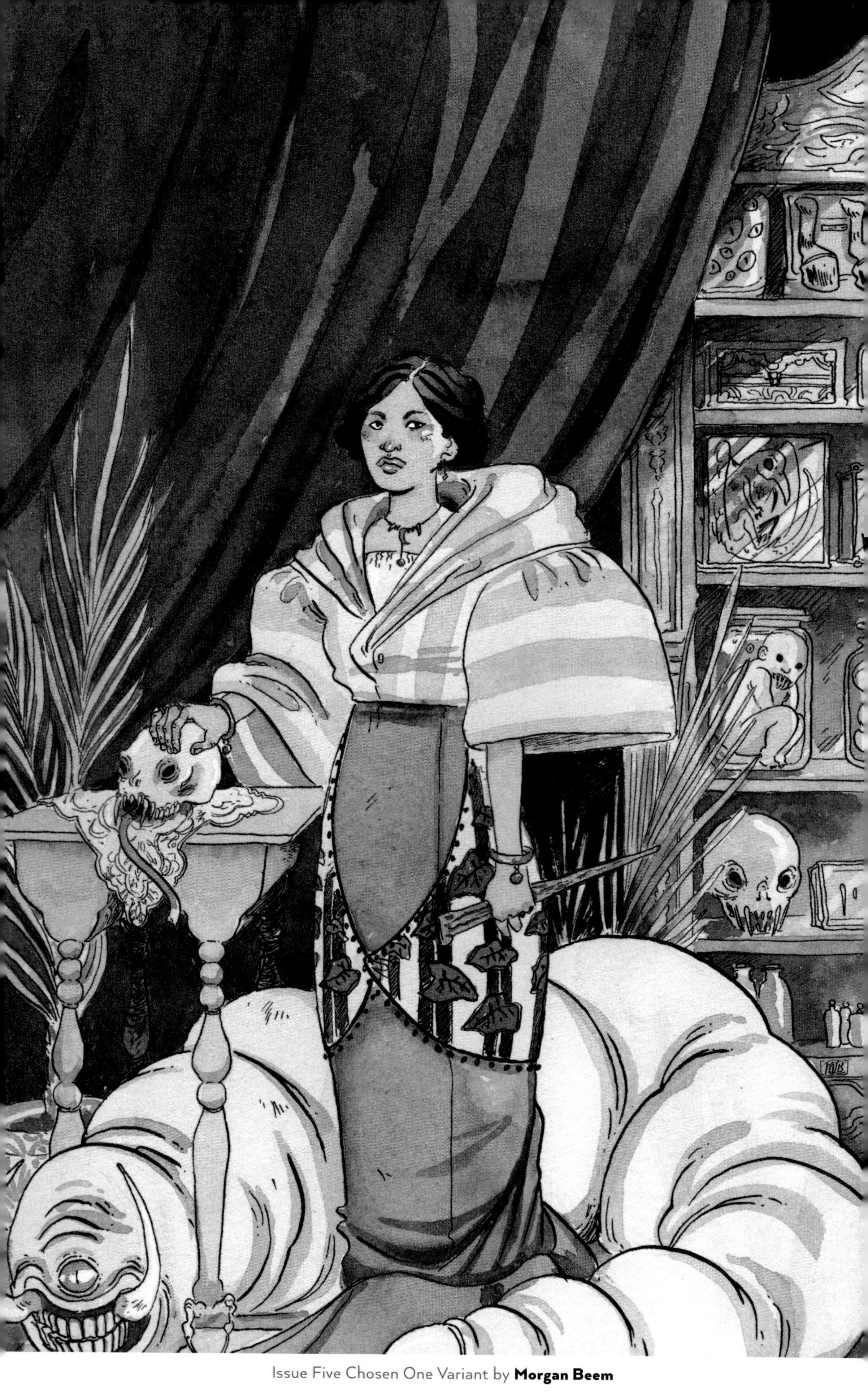

Issue Five Chosen One Variant by **Morgan Beem**

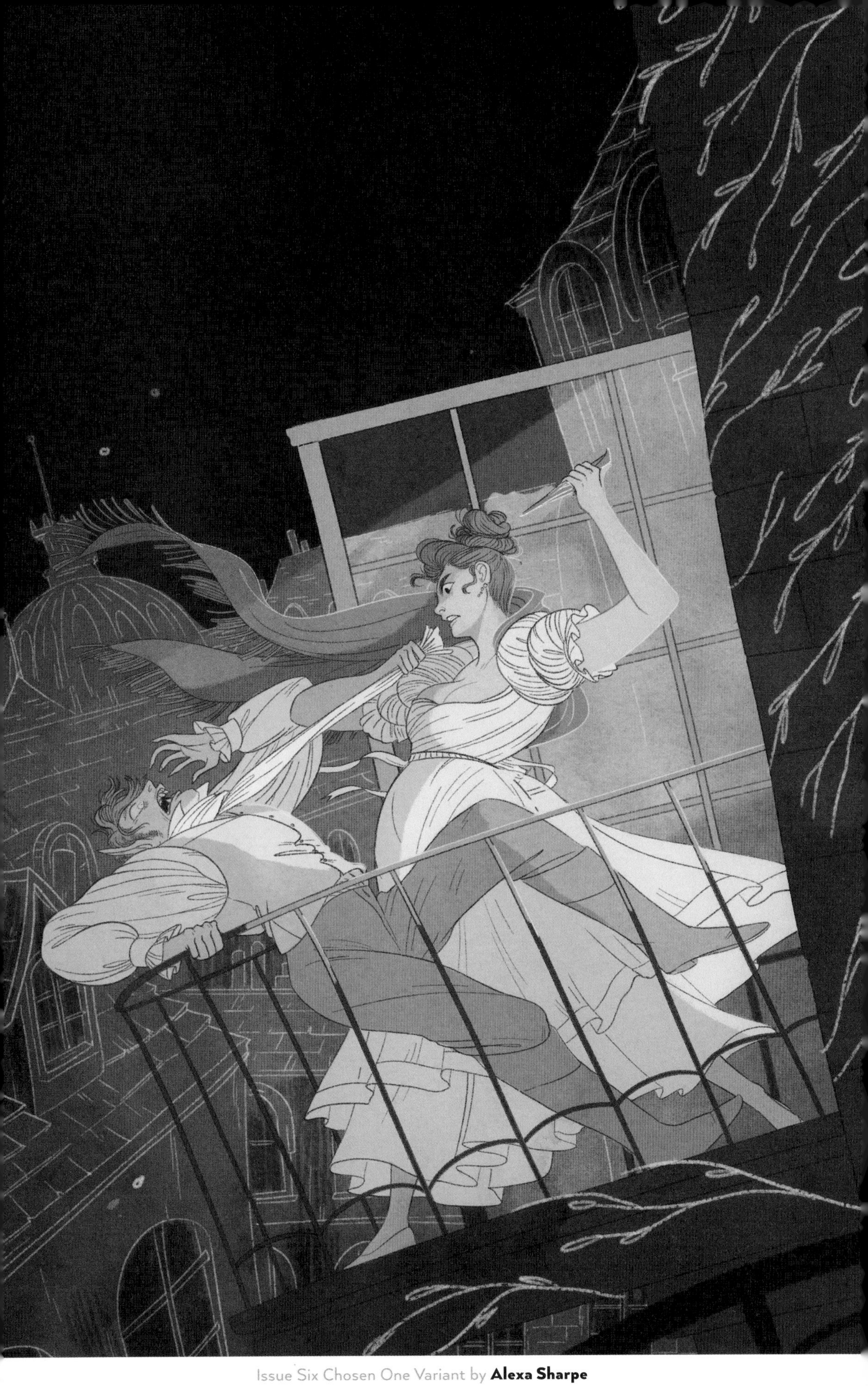

Issue Six Chosen One Variant by **Alexa Sharpe**

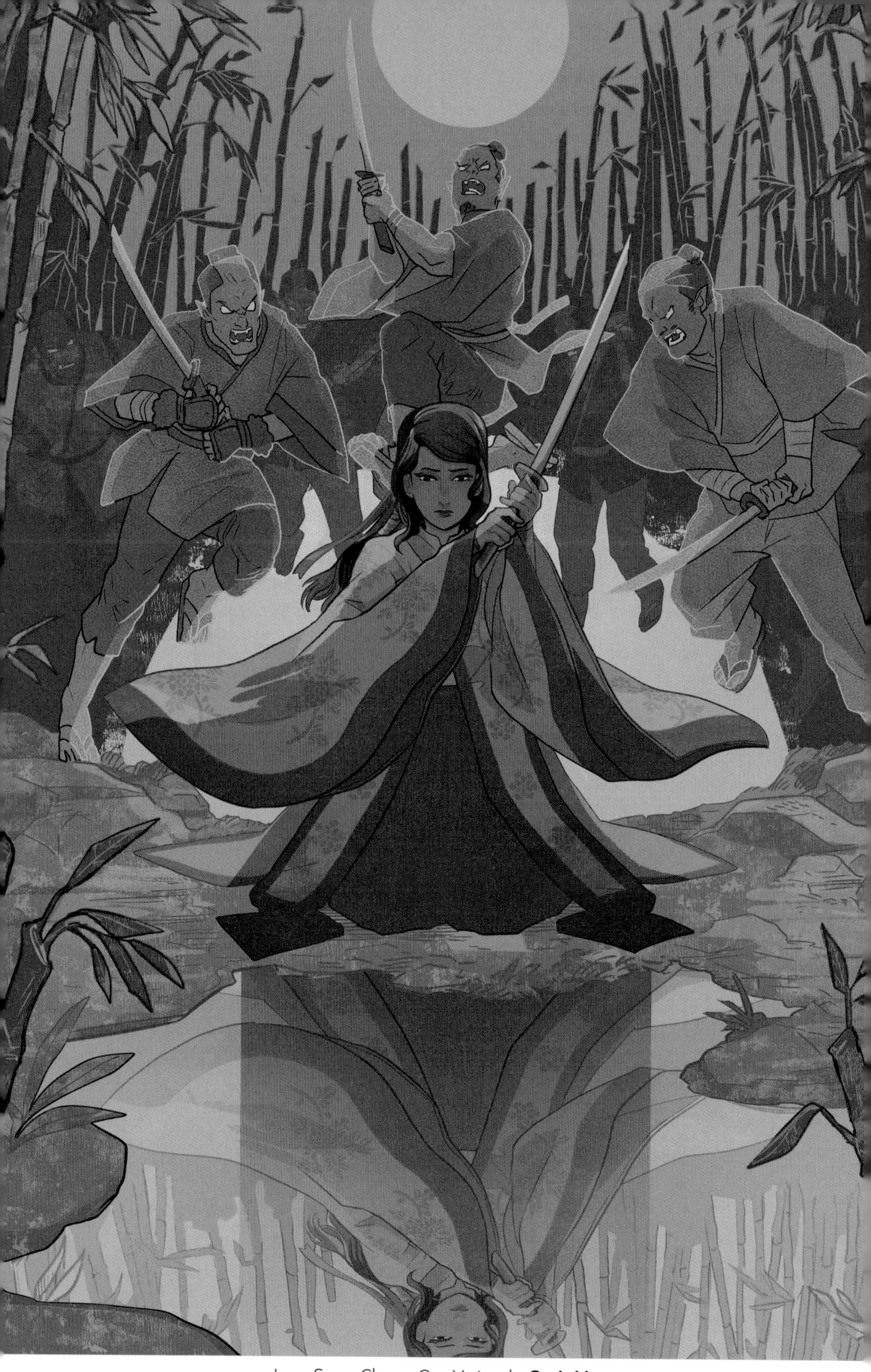

Issue Seven Chosen One Variant by **Sonia Liao**

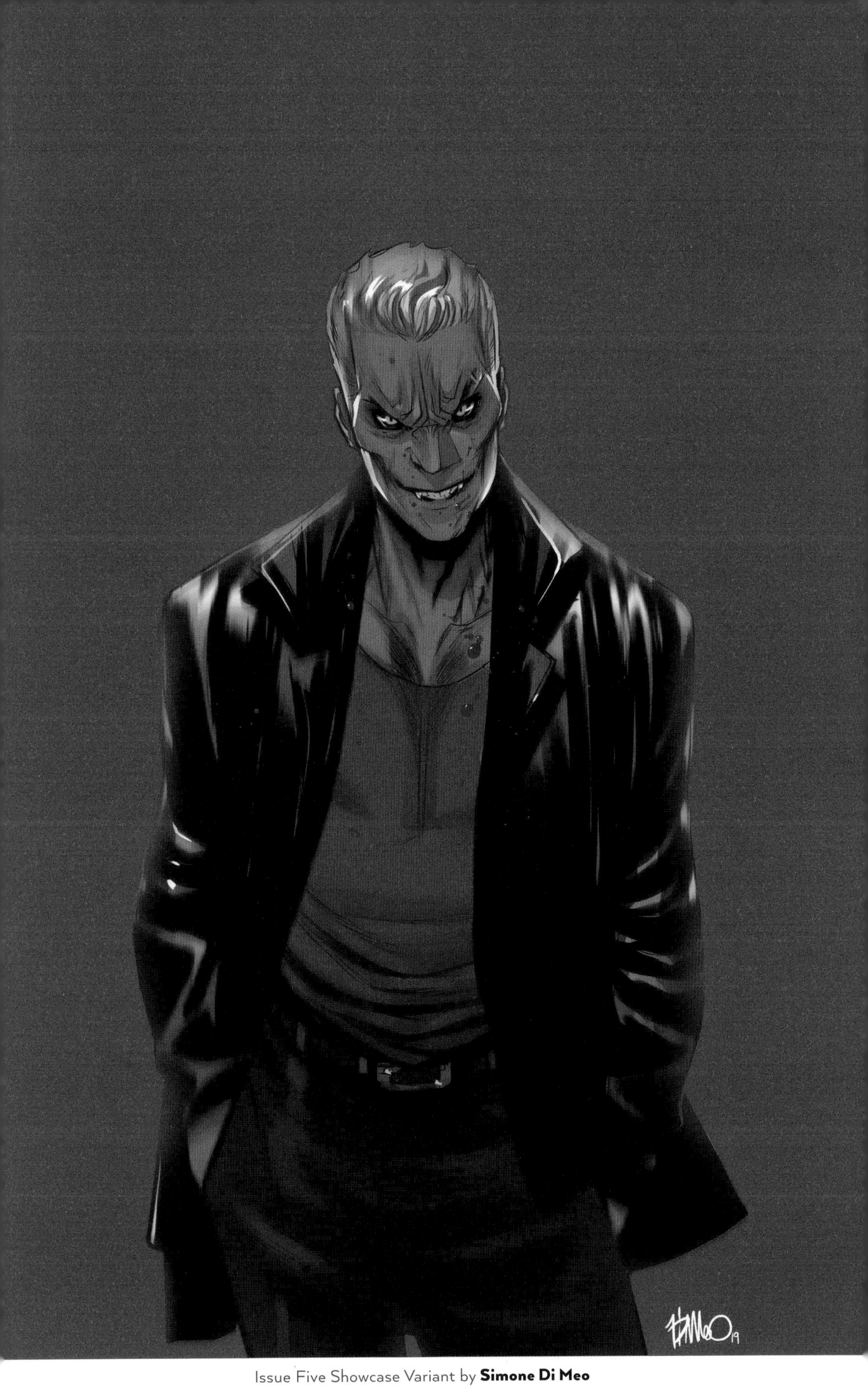

Issue Five Showcase Variant by **Simone Di Meo**

BUFFY THE VAMPIRE SLAYER

DOPPEL GANG LAND

Issue Five Episode Variant by **Becca Carey**

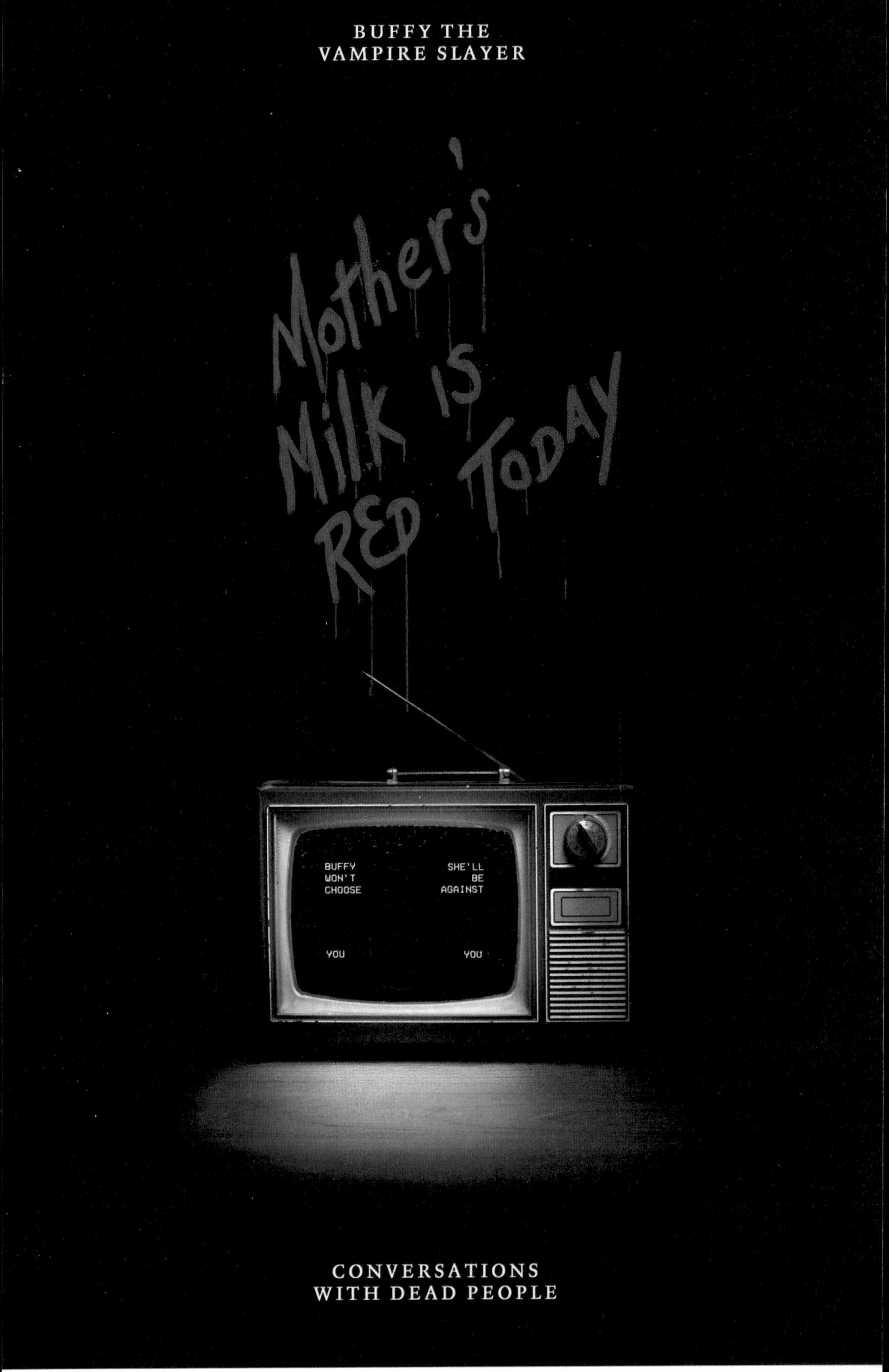
BUFFY THE
VAMPIRE SLAYER
Mother's Milk is RED Today
BUFFY WON'T CHOOSE YOU
SHE'LL BE AGAINST YOU
CONVERSATIONS
WITH DEAD PEOPLE

Issue Six Episode Variant by **Becca Carey**

Buffy the
Vampire
Slayer

The
Body

Issue Seven Episode Variant by **Becca Carey**

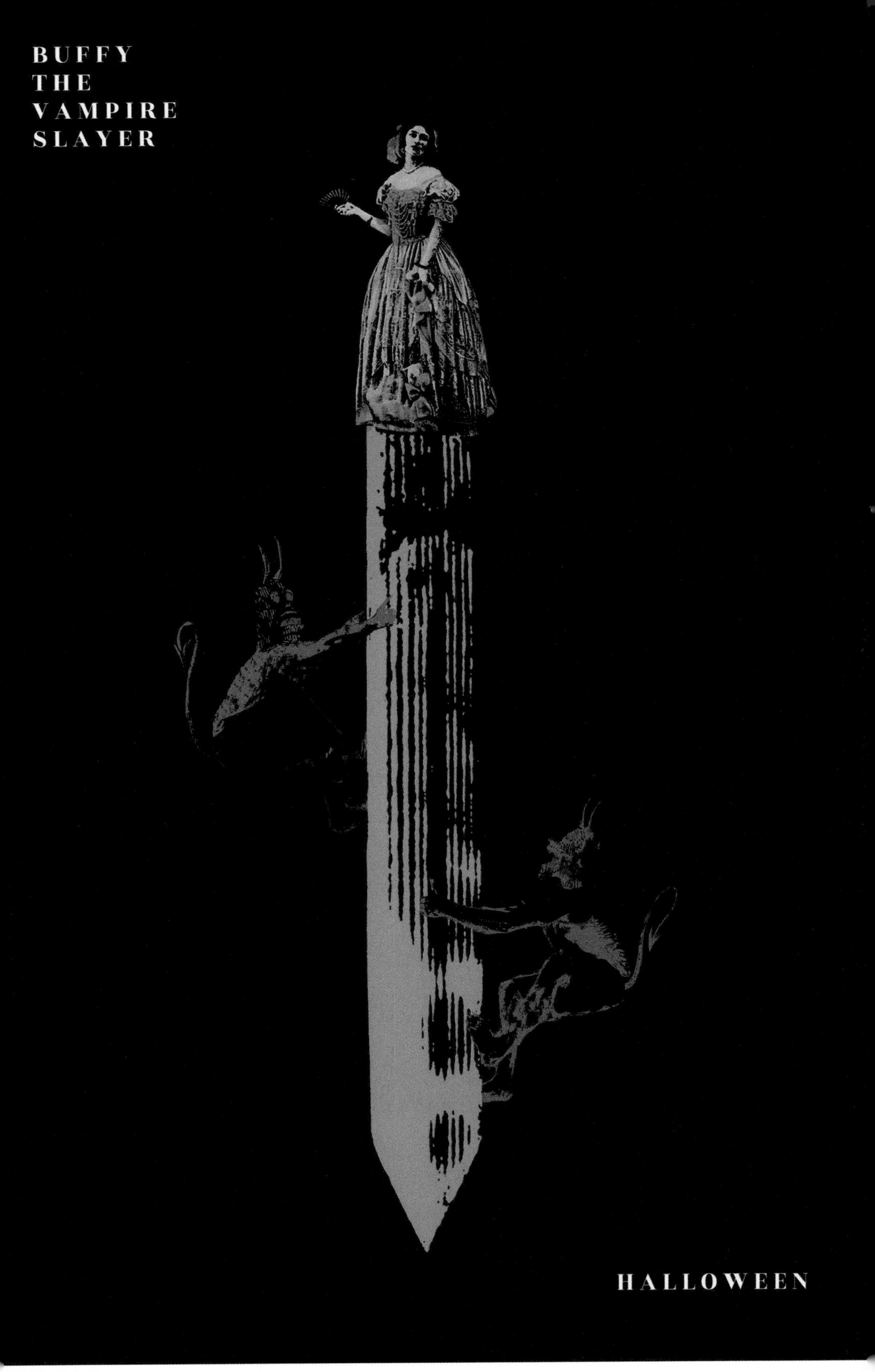
BUFFY
THE
VAMPIRE
SLAYER
HALLOWEEN

Issue Eight Episode Variant by **Becca Carey**

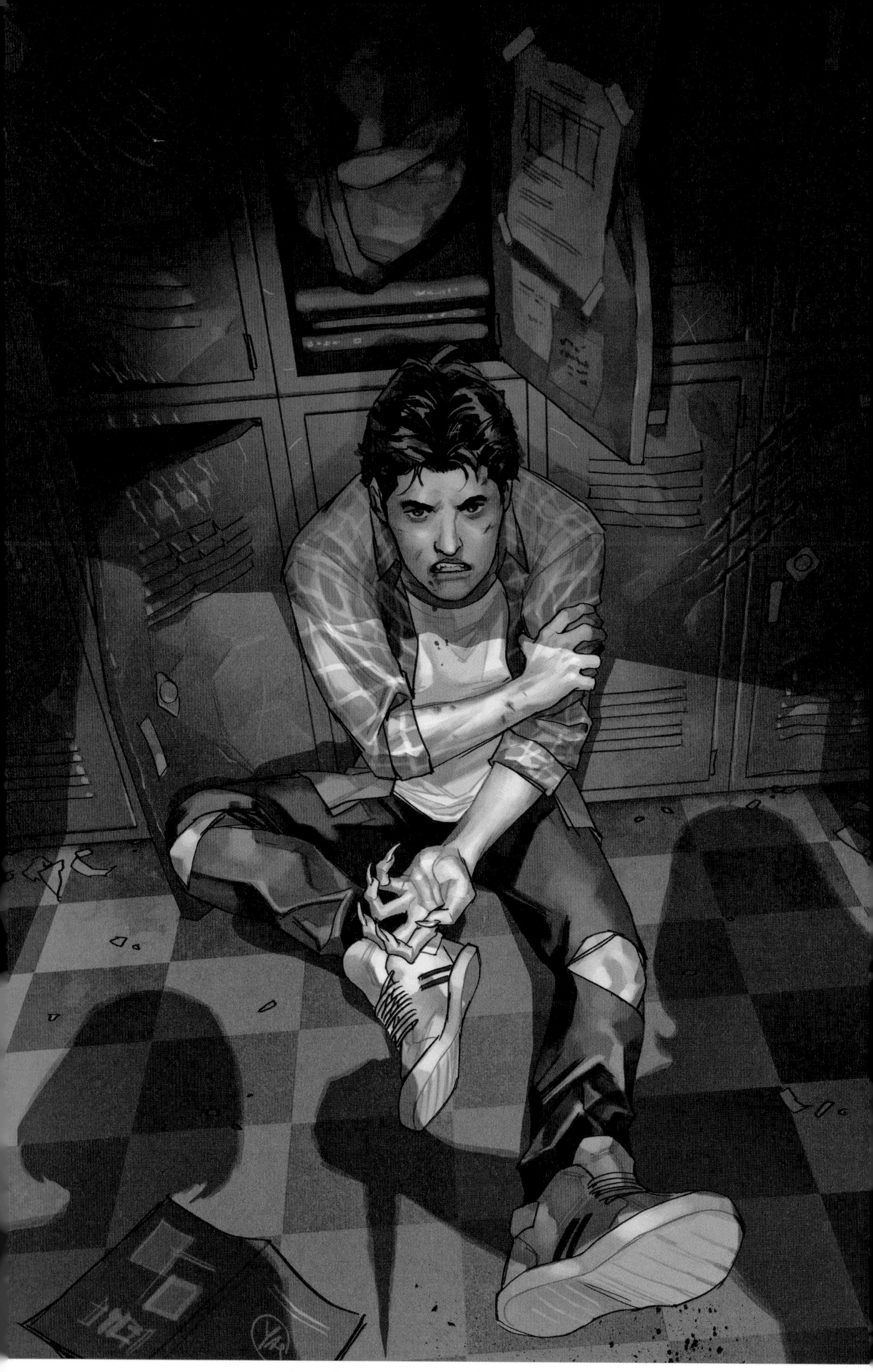

Issue Five Incentive Cover by **Yasmine Putri**

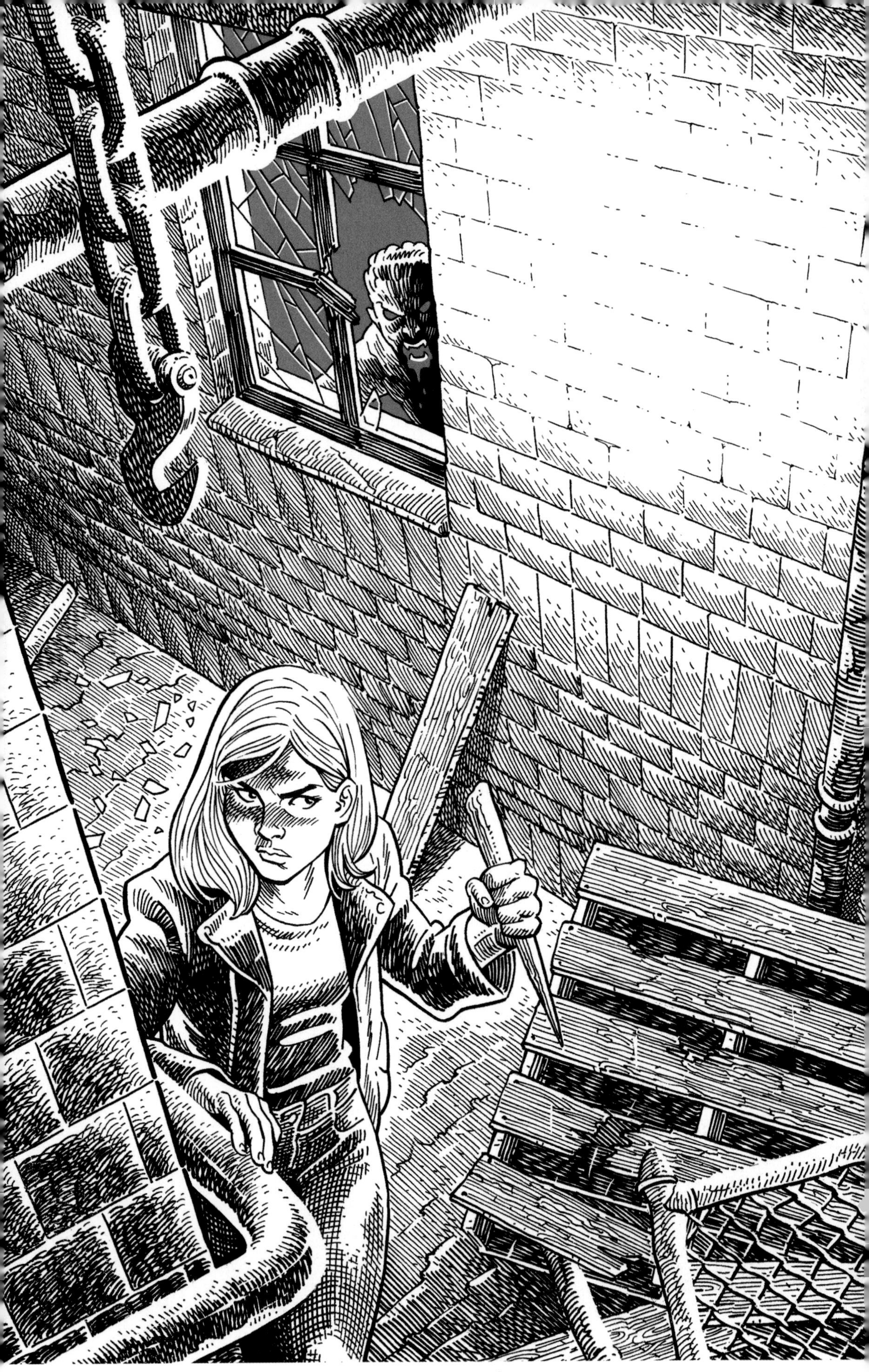

Issue Six Incentive Cover by **Ethan Young**

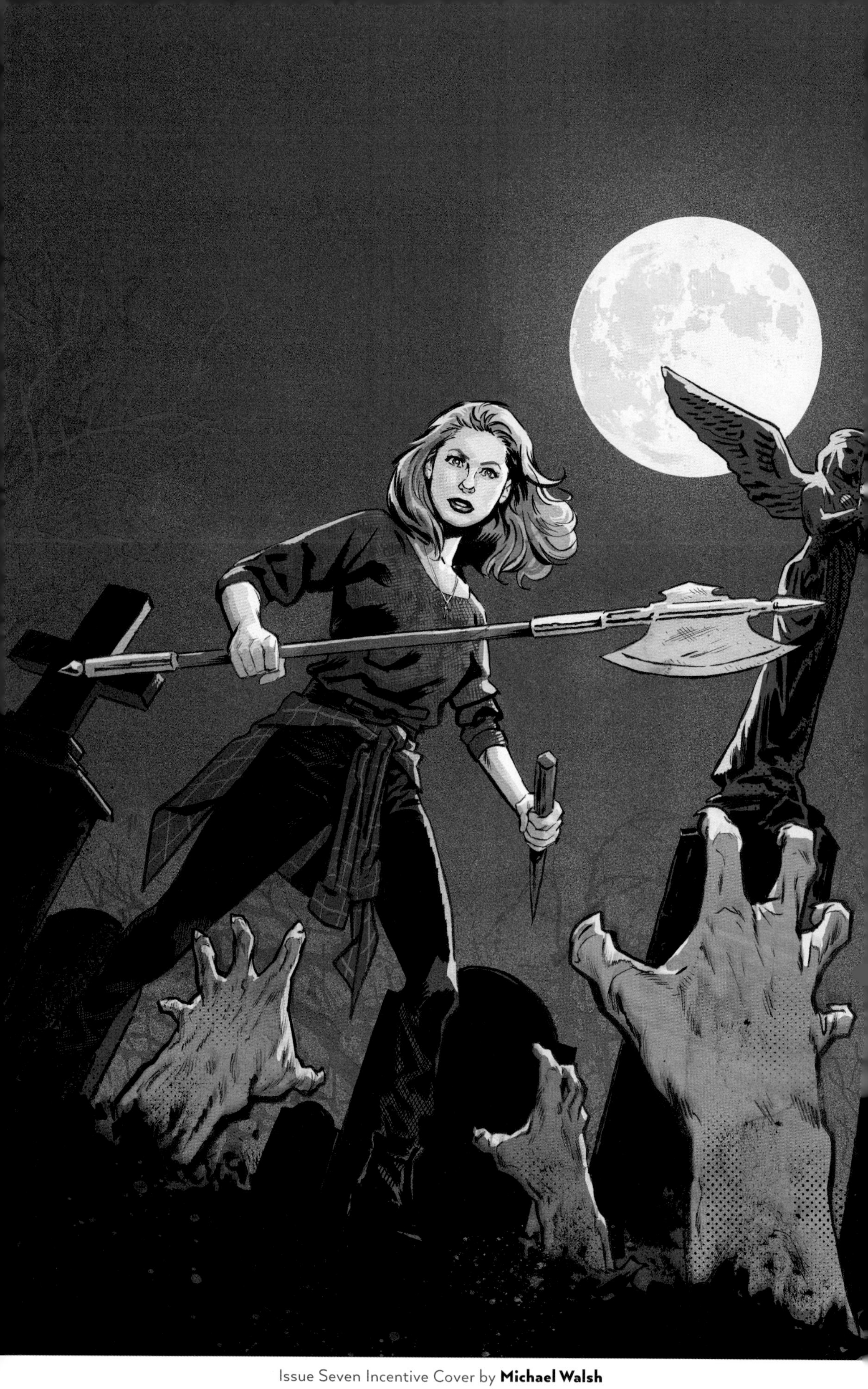

Issue Seven Incentive Cover by **Michael Walsh**

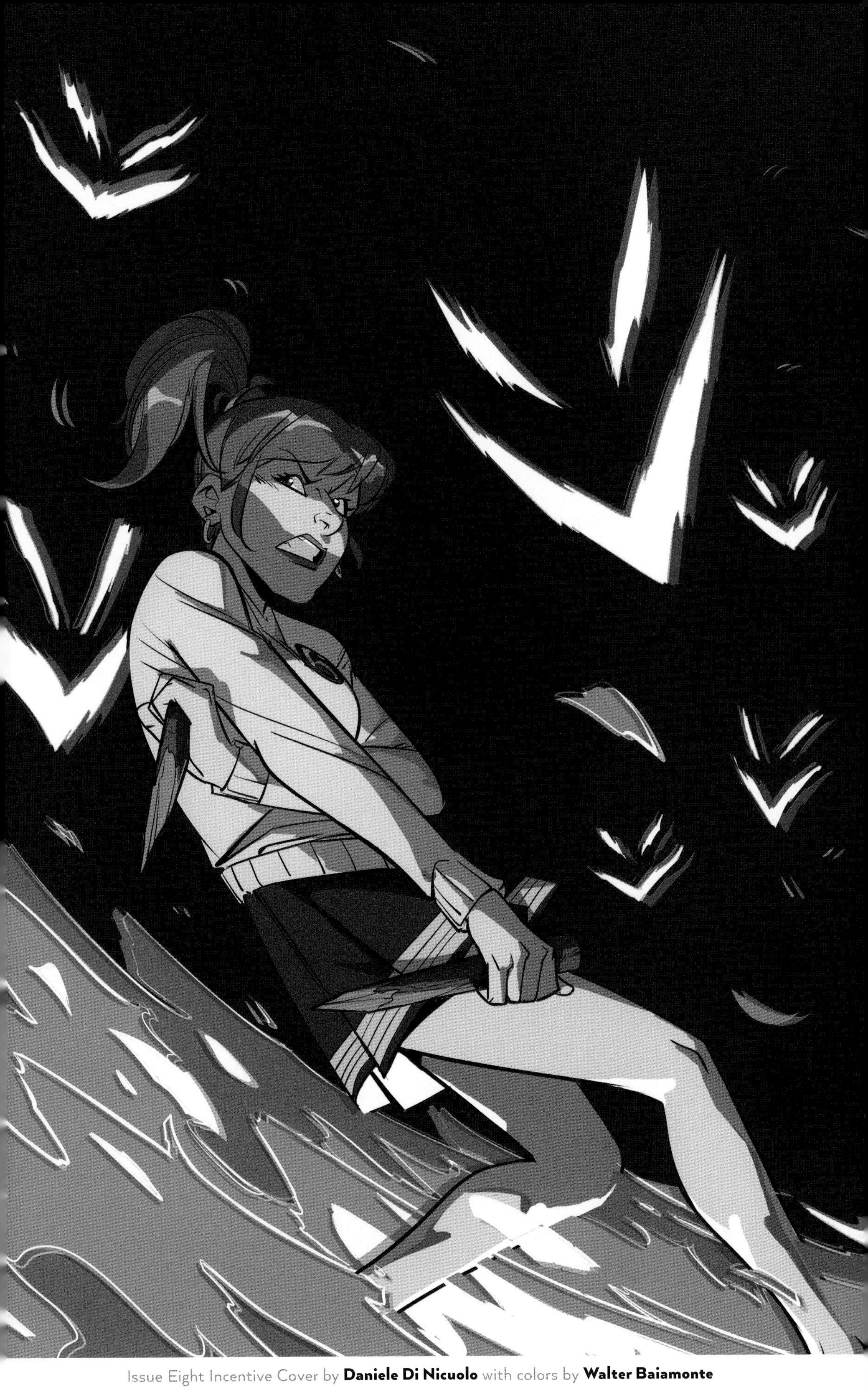

Issue Eight Incentive Cover by **Daniele Di Nicuolo** with colors by **Walter Baiamonte**

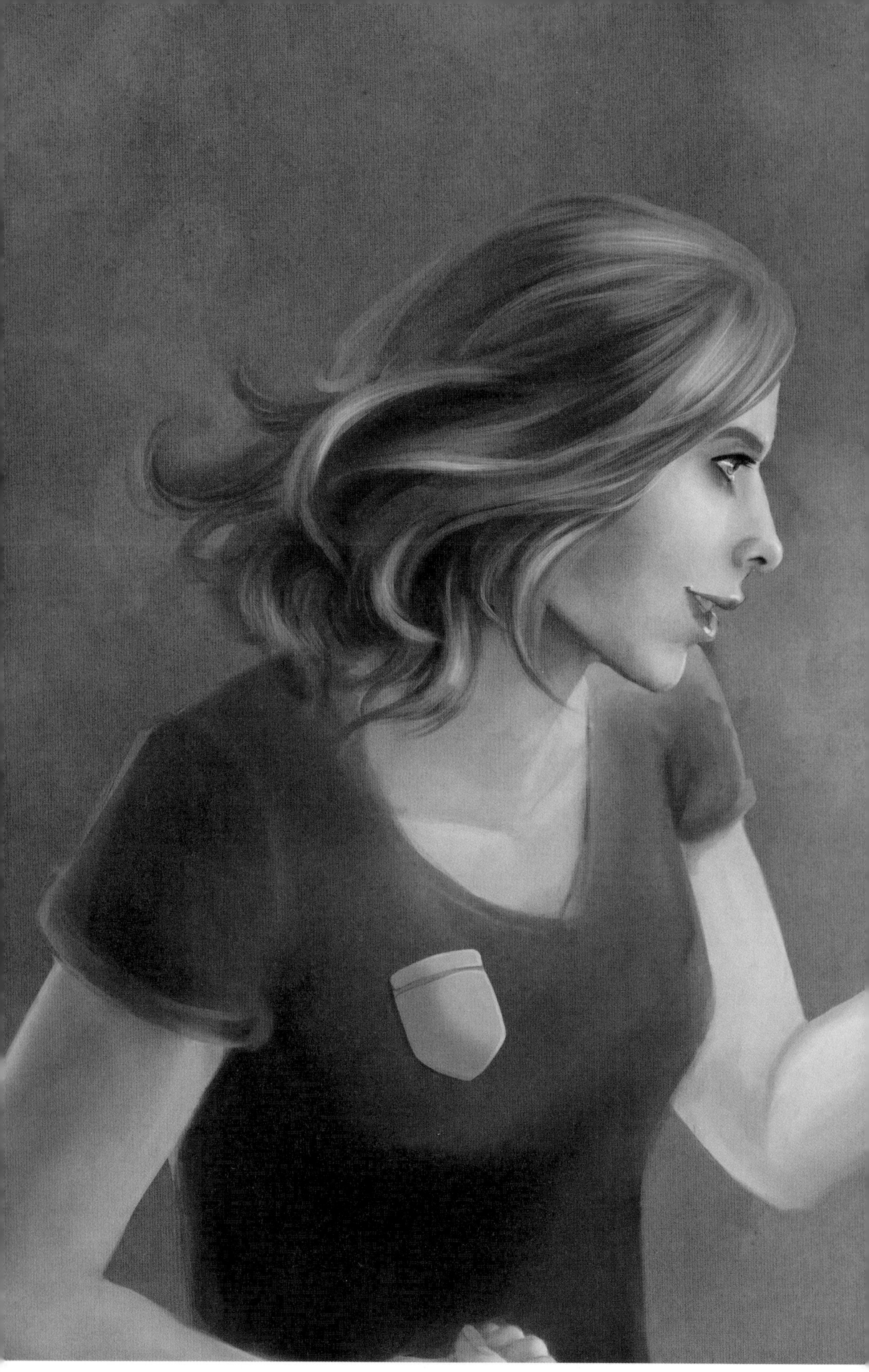

Issue Five Choose Your Side Slayer Variant by **Kaiti Infante**

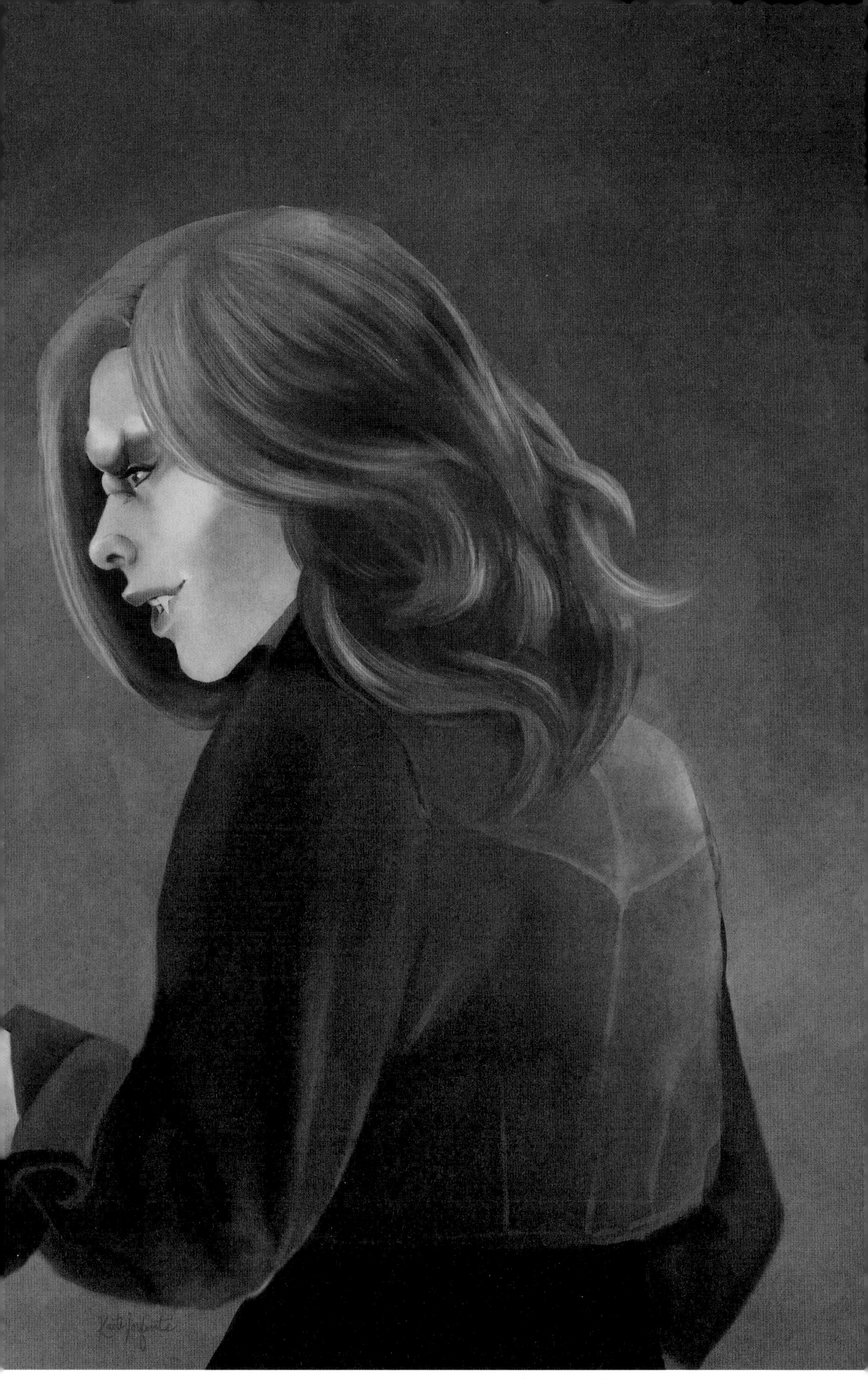

Issue Five Choose Your Side Vampire Variant by **Kaiti Infante**

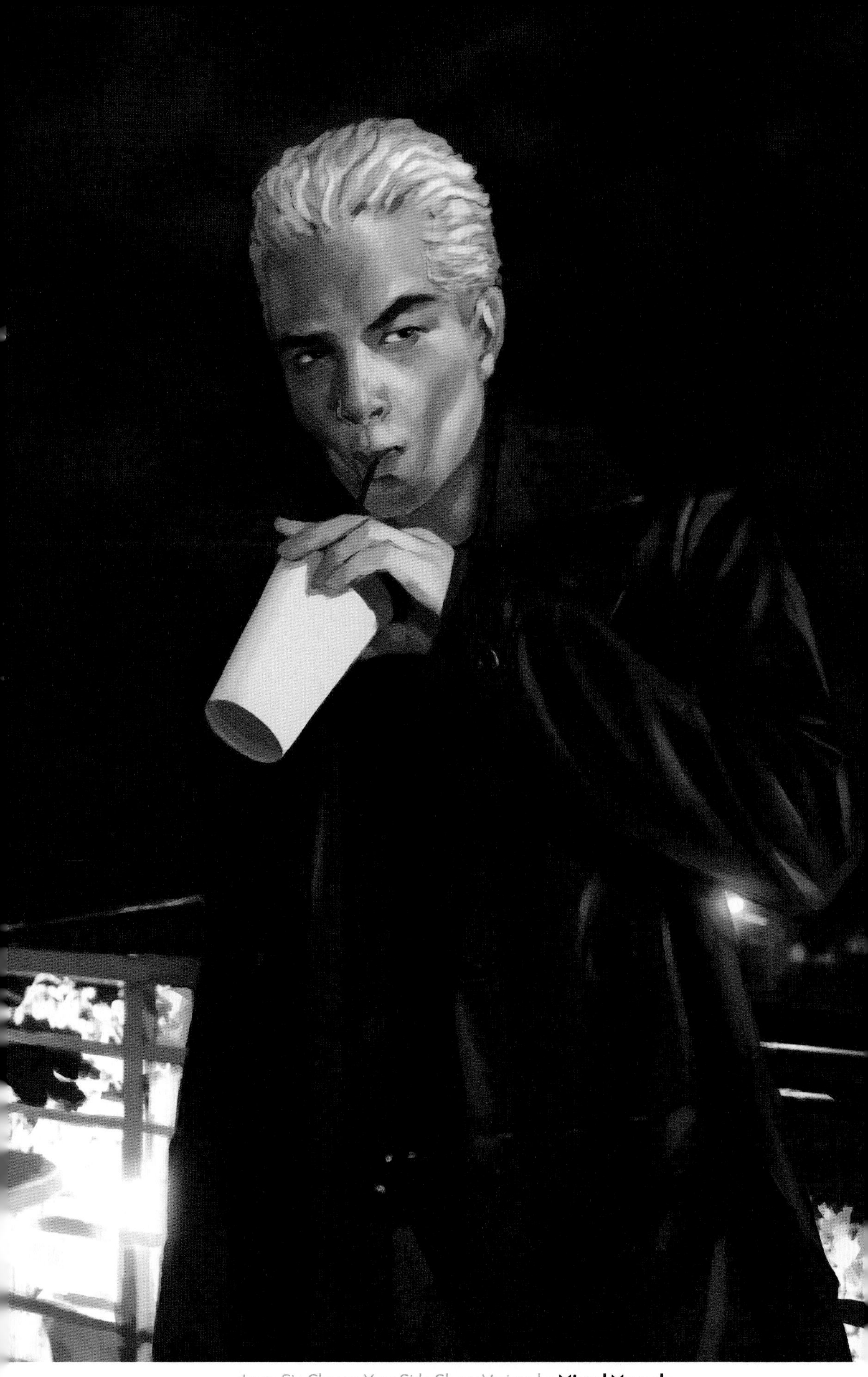

Issue Six Choose Your Side Slayer Variant by **Miguel Mercado**

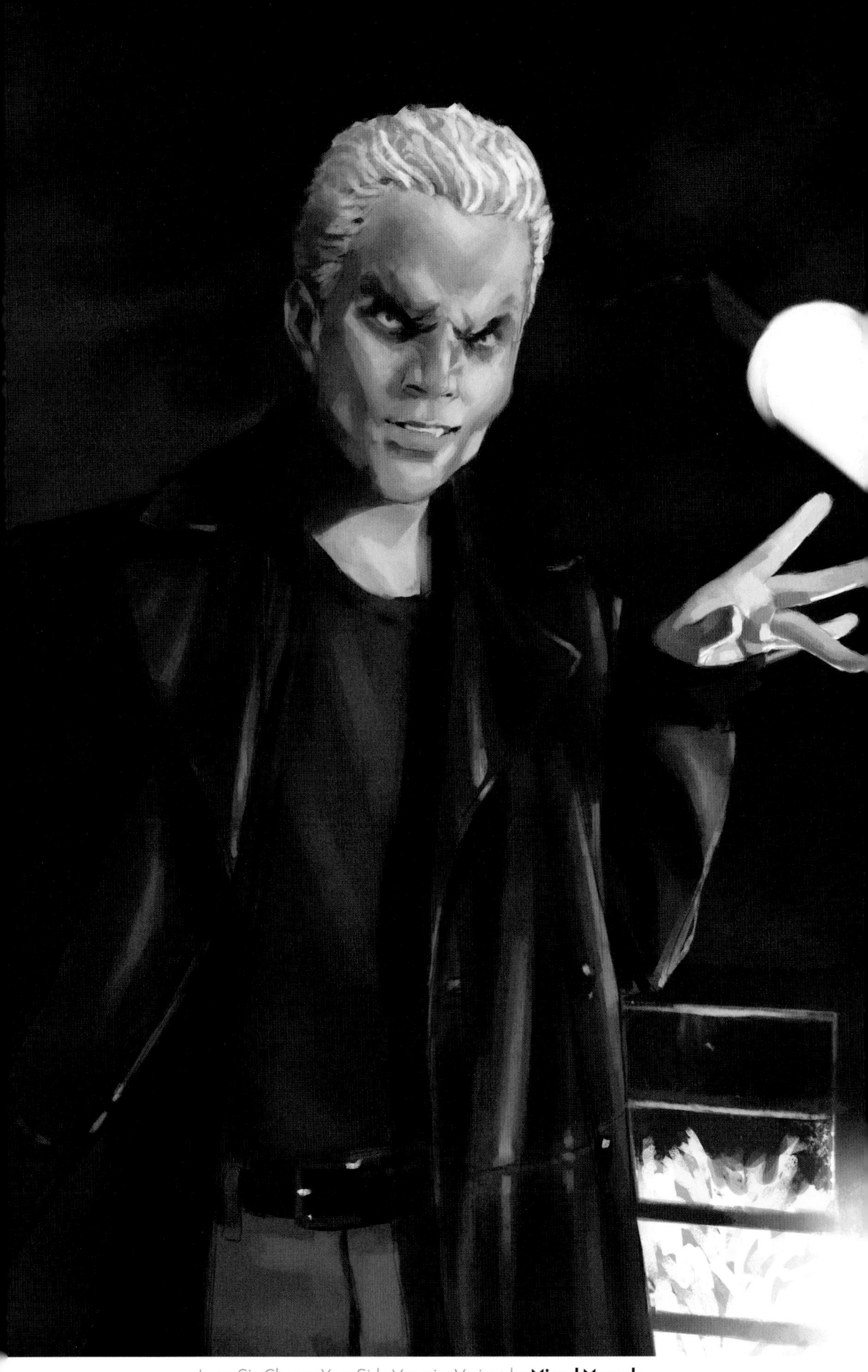

Issue Six Choose Your Side Vampire Variant by **Miguel Mercado**

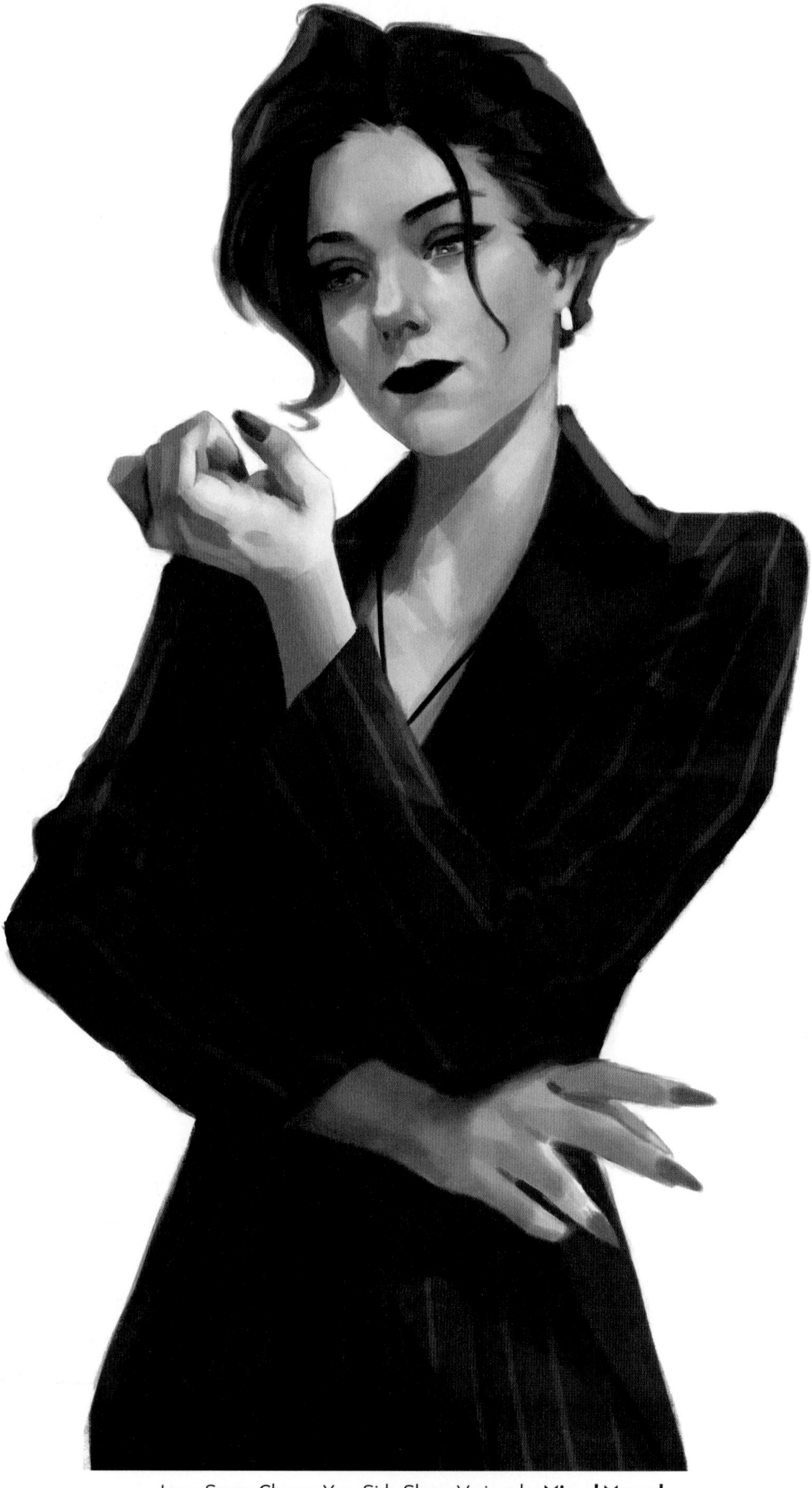

Issue Seven Choose Your Side Slayer Variant by **Miguel Mercado**

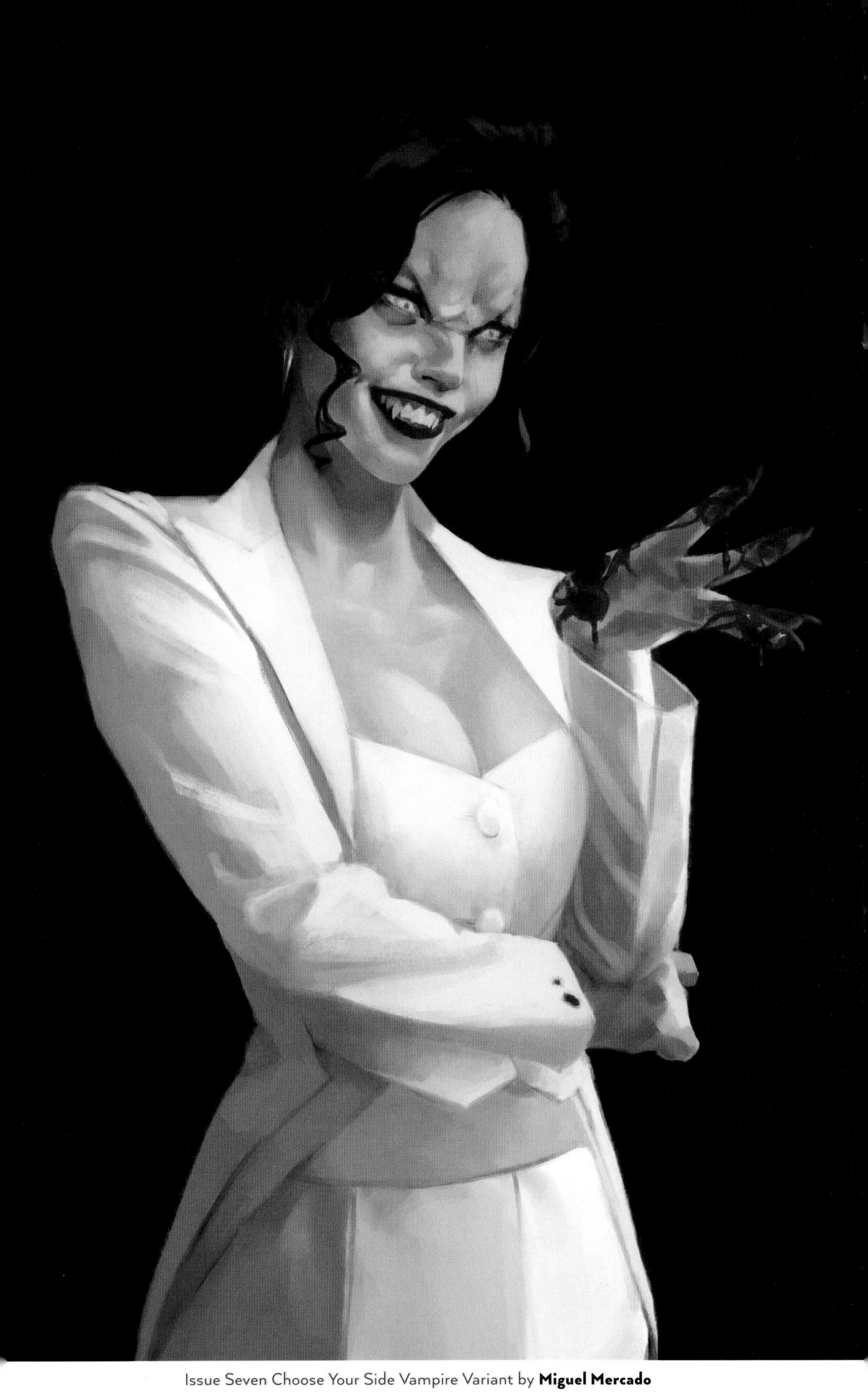

Issue Seven Choose Your Side Vampire Variant by **Miguel Mercado**

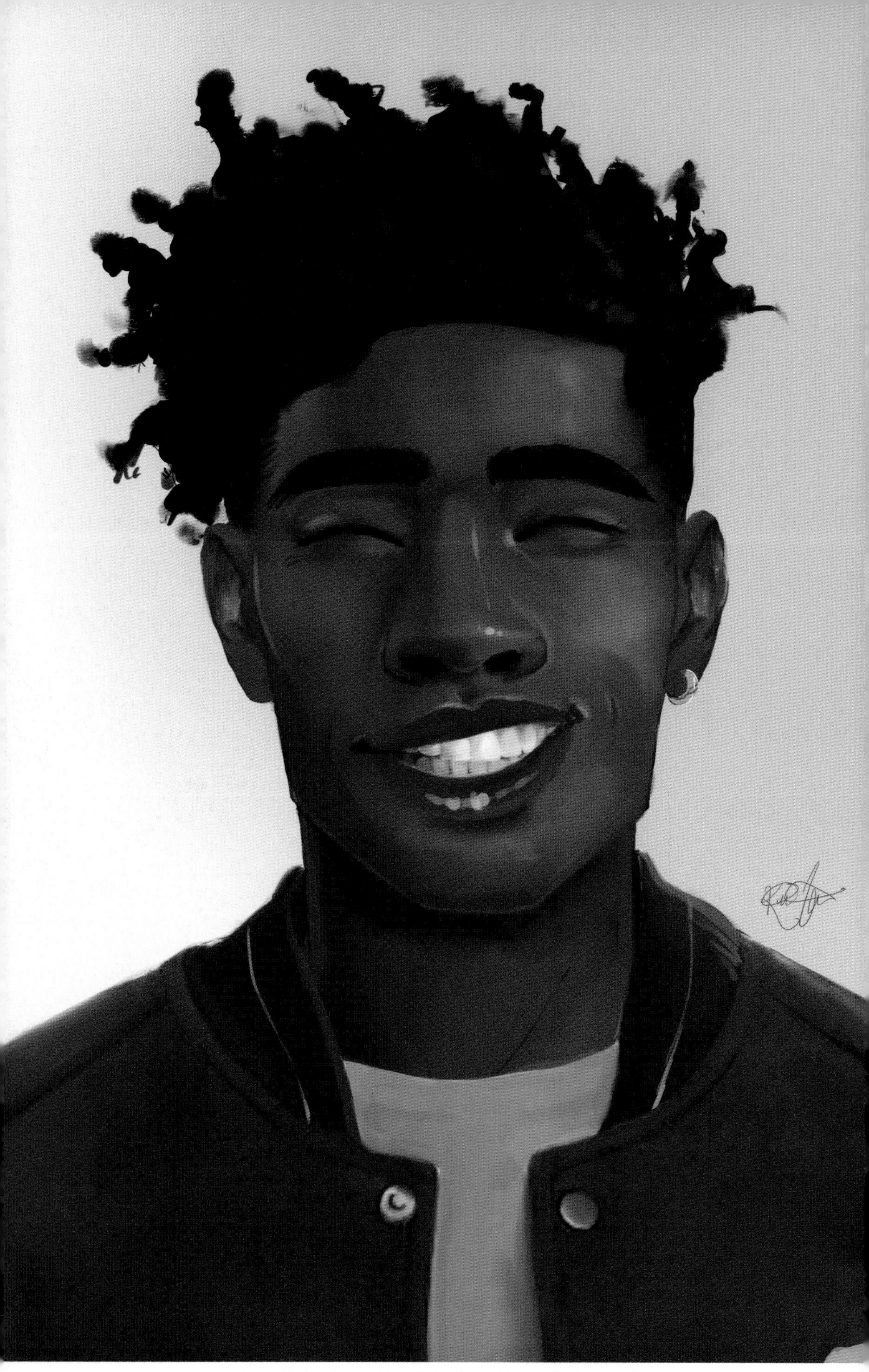

Issue Eight Choose Your Side Slayer Variant by **Kaiti Infante**

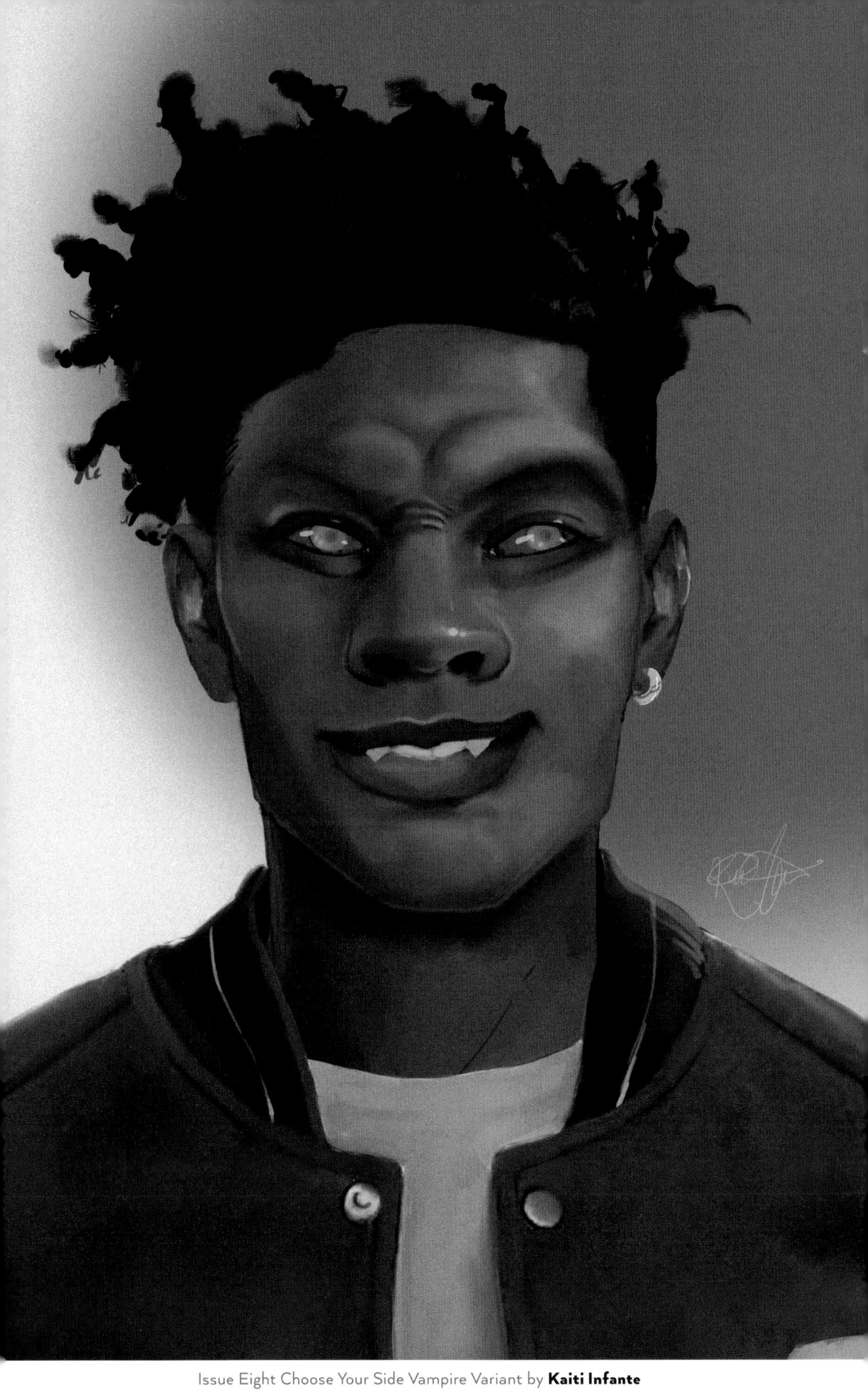

Issue Eight Choose Your Side Vampire Variant by **Kaiti Infante**

DISCOVER
VISIONARY CREATORS

THE WOODS
JAMES TYNION IV • MICHAEL DIALYNAS
VOL. 1
THE ARROW

"The Spire is fantastic! My kind of genre free-for-all."
—BRIAN K. VAUGHAN (Saga)
THE SPIRE
SIMON SPURRIER
JEFF STOKELY
ANDRÉ MAY

MARK WAID • PETER KRAUSE
IRREDEEMABLE
AFTERWORD BY GRANT MORRISON

MARK WAID • JEAN DIAZ
INCORRUPTIBLE

MICHAEL ALAN NELSON
DAN MORA
GABRIEL CASSATA
HEXED
THE HARLOT & THE THIEF VOLUME ONE

ABNETT & CULBARD
WILD'S END
FIRST LIGHT
"IT'S REALLY, GREAT!"
JEFF LEMIRE

James Tynion IV
The Woods
Volume 1
ISBN: 978-1-60886-454-6 | $9.99 US
Volume 2
ISBN: 978-1-60886-495-9 | $14.99 US
Volume 3
ISBN: 978-1-60886-773-8 | $14.99 US

The Backstagers
Volume 1
ISBN: 978-1-60886-993-0 | $14.99 US

Simon Spurrier
Six-Gun Gorilla
ISBN: 978-1-60886-390-7 | $19.99 US

The Spire
ISBN: 978-1-60886-913-8 | $29.99 US

Weavers
ISBN: 978-1-60886-963-3 | $19.99 US

Mark Waid
Irredeemable
Volume 1
ISBN: 978-1-93450-690-5 | $16.99 US
Volume 2
ISBN: 978-1-60886-000-5 | $16.99 US

Incorruptible
Volume 1
ISBN: 978-1-60886-015-9 | $16.99 US
Volume 2
ISBN: 978-1-60886-028-9 | $16.99 US

Michael Alan Nelson
Hexed The Harlot & The Thief
Volume 1
ISBN: 978-1-60886-718-9 | $14.99 US
Volume 2
ISBN: 978-1-60886-816-2 | $14.99 US

Day Men
Volume 1
ISBN: 978-1-60886-393-8 | $9.99 US
Volume 2
ISBN: 978-1-60886-852-0 | $9.99 US

Dan Abnett
Wild's End
Volume 1: First Light
ISBN: 978-1-60886-735-6 | $19.99 US
Volume 2: The Enemy Within
ISBN: 978-1-60886-877-3 | $19.99 US

Hypernaturals
Volume 1
ISBN: 978-1-60886-298-6 | $16.99 US
Volume 2
ISBN: 978-1-60886-319-8 | $19.99 US

BOOM! STUDIOS

AVAILABLE AT YOUR LOCAL COMICS SHOP AND BOOKSTORE

To find a comics shop in your area, visit www.comicshoplocator.com

WWW.**BOOM-STUDIOS**.COM

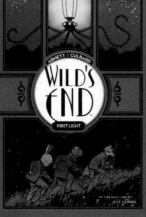